Tramp Printers

FOURTH PRINTING, 2013

Tramp Printers

A history of printing and of those
itinerant artisans who traveled the world
to create printed words
from metal type.

. . . it may be,
that I am among strangers,
and sing the glories
of a forgotten age
to unfamiliar ears...

— Mark Twain

TRAMP PRINTERS

by

John M. Howells, M.A. and

Marion V. Dearman, Ph.D

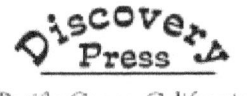

Pacific Grove, California

Published by
DISCOVERY PRESS
382 Central Ave. #1
Pacific Grove, California 93950
(831) 375-7698
e-mail: **johnhowells40@gmail.com**
http://discoverypress.com/trampweb

Copyright 2013
John M. Howells, M.A. and Marion V. Dearman, PhD

All rights reserved. No form of reproduction of any part of this book shall be made without written permission of the copyright holder, except for brief quotations embodied in articles and reviews.

Printed in the United States of America
First published in 1996 – Fourth printing September 2013

ISBN 0-9650979-0-0

All labor donated by ex-ITU members.
Roy Carter, Don Cleary, and Le Hanesworth, associate editors

Contents

INTRODUCTION	11
INVENTION OF PRINTING	19
PRINTING TRADITIONS	29
PREMATURE OBITUARIES	37
SUBSTITUTE SYSTEM	55
JOHN BARLEYCORN	63
LEGENDS IN THEIR TIME	73
WOMEN PRINTERS	103
CIVIL WAR TO WWI	123
TRAMPING IN THE 1920s	135
THE GREAT DEPRESSION	153
POST-WAR BONANZA	179
FRIENDS AND ENEMIES	205
PRINTING POTPOURRI	221
EL PASO, TEXAS	243
END OF THE TRAIL	255
SOCIOLOGICAL POSTSCRIPT	265
GLOSSARY	273
BIBLIOGRAPHY	283
INDEX	285

Acknowledgments

The following individuals assisted in the production of this book, either by contributing their writings, their experience or simply their support and encouragement. Of course, any time that so many people are involved in a project such as this, some will be overlooked. Please contact the authors if we've skipped over your name. Oversights and errors will be rectified in the next edition of Tramp Printers.

Albert H. Ahr	Charlie Fisher	John P. Koonce	Peter Platts
Paul Fermin Austin	Bob Fladd	Thomas W. Kopeck	Chester Pyle
Leo Baker	Dick Fleming	Arlond Korff	A.O. Reed
Gerold F. Barnitz	Melvin Franz	George Libbey	Jack Reuter
Leo J. Barry	Chris Frishe	Mike Librik	George Rollbusch
J S. Barton	Gordon Froud	Eddie Little	John Rote
Don Bosworth	Robin Gail	Sharon Longley	Herb Russ
Kenneth A. Brisse	Geraldine Galbraith	Charles F. Lottes	Clem D. Russell
Clay Brownhill	Anthony G. Ganss	Fred MacDonald	Dustin G Reyer
Lou and Del Brueske	Denny Gatzmeyer	Ralph Majak	Leonard Sandick
Edgar L. Burr	Bob Gieske	Robert H. Mason	Fred Schmidt
John Burt	Frank Graham	Stella L. Maxim	Jeannie Schultz
Andrew Carroll	Frank Granger	Mary McCarthy	Faye Shaw
Charles R. Carter	Dick Gray	Chris McEwen	Bill Silver
Roy Carter	B.G. Griffith	Steve V. Medigovich	Reuben F. Slattery
Charles Cartwright	A. Gudjohnsen	Paul Melvin	Louis Smasal
Bert Crampton	Roger Halls	Edward. H. Michelson	Ron Smith
Albert P. Chandler	Red Haloran	Dick Mohler	Gary Stiggers
George A. Clark Sr.	Le Hanesworth	Richard Mollman	George Story
Don Cleary	Jerry Hansen	Lloyd Mooney	Rocky Stremming
The Cleers	Win Hardisty	Ted Morse	David Stryker
Jim Coates	Joe Harnik	Robert F. Neff	A.J. Taylor
Elmo Collins	H.J. (Mose) Hartley	Arnold Nevers	Robert Taylor
Lonnie Coleman	John Hatfield	Merle Nimbar	Wm. W. Taylor
Bryan Maloney	David Hawk	Horace B. Norvill	Bob Troupe
Bob Conboy	Eddie Hayes	Lance Nygard	Ed Vandever
Cliff Cos	Len Henderson	Wild Bill O'Keefe	Robert Voorhees
John Mason Cox	Thomas W. Holson	Ed O'Rourke	Junius P. Welch
Ed Cox	Eugene Hubrich	Wesley H. Ott	Jim White
Forrest Daniel	Robert Johnson	Malcolm Pace Jr.	Art H. Whitted
Fritz De La Fleur	Bob H. Johnson	Bob Parker	Alvin Wier
Marion Dearman	Jewelie Johnson	Mary C. Penland	W.O. Wildman
O.T. Dixon	Robert A. Johnson	Richard D. Philips	Fred Williams
George Duncan	Donna R. Jones	Michael Phillips	Sunshine Wilson
Richard Ellian	Jim Kapplin	Chuck Phillis	H. Yahn
James D. Ferguson	Joe Kempe	Lawrence E. Piazza	

A Race of Men

There's a race of men, that don't fit in
A race that can't sit still.
So they break the hearts of kith and kin
And roam the world at will.
They range the field and rove the flood,
And they climb the mountain crest;
Theirs is the curse of the gypsy blood,
And they don't know how to rest.

If they just went straight they might go far —
They are strong, and brave and true;
But they're always tired of things that are
And they want the strange and new.
They say, 'Could I find my proper groove,
What a deep mark I would make.'
So they keep on going and each new move
Is only a fresh mistake.

—ROBERT W. SERVICE

A short take of handset type from Johann Gutenberg's first typesetting job: the Bible.

INTRODUCTION

T HIS IS A PIECE OF HISTORY that needs to be set in type before it vanishes into the dusty corners of time. The story's theme is printing—the "art preservative of all arts." But the focus is on a group of legendary characters who called themselves *tramp printers,* craftsmen who traveled the world at will, wandering from town to town—sometimes from country to country—as freelance artisans of typography. Pride, dignity and uncompromising independence were their badges. Skills, artistry, and solidarity with fellow printers, were their tools.

As years increase the distance between old, traditional printing methods and new, computer-generated photographic or laser beam techniques of producing printed material, the secrets, traditions and close-knit fraternalism of printers are fading into the past. Since "hot type" printers have all but disappeared, it's not surprising that itinerant tramp printers are also extinct.

Before we go any farther, let's define the term *tramp printer.* The origin is obscure, but please understand that "tramp printer," has nothing in common with the terms "hobo," "bum," or "tramp" in the sense of someone who doesn't work, can't work, or won't work. On the contrary, a tramp printer was a craftsman who traveled about the world in *search* of work.

In the United States and Canada, for over a century and a half (possibly even longer) the term "tramp printer" described an itinerant typesetter who preferred to travel from print shop to print shop, rather than work at the same job for life. For many of them, this was a temporary pursuit, for oftentimes a good job would tempt them to abandon traveling.

Typically, a tramp printer was highly skilled, capable of demanding high wages, and above average in literacy. He was the archetype of Robert Service's "race of men that don't fit in." Many were addicted to drink, as well as travel, and held a cavalier attitude toward responsibility. For any frivolous reason, tramp printers could quit a job, and move on, because they were, as Robert Service so correctly pointed out, "always tired of things that are, and want the strange and new."

An interesting aspect of this free spirit was that membership in the typesetters' labor organization, the International Typographical Union, made traveling almost absurdly easy, yet all tramp printers were not union members. Non-union workers—particularly those skilled in "country-weekly" publications—also enjoyed the freedom, mobility, and dignity their trade provided. They had the additional advantage of knowing all phases of printing, for in a small shop one needed to be skilled in presswork, stereotype, and bookbinding—as well as knowing how to run and repair a Linotype. They proudly called themselves "all-round printers." Since smalltown weeklies were chronically desperate for help, printers knew full well they could quit one job and find another one without missing a day's work. Country printers also held a bargaining position and power over their employers; if the only printer in a one-man printshop quit, a publisher knew he'd find himself in deep, deep trouble. Consequently country printers were usually accorded great respect from employers.

Early Travelers

Rarely if ever in the history of work and labor has a group of craftsmen enjoyed as much freedom, dignity, and mobility as those engaged in the art of printing. From the very beginning, starting with the introduction of movable type by Johann Gutenberg in the 15th century, the notion of "journeyman" embedded itself in the curriculum of learning to be a printer. To properly master the art of printing—after finishing several years of apprenticeship—it was almost obligatory to journey from one shop to another, preferably from one town to another, even between countries. He was expected to leave the shop where he learned the trade, to make room for another apprentice. The more print shops a journeyman worked, the more techniques and "tricks of the trade" he learned, and the more rounded a craftsman he became. Only after he'd acquired a full proficiency of the trade could he proudly call himself a "journeyman" printer.

From the earliest times, the art of printing enabled a worker to go anywhere in the world he pleased. He could easily find work for a master printer or—with minimal investment—could establish his own printing shop and become a master printer himself. Demand for the printed word increased geometrically with the proliferation of the technology. Jobs and opportunities expanded with each new print shop established. Printers knew they were in demand and were tempted to change jobs frequently, knowing they could travel from place to place with ease.

This book focuses, therefore, upon just one aspect of the printing trade, one which disappeared with the advent of computer technology: the traveling typesetter or tramp printer. We'll look at the historic mobility of printers over the past century and a half, and try to document that carefree lifestyle of tramp printers. We'll look at personalities such as Rabbit Ormand, "Gulf Coast" Guy Foley, Sam Ball, Sunshine Wilson and Big Marie Emory. These names are meaningless to most people, but to old-time printers, they are legendary. Few personalities in this book are still alive at time of publication, but all deserve to be remembered.

Eventually, with the funeral of the last of these tramp printers or "knights of the road," as they often called themselves, all memories of them will dissolve. Therefore, we dedicate this book to the memory of those traveling journeyman printers who made their living over the past five centuries through the ancient art of typography.

Ironically, this book about metal type—and those who composed it into books, magazines, programs and business cards—is *not* set in metal type! The humiliating truth is that the typesetting was done on a Pentium-based computer, using a word processing program called XyWrite, with Ventura Publisher (developed by the Xerox Corp.) as the desktop publishing program. The body type is Galliard, generated by the computer as a descriptive language and output on a Hewlett-Packard laser printer. The method of printing the words on paper wasn't even a traditional letterpress or offset, rather these pages were output on a high-speed copy machine. It may be a saving grace to note that the computer typesetting was done by a 42-year member of the International Typographical Union (or rather what is left of the Typographical Union) and his dues are currently paid up until the first of January, 1997.

In laying out a structure for this book, a great deal of time was spent analyzing questionnaires and data returned to the authors by correspondents. We read our way through stacks of letters and stories from tramp printers over the past 25 years, who supplied copy for a newsletter titled, *When Printers Worked with Real Type*.[1]

Our original goal was to create a sociological statement about tramp printers, their work traditions, values, and position in the history of the North American work force. Surely, this group was unique among the workers and tradesmen. To our knowledge, no other industry operated the way the printing trade did. Few workers enjoyed the freedom of movement and autonomy available to printers. Unusual work practices, rigid adherence to centuries of tradition, a high degree of literacy, and complex social relationships traditionally placed printers in a unique category in America's labor movement. Tramp printers formed a distinct subcategory within the working community. Their "education" placed them in the forefront of labor leaders.

It may be of interest to the reader to learn that this book's authors are both ex-tramp printers. Like many tramp printers, they used the knowledge and experiences gained from touring the country to forge ahead in their printing careers, and to later move on into other spheres of interests. One author earned a doctorate in Sociology, the other a master's degree in Anthropology.

Therefore, as social scientists, our original intent was to publish this study as a contribution to the field of Sociology of Labor. Our goal was to produce an academic study of the phenomenon of tramp printers. After many hours of surveying voluminous research material, it became clear that a monograph of objective, analytical, and scientific descriptions of Tramp Printers and their place in the Sociology of Labor could wait. More urgent was the problem of getting the story in print while some tramp printers were still alive to relate their experiences.

---

[1] Published from 1982-1985 by John Howells, at San Jose California

Therefore, this volume intends to address the subject in a more entertaining manner, hopefully in a way that will encourage broad readership and induce an appreciation of tramp printers in a wider audience. Were this study to be rigidly academic, many negative facets of the lives of tramp printers would need to be detailed and the dysfunctional aspects emphasized. Without doubt, the consequences of drifting from town to town, job to job, affected some tramp printers in adverse ways. Some never put down roots, they abused alcohol, left broken families, and generally "broke the hearts of kith and kin."

Although severely dysfunctional individuals were in the tramp printer minority, these individuals tended to be the most colorful, the best remembered, and the most envied by "homeguards" who felt trapped in their humdrum, staid and safe jobs.

Unlike most workers who misuse alcohol and shun responsibility, dysfunctional tramp printers suffered little damage from getting fired. When a printer was sacked for drinking on the job, he didn't have to become a beggar on skid row; another good-paying job waited across the street, across town, across the state, or across the country. However, as will be explained later, drinking was so common on so many newspapers (among editors and reporters as well as printers) that drinkers often were not fired unless drinking interfered with their ability to keep up with the composing room's production standards.

The fact is, most tramp printers were not alcoholics or derelicts. At any given time in history, the majority of them were temporary "tourists." In good times, they were tramp printers by choice, and not by necessity. In depression times, it was necessary to travel to find work—until jobs opened up back home. Traditionally, young fledgling printers took time at the end of their apprenticeships to enjoy the adventure and freedom of traveling, or "tramping" while they searched for an ideal place to settle down. Many eagerly looked forward to the completion of their apprenticeship so they, too, could "tour" the country and enjoy the luxury of working where and when they pleased after an onerous obligation of six years working in the same place. Some tramp printers (like the authors) traveled with their families, sometimes living in house trailers or renting apartments close to the printing plants where they worked.

Of course, a number of printers and employers in the printing industry during those halcyon days of tramp printers did not view tramps with fondness. Some union members disliked tramps because they forced regular workers to "give out their overtime" (explained later). Some employers resented tramp printers' lack of loyalty to the company and often arrogant attitudes when dealing with management. The irresponsible, alcoholic tramp printers were well remembered, and those who behaved normally were forgotten. These negative viewpoints will be recorded insofar as we've been able to collect them.

Therefore, after long consideration we (the authors) succumbed to our personal biases and happy remembrances of the positive aspects of being tramps. We fondly recall the euphoric sense of freedom; the reinforcing bond of camaraderie with other printers, and adventures to be discovered by taking whichever fork of the road appeared to be the most romantic. Our decision is to concentrate on presenting stories, anecdotes, and observations of those who enjoyed this way of life. Rather than a traditional ethnographic description of function, role, solidarity, and such, from the viewpoint of the observer—that is an "etic" view—we prefer to take an "emic" approach. We will describe the lives, customs, and behavior of tramp printers from *their* perspective rather than from the judgmental viewpoint of an observer. In other words, the views in this book are from the participants' observation.[2] So, those of you who are looking for something scientific rather than entertaining, better wait for the scientific dissertation, which may or may never be published.

Sources of Information for this Book

The core of this book about tramp printers was written by tramp printers themselves. The majority of the contributors to this book are

---

[2] For those readers who are interested, the Etic/Emic distinction is as follows: Etic statements depend on phenomenal distinctions judged appropriate by scientific observers. Emic statements, on the other hand, depend on contrasts and discriminations judged as appropriate by the actors themselves. Emic study looks not only at the culture and behavior, but attempts to understand individual actors in a life-drama, their attitudes, motives, interests, responses, conflicts, and personality development. (See *The Rise of Anthropological Theory,* by Marvin Harris, Columbia University, 1968.)

now dead. You will be reading stories sent to us over a 20-year period—you'd find transcripts of conversations and interviews plus personal experiences and observations written *by* tramp printers, *about* tramp printers.

We've deliberately refrained from over-editing this material for fear of losing the impact of the actual words of the tramp printers and their contemporaries. You may even find typographical errors sprinkled among these pages, but we don't apologize; we are in a hurry to publish. Those very few remaining ex-tramp printers are anxiously awaiting publication of this book. They need to see their handiwork before they too, join their brother and sister printers.

The idea for this project began back in 1972, when the authors began collecting information from other tramp printers. We intended to publish a paper for the *California Sociologist,* a journal published by California State University at Los Angeles. We became sidetracked by other projects, however, and never got around to doing much more after completing one paper on the Sociology of Labor, and one paper on the effects of automation on newspaper workers.

While we were deciding what to do with the information, John Howells decided to issue a "tramp printer's newsletter" and circulate among a mail list of ex-tramps. This publication had two names: *When Printers Worked With Real Type* and *Tramp Printers' Newsletter.* It was published on a more or less regular basis for about three years.

Many stories, anecdotes, and incidents related in this book came from those early contributors. These memories came from printers who traveled between the years of 1920 to 1970. Unfortunately, most, if not quite all of these respondents have passed away during these two decades of procrastination. Then in 1994, fired with a resolve to complete our project, we issued a new call for information through the pages of the *CWA News* (a newspaper issued by Communications Workers of America) and *The Printer* (a publication for printing historians and hot-metal printing buffs).

A new wave of information flooded us, with stories and memories of a later group of traveling printers: those who became printers after World War II. Their traveling years were of a different quality and experience from their counterparts who went through the depression. The newer breed enjoyed one of the more idyllic periods of printing history in that they rode a wave of continual prosperity and full employment—that is, until the new processes abruptly ended forever the careers of tramp printers.

Another very valuable source of printing history came from the book *Adventures of a Tramp Printer* by John Edward Hicks. A very well-traveled printer, Mr. Hicks drew on his experiences as a tramp printer in the 1880's and 1890's to produce a very readable collection of vignettes about tramp printers. He traveled the country from the Atlantic to the Pacific, worked on big city dailies, country weeklies, and job printing shops. His experience in traveling about the country enabled him to become a field representative for the International Typographical Union. Hicks eventually settled in Kansas City where he published his book with nationwide help from editors, newswriters, historians, and of course, other tramp printers. He must have been in his 90s at the time of publication.

INVENTION OF PRINTING

"We should note the force, effect and consequences of inventions which are nowhere more conspicuous than those three which were unknown to the ancients, namely, printing, gunpowder, and the compass. For these three have changed the appearance and state of the whole world."

—SIR FRANCIS BACON, 15th Century

EVEN THOUGH THE COMPASS enabled sailors to explore the world, and gunpowder empowered soldiers to force their nations' will upon those lacking sufficient firepower, printing was the most revolutionary invention of all. Printing made possible a widespread distribution of information, ideas and theory. It proved to be an efficient and inexpensive way of preserving knowledge for posterity. After printing dramatically slashed the cost of books, libraries grew in body and complexity with each succeeding generation. As information accumulated, new inventions and technology developed from this growing reservoir of data. Science and technology expanded at an ever increasing rate. Eventually even gunpowder became obsolete, replaced by nuclear weapons. Compasses have been made obsolete by electronic devices that can mark your place on the earth with an accuracy of a few feet. None of this could have happened unless scientists had access to printed books, technical journals, dissertations and reports available in libraries.

Without easy access to this storehouse of information, recording of events, discoveries and technological breakthroughs, the world would surely be a different place today. At least 80 percent of what we know comes from printed words. Political writings have prompted far more historical changes than gunpowder.

From Manuscript to Metal Type

Long before movable type was invented, craftsmen produced books which were laboriously copied by pen and brush. But the process of printing from engraved wood blocks was well known. Those who inked these engravings and imprinted them, using a wine-press type of device, were called *pressmen*. They often imprinted sheets of parchment with illustrations and decorative initial letters. These pre-printed parchments were filled out with hand-lettering by the *scribes*. Those who assembled the manuscripts and encased them in leather bindings were called *bookbinders*. Therefore, even before movable type made high-production possible, there was a division of labor between pressmen, scribes and bookbinders.

The shakeup began with the invention of movable metal type—by a German watchmaker by the name of Johann Gutenberg (nee Gensfleisch)—introducing a revolutionary new technology, a new and inexpensive method of producing books. Skilled in working with brass, Gutenberg designed a process to engrave an individual letter onto a brass matrix and then use this mold to cast type with a special lead alloy, which he also perfected. Until that time, printing was very rudimentary and tedious; words and illustrations were either carved into wood blocks or inscribed on stone. It was quicker by far to hand-letter pages of a book, as did the church scribes.

With this new process, individual letters in pieces of metal could be assembled into words, sentences and pages. The composed type was then inked and impressed on paper. Instead of a scribe laboriously creating one copy of information, a printer could create thousands of copies in the same amount of time. He could also do it at an infinitely lower cost per volume.

Shortly after Gutenberg's invention, printing plants proliferated all over Europe. Although many tried to keep the process a secret, they were singularly unsuccessful. Churches and monasteries lost their monopoly over book production rather quickly as newly trained workers left their employ to start their own print shops. Within decades, printed books became commonplace. Type founders designed new type faces and found no lack of enthusiastic buyers for their type fonts. Shortly after the Americas were discovered, printing offices flourished there. It's interesting to note that one of the first thing printers in America did was to form unions, the first in the New World. Unlike the European guilds, the American printing unions tended to exclude employers from their ranks.

The new concept of printing involved many intricate steps: casting type, composing individual characters into pages, pulling the press handle to make an impression from the type, and finally binding the finished product. Printing artisans drew upon a deep reservoir of accumulated knowledge, skills, and "tricks of the trade." Thus, quite correctly, printers proudly referred to their craft as the "art preservative of all arts." Just as an artist learns from observing techniques of other artists, the art of printing was passed along from journeyman to apprentice by demonstrating techniques and secrets of the trade. These secrets were jealously guarded over the centuries, with guild and union printers swearing an oath that their craft be kept secret from outsiders.

Apprentice printers, called *devils* back then, learned to manipulate type and arrange it into eye-pleasing combinations through verbal instructions from a journeyman or a master printer. They discovered which type designs were appropriate to a particular project or "job" by imitating the experts and by experimenting on their own. Sometimes they needed to know how to operate a printing press, mix inks, bind books and other skills involved in the total process. Even when printers worked exclusively with type, a knowledge of the entire process was essential.

Ironically, very little of this information was passed along by way of the printed word. Tradition, customs and techniques were orally transmitted, not printed. Newcomers to the trade listened and imitated as older workers handed down knowledge that began accumulating in the late 1400s.

Printers in general always had reputations for being independent and condescending toward their employers. Since their skills were completely portable, it didn't take much to convince a printer to walk off the job and go work for someone else. Therefore, when printers organized a guild or a union, their monopoly over the skills necessary to produce printing, and their tight organization earned them a reputation for militancy, strength and support for their members.

Unions—or guilds, as they were called earlier—also predated the invention of movable type. The ancient scribes—while they worked almost exclusively for churches or religious establishments—were secular, and they organized guilds to regulate working conditions and pay for their skilled work. Seated in rows, the scribes laboriously lettered the text in response to the reading by one of their members who sat in a chair in front of the assemblage, hence he was called a "chairman," or sometimes the "chapel father." The scribe guild members referred to themselves as "members of the chapel." The chairman or father was traditionally the head of the guild in that chapel, a kind of early day shop steward. One of his duties was to see that all artists were treated fairly and that working conditions were maintained.

When typesetting replaced hand-lettering, scribes were naturally the first to learn the new process. Type cases, imposing stones and presses replaced the rows of desks. And the scribes' guilds became printers' guilds, and later printers' unions. Tradition hung on tenaciously. In the late 20th Century, the remaining union composing rooms in English-speaking nations still are called "chapels." The union representative is referred to as the "chairman" or the "father" of the chapel. Like the earlier chapel chairman, his job is to adjudicate differences between members, to see to it that all chapel members were treated fairly, and to enforce the contract and working rules.

Early printing guilds were strong and militant. At one time, in the early 1500's, the guilds convinced British Parliament to pass restrictive laws that made it illegal for any more than 500 impressions to be pulled from one typeset form. The type had to be distributed and reset for the next 500 copies. (Early-day bogus[1] rules.)

---

[1] Throughout this book you'll find numerous instances of printers' jargon, and special jargon used by tramp printers. We'll try to explain crucial words and phrases, but a glossary is included at the end of the book for the convenience of non-printers.

Tradition played an extremely important part in the process of passing along the techniques of printing technology. Certain ways of working could not be questioned. Even the words one spoke in a print shop (or could not speak) were controlled by custom. Printers' jargon reflected century-old traditions, bewildering and sometimes meaningless to the outsider. If you asked a printer why he called the long metal trays that held type a "galley," why the drawers that held type were called "cases," or why type faces were called "fonts," you'd probably receive a look of pity from the printers in a composing room. Outsiders who didn't know the jargon were ridiculed when they attempted to infiltrate a print shop. You could always tell an outsider or beginner by the way he spoke. Printers who violated the rules, such as the ban on whistling in the shop, fighting, or any other infraction were fined by the chapel (often payable in beer). For more serious infractions, the offender could be "sent to Coventry." That is, he received the silent treatment for a given period of time, after which he could buy his way back into good graces by purchasing an amount of beer for his fellow chapel members. Some jargon continues even today, carrying over into the field of digitized typesetting. But, as we shall see later on in this book, tramp printers evolved their own special jargon, the meaning of which is quickly disappearing as tramp printers die off. A special glossary is included in the back of this book to explain some of the more obscure terms.

Logically, all those engaged in printing offices—pressmen, bookbinders and typesetters—could be called "printers," but in fact only those who worked with type were known as such. This probably evolved because, while the master printer needed to know all aspects of the trade, he was invariably a typesetter first and foremost. Typesetting required the most education; skill and dexterity, while presswork involved brute strength in the early days of hand presses and pressmen were hired because of size. Furthermore, pressmen and bookbinders traditionally learned only their segment of the trade, and received lower wages and social status than a printer. Therefore, in this book, when the term *printer* is used, please interpret this as meaning: a typographer or composing room worker who performs tasks such as typesetting, imposition, makeup or any of the numerous skills involved in typography.

A Second Revolution

Although the invention of movable type spread quickly from country to country, innovations and improvements in technology were slow in coming. For the next four centuries, the state of the art in typesetting basically consisted of hand-picking each individual letter from a wooden "case" and placing it in a "stick" until a line of type was complete and then "justified" (spaced out to an even length). After the "job" was "set" it was placed on a "stone," "locked" into a "chase" with "quoins", leveled with a planer-block and mallet, and finally turned over to a pressman.

Typesetting production was limited to the speed a printer could assemble type by hand. A few exceptionally proficient workers, known as "swifts" were proud of their speed; but there was a definite limit to their dexterity. Presses changed little over the centuries, as well. Until the middle 1800s, most newspaper presses were still hand powered, using a screw-and-lever technology developed in the Dark Ages for pressing wine, and later for making paper. Some foot-powered printing presses, mostly used for small commercial or "job" work, sped up production, but newspaper presses were exceedingly slow until the introduction of steam-powered cylinder presses, beginning in the early 19th century.

By the late 1800s, several inventors were struggling with the concept of mechanical typesetters. Since presswork efficiency had improved dramatically, an advancement in composition techniques was sorely needed. Among others, Samuel Clemens (Mark Twain) invested heavily in a keyboard-operated typesetting machine. Suddenly, in 1886, a tremendous breakthrough occurred when Ottmar Mergenthaler, a German immigrant installed his invention—the *Linotype*—at the *New York Tribune*. His Linotype took the country by storm. By 1890, newspapers and book publishing plants all over the country had purchased this miracle machine. Within a few years, virtually all major newspapers replaced handset type with Linotypes, the first successful attempt at automation in the printing industry. Boosted by even faster, more efficient presses, printing production increased fantastically.[2]

---

[2] See Carl Schlesinger's book, *The Biography of Ottmar Mergenthaler*

At first printers felt extreme dismay toward new innovation; it looked like the end of an era. One Linotype operator could produce almost as much type in a day as a good hand compositor could in a week. At Horace Greeley's *New York Tribune,* 28 operators cranked out the equivalent production of 100 hand compositors. To add to workers' worries, many publishers were reluctant to retrain printers on the new machines. They preferred to go "outside" the trade, assuming that neophytes might not develop the independence and intransigence of traditional printers. Women were considered ideal trainees, because they worked for lower wages and were considered more easily manipulated than men.

This didn't prove to be the case, because the newcomers quickly assimilated the traditional behavior of the print shop, becoming just as inflexible and bull-headed as the old-time hand compositors. Women clamored to join the union, and the ITU insisted on equal pay for women. (Not so much because printers were concerned about equal rights, but because they feared unfair competition from low-paid women.) Another factor was that experienced hand compositors learned to operate Linotypes more quickly than people without printing backgrounds. They transferred their skills and expertise to the new process and became "swifts" on the new machines. In addition, the International Typographical Union insisted on total jurisdiction over the new process; it prohibited its members from working in plants where non-union Linotype operators or machinists were employed. After several bitter strikes, most publishers decided it was easier to work with the union than to fight it. The ITU's membership grew and prospered far beyond its earlier years.

The printing industry flourished. Daily newspapers replaced weekly newspapers, and new publications popped up all over the country. A flood of books rolled off the presses in astounding numbers. Country weeklies changed from four-page editions to eight or sixteen pages. Ever more workers were needed to cope with the greatly increased volume of work. As printers perfected their skills on the Linotype, they minted fresh jargon that dealt with the new "mills."

Mergenthaler's invention was an engineering marvel. Very

complicated, with as many as 5,000 moving parts, the Linotype was also reliable and easy to maintain, since components were interchangeable—a relatively new idea at that time. In fact, it was so well-designed that when the Linotype went out of production nearly a century later, the design was virtually unchanged. Ottmar Mergenthaler would have easily recognized the latest model, and would have little trouble repairing it. The brass matrices which cast the lines of type, the spacebands which spaced between words and the cams which operated the marvel were essentially the same as those used on early versions of the machine.

The Linotype, with its 19th century technology, ruled as king for many years, while inventors struggled to achieve the next breakthrough with a new technology. Publishers, eager to break the ITU's stranglehold on their composing rooms, poured money into inventions which would permit relatively unskilled workers to replace printers. Most efforts failed miserably. Teletypesetters (known as TTS), which was a system of operating a Linotype with punched paper tape, gained popularity and worked its way into most newspapers by the late 1960's. The advantage to TTS was supposedly that a semi-skilled operator could punch tape and bypass unionized or highly paid workers. Unfortunately, the idea of automating an already automated machine turned out to be inefficient and productivity was low. In most cases, expenses and personnel increased. Printers smugly watched these efforts to bypass them and felt secure. "As long as there is printing, they'll need printers" was a common saying.

But printers were in for a painful surprise. Change rolled in on a tide of computers and software. Starting in the late 1960s, gaining momentum year by year, the final breakthrough came ten years later with the perfection of photocomposing machines and computer terminals. Newspapers began scrapping batteries of Linotype machines, replacing them with computer-operated photo-typesetting machines or laser printers. Linotype and TTS operators were replaced by newswriters using video terminals in the newsrooms to write the stories and send them directly to the computer-operated photo-typesetting machines. Reporters and editors took over the job of typesetting, bypassing the traditional composing room workers. The newspaper business returned to where it started two centuries earlier, with newswriting and typesetting being done by the same individuals. Printers found their numbers shrinking, their skill levels lowered, and job opportunities vanishing.

By the late 1980s, many newspapers eliminated their entire composing rooms. Others maintained skeleton staffs, performing marginally skilled tasks. Many union workers were covered by "lifetime jobs" and were kept on until retirement—but not replaced. Non-union workers were laid off permanently, without apology.

Adding to the typographer's demise was the development of computer software which came to be known as "desktop publishing." Suddenly the capacity to set type and produce professional looking printing was in the hands of anyone who owned an inexpensive IBM clone computer. Simply by calling up the program on the screen, the novice was presented with a selection of typefaces and type sizes that wasn't to be matched in even the most modern printing plants. This spelled the end for those printers who still held jobs in commercial printing plants. Customers began bringing in their own typeset material to be put on the press. A secretary could do her own typesetting. Commercial printers began eliminating their composing rooms en masse.

The International Typographical Union, which had been the oldest, the strongest, the most active labor union in the history of the American labor movement, threw in the towel. Faced with a drastically shrinking membership, the international officers sought merger with whichever organization would have them (and presumably take best care of the officers). After flirting with the Teamsters Union and the Newspaper Guild, the once great Typographical Union finally became a subsidiary of Communications Workers of America.[3] After 134 years, the International Typographical Union faded into history, and before long, a gossamer memory.

---

[3] Originally a telephone workers' union which dealt with AT&T, but began expanding into various branches of communication.

PRINTING TRADITIONS

ALTHOUGH THIS BOOK chronicles the tramp printer, it's necessary to take another look at the history of printing in general, with a view toward printing customs and traditions to understand how the phenomenon of tramp printers evolved. The notion of a craftsman being "footloose and fancy free" is not a common one in the history of labor. Most workers crave stability, placing high value upon steady employment. But from the very earliest days of printing, the notion of moving from job to job seemed only natural.

An indication of a fully trained craftsman's mobility is the title of "journeyman," which was awarded upon completion of training. The name probably derived from the French word *journeaux* for a day's work, yet it also involved the concept of travel, for once an apprentice finished his term of indenture (usually six years), he was expected to leave his employment to make room for a new apprentice. He then traveled about the country until he found a suitable position as a fully qualified journeyman.

In a real sense, the concept of traveling printers originated with the invention of movable type and the art of printing. From the very beginning, when an individual mastered the secrets of this new method of book production, he realized the potential for personal advancement and moved on to another city or country to establish his own printing office. In turn, his apprentices stayed just long enough to develop their skills, and then move on to repeat the process. This international movement of artisans was the mechanism that spread printing and publishing so rapidly across Europe and eventually the world. Within a few decades, print shops dotted Europe and before long, the New World.

As time went on, printing plants grew larger and capital investment requirements became more onerous, but the number of journeymen required to man these plants increased as well. It seemed there was always another printing job waiting for the restless journeyman. In short, traveling has always been one of the benefits of being a printer. They took full advantage of it.

Traveling from town to town, working in a number of printing establishments, workers found opportunities to pick up more "tricks of the trade," strategies for performing his work faster, more efficiently, with greater artistic flair. Thus the more widely traveled printers earned reputations for skill and artistry. Their talents were highly prized by the master printers who owned the print shops. When the opportunity arose to start their own printing plant these skills served them well.

Guild Tradition

Many early traditions in those newly established print shops derived from common practices in industrial and commercial guilds so powerful in Europe at the time: guilds such as textile, ceramic, and metal workers. An important component of guild organization was that of *master* (the owner or proprietor), *journeyman,* and *apprentice,* which fit nicely into the new industry of printing. As mentioned previously, when an apprentice completed his training, he was expected to "journey." The new journeyman typically wandered from town to town in search of work, picking up a day's work here and there until he encountered a "situation" in a place he liked, where he could work as long as he cared to. Other traditions borrowed from guilds regulated behavior among workers, demanding loyalty to guild members and establishing fines for infraction of guild rules.

A major source of tradition came naturally from the church scribe guilds who regulated work before movable type came on the scene. Since they changed from calligraphy to typography, they kept the same guild structure to regulate working conditions and traditions which were unique to their craft. As we discussed earlier, the guild's organization was called a "chapel," no matter where the work was performed, and the chapel member who read the copy was called the chapel "chairman" or "father." In all probability he was elected from the chapel members and was responsible for settlement of disputes and the general well-being of the members, just as his successors in composing room "chapels" were to do.

This concept of chapel continued on through the centuries, with union printers' bargaining units called chapels, the elected chapel representative was called the chapel chairman, and sometimes the chapel father. The chapel voted on rules and regulations governing conduct of chapel members, and sometimes voted to confirm or deny the justification of a printer being fired by the foreman.

Early Day Traveling Printers

Printers were among the earliest craftsmen to emigrate to the New World, bringing their presses, foundry equipment, and skills with them. Presses were transported as hardware, with wooden beams hewn from local trees making up the massive part of the presses. Soon, print shops and newspapers cropped up in all parts of the Colonies.

As you might expect, printers brought guild traditions with them, and they quickly organized informal printers' societies, springing from the solidarity of printers. Since they were opposed by proprietors, these early organizations were often surreptitious, with union and chapel meetings held in private homes, often in secret, and reinforced the solidarity feeling with rituals, symbols and secret handshakes. Printers were fiercely proud of their traditions and jealously guarded the secrets of their craft. They tended to associate exclusively with other printers, and union members were discouraged from cooperating with non-union workers and prohibited from disclosing trade secrets. Violators were punished by fines, ostracism, and even bodily harm. It became unthinkable to cooperate with outsiders, who hadn't served apprenticeships. The master printer also had an interest in protecting trade secrets, and cooperated with the chapel organization, not interfering with its structure (as long as chapel members didn't openly agitate for higher wages).

An organized printers' strike occurred in New York City as early as 1776, and a formal typographical union was formed in 1798 in that city. By 1839, a national organization was formed, and passed the following regulation: "... It shall not be lawful for any local society to permit members of said society to work in any office where boys may be taken as apprentices for a less period than five years." The organization also made it illegal for any local society to consider an applicant for membership unless he had served five years as a regularly indentured apprentice.[1]

Until 1848, when Horace Greeley helped form the New York Typographical Union, most local printers' unions that were organized either disappeared after gaining their immediate goals and or they became benevolent societies. Starting that year, however, printing unions in the United States began to build a stable base, and two years later formed what was to become the International Typographical Union. By 1860, 34 unions belonged to the ITU, and by 1873, 104 locals.

Solidarity among craftsman was paramount among the functions of early printing unions. A major concern was the welfare of other printers, particularly unemployed journeymen. Often a fund was maintained, under control of the chapel chairman, which provided monetary relief for traveling printers who found no work available. Some print shops set up a system whereby a journeyman printer seeking work could be hired by individuals if the printing establishment didn't need an extra hand. Because of the long hours traditionally worked by printers, a substitute was often welcomed by regular workers as an excuse to take a day off.

Under the Typographical Union, these customs evolved into a system of work-sharing involving substitute printers. Substitutes could work from day to day, and show up for work wherever they thought they could best catch work. Were it not for this system of easy traveling, the phenomenon of tramp printers couldn't have existed. This ability to hire a substitute at will gave printers an unusual freedom and feeling of independence. It also gave substitutes

---

[1] *History of New York Typographical Union Number Six.*

employment and the freedom to seek work wherever they pleased (during good times) and the chance to seek jobs elsewhere when necessary (during bad times). Many chose to work in the Southern states during the winter months, then traveled to the Northern states for the summer. For this reason, traveling substitutes were often called "snowbirds."

Tramp Printers
by Marion Dearman

Although I spent almost exactly equal parts of my adult life first as a printer then as a sociologist—25 years journeyman membership in the ITU and another 25 years in academia, I think of myself primarily as a printer. In this regard, I identify with Benjamin Franklin who, despite his innumerable accomplishments (writer, wit, statesman, inventor) and his immense erudition, nevertheless wished his epitaph to say simply "Benjamin Franklin, printer." But sociological training and insights may be helpful for understanding the long and impressive history of the craft of printing and tramp printing itself. I will strive to keep my comments as free as possible from sociological gobble-de-gook and soshspeak. We hope to present a more academic approach in a future edition designed for a different audience.

There are several sociological systems which could profitably be applied to the institution of tramp printing— conflict theory, exchange theory, and interaction theory, for instance. But the most useful perspective, we believe, is one shared by both sociology and anthropology and which makes sense to the uninitiated as well as social science cognoscenti. That perspective is structural-functionalism, which views whatever relevant institutional complex being studied as a structure composed of parts, each of which function toward maintaining the viability, strength, and adaptation of the organization as a whole. It's very much like the Linotype operator or machinist who must understand how the different parts of Merganthaler's marvel work together to do what the machine was designed for. As we know, the keyboard, first elevator, second elevator, distributor bar, magazines, mats, etc. must work in unison for the Linotype's work to be done. Clean space bands liberally coated with graphite are "functional" for the machine; anything causing a squirt, on the other hand, would be "dysfunctional," i.e., would interfere with the positive functioning of the machine.

A good place to start is to ask whether tramp printers had a positive (functional) or negative (dysfunctional) effect on the Union's structure and its efforts to construct a powerful organization for protection of the welfare of its members. The evidence throughout these pages, we believe, illustrates that despite some negative features—high alcohol consumption, little loyalty to local unions, offensive personal habits frequently—on the whole, the functions of the tramp printer were extremely useful to the ITU, the homeguards, and to their employers. Some of these positive functions are as follows:

1. It alleviated the problem of chronic under- and over-employment. By its very nature, printing is cyclical, with big surges periodically. This is especially true in the newspaper industry, with the highs coming in Spring and Fall. Travelers were also needed to cover vacations in Summer. At Christmas, those on the bottom of the board got layoffs for their Christmas presents. With a traveling card, the sub could go to where the work was rather than passively waiting for it to come to him.

2. It enabled homeguards to take time off work for short or long stints. He could hire a substitute without the foreman's consent.

3. Both homeguards and tramps were more free to work or not work—the tramp by turning his slip and the homeguard by putting a sub on to work for him.

4. It helped bring about shorter hours and discouraged overtime hogging.

5. The practice of tramp printing helped cement the hundreds of locals together into a cohesive whole. Instead of solitary locals, isolated and perhaps competing with each other, travelers constantly reminded homeguards that they were the International Typographical Union, not just Indianapolis #1, or Detroit #18, or San Francisco #21, and so on.

6. Tramp printers continually reminded homeguards of their options in employment. The local printer never had to feel that he was owned by his employer. Freedom to travel was as near as the

local secretary's office, where the traveling cards were issued.

7. Long before it was an option in other industries, tramp printing already practiced sharing jobs, worked much shorter hours than is common in any other industry, and practiced a form of sabbatical (with hires to lay off overtime).

8. Skills and tricks of the trade were transferred throughout the ITU by traveling printers. At the same time, homeguards could compare their knowledge and ability with those who had worked in many shops and tramps could test themselves against all kinds of printing conditions.

9. Tramp printers greatly strengthened the ITU's system of laws. They were knowledgeable about the laws, out of self-preservation perhaps, and zealously saw to their observance.

While these may be considered positive functions of tramp printing by some, not all would agree. It depends, as they say, on whose ox is being gored. For the homeguard in dire financial straits, getting his overtime bumped or even working shorter hours may not seem desirable or positive. Nor would employers, and their representatives in the composing room—the foremen—be expected to applaud the ITU contractual clauses requiring hiring of subs to set repro ads or allowing regulars to hire their own subs without office involvement. In the short run, good practices may seem bad; but, in the long run, many elements of the institution of tramp printing certainly had positive effects, not only for the ITU and the printing industry in the near past, but since the invention of movable type in the 15th century. The spread of printing could not have happened without the traveler, either in its early days in Europe or in the spread of population during settlement of the United States.

As the entries in this book demonstrate, social relationships between tramps were generally cordial. They respected each other's skill and experience and took great pride in the extent and duration of their traveling. At work and over drinks a genuine sense of camaraderie existed among these "knights of the road." They helped each other over hard places, loaned each other money, advised each other about where the work was, who the bad foremen were, and which shops had cash-in men. Between tramps and homeguards, feelings were more ambivalent.

❄ ❄ ❄

Not all, but a substantial proportion, of tramp printers were multifaceted, highly intelligent, often extremely literate individuals — a far cry from the stereotype that the term "tramp" would seem to connote. Many of us have been passably successful in other endeavors, your authors for instance. John Howells has published a dozen successful travel books, as well as a scholarly book on the social change in Russia since Glasnost, and has published in academic journals. He has a BA in Anthropology and an MA in Ethnic Studies from San Jose State University. Marion Dearman has a BA (with great distinction) from San Jose State and an MA and PhD (Sociology) from the University of Oregon. Both authors got their university degrees while working members of the ITU. We don't believe that we are particularly exceptional tramp printers. The crucible that produced us molded a host of successful people.

PREMATURE OBITUARIES

THE DEMISE OF tramp printers has been prematurely predicted several times in the past. When the Linotype burst upon the scene in the 1890s, a general feeling of malaise filled composing rooms all over the continent, with everyone agreeing that printing would change and itinerant compositors were a thing of the past. This of course didn't happen. Again, when the 1930s depression hit, things looked gloomy for workers in all sectors of industry. Yet tramp printers increased, forced to travel to survive. But today, it isn't necessary to predict the future of tramp printers; they can truly be described in the past tense. The following essay was written in the 1890s, during the depths of Linotype pessimism. The author is unknown.

Vanished from the Scene

"The story of the tramp printer now is a tale that is told and has passed into legend. Once in their myriad numbers they covered this country... from coast to coast and from the lakes to the gulf. But now they come no more to their accustomed haunts. One of the most picturesque and interesting characters in the annals of America's folk history has vanished from the scene. The most romantic page in the history of American journalism has been written by these flitting troubadours, who came with a story in lieu of a song, stayed their little day or two and vanished into the mists, even as now their entire tribe has vanished, save in the mists of memory...

"Essentially poets at heart, theirs was a puckish attitude toward life and its responsibilities. Shrewd they were and frank in their appraisal of men, yet they had in their makeup a little of the child, artless and whimsical; something of the philosopher, disillusioned and made cynical by their experiences; careless alike of their manner of living and the manner of their dying, they were gentle stoics and tender cynics to the end.

"That vast and vagulous army is no more. Those carefree artisans are vanished from their old haunts, while the paths they wandered now are trod only in the dreams of old men's retrospection . . . they come no more."

Tramp printers can be described many ways, depending upon where in the printing industry one was situated. Publishers, print shop owners, and some homeguards will have diametrically opposed recollections from the fond memories of traveling printers themselves. Since both authors of this book were tramp printers, the reader can expect to see a more romantic, idealized version of our old compatriots. This is only natural, and we do not apologize for our biases.

The section below, adapted from John Edward Hicks' *Adventures of a Tramp Printer,* probably sums up many rank and file printers' opinions of itinerant typesetters around the turn of the century. The characterization, although somewhat idealized, describes profiles of traveling printers of a hundred years ago, but the description would be not much different when the era ended in the 1970s.

The Day of the Tramp Printer

describing the era from 1880 to 1910

In those days, a printer was not really considered bonafide—his education was not considered complete and he was not accepted by his fellows—until he had done some wandering. The days after the Civil War to the end of the century were the day of the tramp printer. The tales of travel related by the veteran tramps glittered with romance and were listened to with eager ears by the novice, who was filled with a longing for adventure.

For the most part, those were days of class struggle, with proprietors and publishers always striving for lower wages, with printers determined to maintain working conditions as best they could. Foremen were often dictatorial and without restraint. A tramp printer's insurance policy was solidarity with other tramp printers and his brother typositors who held steady jobs.

The traveling printer, as a usual thing, did not marry early, but if married, he had things so arranged that he could make his departure from town without delay, and when things became disagreeable he left quickly, without even a good-by. His home was wherever he happened to be—a convenient hotel, a boarding house—and a steady job was merely a matter of temporary convenience. He didn't own anything, never expected to, and wouldn't know what to do with it if he did. He liked to say, "When my overcoat is buttoned, my luggage is packed."

Two or three days' work in each town was all the tramp printer wanted or would expect. Offers of permanent or semi-permanent jobs were turned down, sometimes scornfully. He was always on the move—going nowhere in particular—but moving, nevertheless. In the old days, he typically arrived in a town on an early-morning freight train, and left the same way, under cover of darkness, a few nights later. In later years, he arrived in an older-model used car, or by Greyhound bus.

Many traveling printers were intelligent and brilliant conversationalists on many subjects, but they often avoided personal history other than a brief resume of their travels, and perhaps to relate an experience or two that gave a hint as to why they preferred the road to a steady job. They were reluctant to tell a great deal about themselves. They seldom mentioned families or revealed anything about their life history. They accepted the world day by day and proceeded on the theory that tomorrow would take care of itself. They lived an easy-going life and made no attempt to resist the lure of the open road.

Tramp printers were usually masters of their craft. Few "blacksmiths," or "jacklegs" (as poor workmen were called) were among them. A tramp was, quite often, fairly well self-educated; acquainted with the topics of the day; good company either in editorial sanctum, tavern, boarding house or saloon. The "homeguards," as the stay-at-homes were called, were ever glad to see the tramp printer, for he brought many a new story and told of his work on the great daily newspapers and publishing plants. All foremen were "wolves," he said, and editors were ignorant. The thoughts that fashioned commonwealths flowed through his mind and fingers to the public.

❄❄❄

In the early days, when all type was set by hand, the idea that a machine could set type was considered ridiculous. A machine would have to have brains to set type! Of course, they were wrong. Forgetting their defeat by the Linotype, printers adopted the same attitude toward the absurd notion that computers or electronic equipment could possibly replace their skills. Again, they were wrong.

Some tramps confined their travels to one area of the country, seldom staying long in one place, always restless and moving on. Others became well-known in shops from coast to coast. The more celebrated of them acquired nicknames which lived long in the annals of printerdom, and are only now dying out as old-time printers expire. Their travels equipped them with stories unending of varied experiences, and with gossip of the craft, which they often related with much gusto. Such printers were not tramps by necessity, but from choice.

Motivation for travel varied between individuals. When an apprentice printer finished his time, he was urged to "get out and learn something." Printing styles and techniques were slightly different in each print shop; there was much for a fledgling to learn. Some tramps took to the road in order to broaden themselves mentally and to see the country, and savor adventures related by other tramp printers. Others traveled to escape an unhappy marriage or stiff alimony. Some merely found the life of a tramp a convenience, a way to shirk responsibility, to indulge themselves. The first two categories of tramp printers were usually temporary. That last category, permanent.

In the old days, the trade afforded a good living to the itinerant printer when work was plentiful, and at least survival when work was slow. In fact, sometimes tramp printers made more than regulars—those who wanted to work, that is—because they had to "show up" every shift, sometimes twice a day, to catch a full week's work. And regular situation holders were tempted to hire and therefore often worked less than substitutes. Tramps knew where the big money was to be made: at special events like legislative sessions, rodeos, state fairs, or any other place where extraordinary overtime would be required. When telephone books were being prepared, loads of overtime could be counted on.

The tramp printer was a salty character, as interesting as he was salty. He was an individualist, sworn to personal freedom of action. He had an insatiable urge to be on the go. He could not be anchored to a regular job for long. He spent what he earned, occasionally spending what he had not earned. He was irresponsible and profligate. His home was where he hung his hat and coat, and sometimes had not where to lay his head. He was habitually without funds. He was rough and ready, rude and often profane. He drank hard liquor and enjoyed life to the fullest.

Technological Future Shock
written in 1977, from Typographical Journal

When scholars study the history of the International Typographical Union, 1976 will be regarded as the most convulsive, frustrating and heartbreaking year in its existence. This was the year when everything came to a head and the membership faced a technological revolution resulting in Future Shock here and now. Productive men and women in the prime of life found themselves "bought out" for a relative pittance and cast adrift in an uncaring world. Skills painfully built were declared obsolete in an industry convinced the computer was king and profits more important than journalistic content or typographic excellence. Publishers were replaced by businessmen and newspapers became links in a chain—much like sausages. The human wreckage was everywhere, most noticeably the pensioner bereft of a pension, and the unemployed bereft of a livelihood.

❊❊❊

Back in the 19th century, it was common for a journeyman printer to be called to temporary duty as a newswriter or reporter. They would be sent out to cover a late-breaking story or put to work on the telegraph desk, selecting interesting copy for the morning's edition. Many printer-journalists went on to become successful editors, publishers, or authors. Samuel Clemens (better known as Mark Twain) is a prime example of a tramp printer who eventually moved into higher realms.

He spoke of his beginnings in the trade in the following speech to United Typothethae of America during the late 1800's. Clemens relates the duties of the apprentice—the printer's devil—and observes that power of freedom of the press formerly was held by the subscribers, the readers. There is little doubt that this power today is held by advertisers.

Samuel L. Clemens
about 1889

"I am somewhat of an antiquity. All things change in the procession of years, and it may be that I am among strangers. It may be that the printer of today is not the printer of 35 years ago.

"I was no stranger to him. I knew him well. I built his fire for him in the winter mornings; I brought his water from the village pump; I swept up his office; I picked up his type from under his stand, and when he was there to see I put the good type in his case and the broken ones in the hell matter, and if he wasn't there to see, I dumped it all among the pi on the imposing stone—for that was the furtive fashion of the cub, and I was a cub.

"I wetted down the paper Saturdays; I turned it Sundays—for this was a country weekly—I rolled; I washed the rollers; I washed the forms; I folded the papers; I carried them round at dawn Thursday mornings. I enveloped the papers that were for the mail—we had a hundred town subscribers and 350 country ones; the town subscribers paid in groceries and the country ones in cabbages and cordwood—when they paid at all, which was merely sometimes, and then we always stated the fact in the paper and gave them a puff; and if we forgot it they stopped the paper.

"Every man on the town list helped edit the thing—that is, he gave orders as to how it was to be edited, dictated its opinions, marked out its course for it, and every time the boss failed to connect, he stopped his paper. We were just infested with critics, and we tried to satisfy them all.

"We had one subscriber who paid cash, and he was more trouble to us than all the rest. He bought us, once a year, body and soul, for $2. We used to modify our politics every which way, and he made us change our religion four times in five years. If we ever tried to reason with him, he would threaten to stop his paper, and, of course, that meant bankruptcy and destruction.

"Life was easy with us; if we pied a form, we suspended till next week, and we suspended every now and then when fishing was good, and explained it by the illness of the editor—a paltry excuse, because that kind of a paper was just as well off with a sick editor as a well one, and better off with a dead one than either of them.

"All this was over 35 years ago, when the man who could set 700 ems an hour could put on as many airs as he wanted to; and if these New York men who recently on a wager set 2,000 an hour solid minion four hours on a stretch had appeared in that old office, they would have been received as accomplishers of the supremely impossible, and drenched with hospitality beer till the brewery was bankrupt.

"I can see that printing-office of prehistoric times yet, with its horse bills on the walls; its 'd' boxes clogged with tallow, because we always stood the candle in the 'k' box at night; its towel, which was not considered soiled until it could stand alone, and other signs and symbols that marked the establishment of that kind in the Mississippi Valley. I can see also the tramping journeyman, who flitted up in the summer and tarried a day, with his wallet stuffed with one shirt and a hatful of handbills; for if he couldn't get any type to set, he would do a temperance lecture. His way of life was simple, his needs not complex; all he wanted was plate and bed and money enough to get drunk on and he was satisfied.

"But it may be, as I have said, that I am among strangers, and sing the glories of a forgotten age to unfamiliar ears, so I will make even and stop."[1]

❄❄❄

Throughout most of the history of the tramping, the lifestyle of the tramp printer remained recognizably similar. There were variations, of course. For example, the mode of travel changed with technology: they walked, rode horses or wagons, and stagecoaches prior to the appearance of trains, which many of them then rode, either on the rods, in boxcars, or as paying passengers.

The development of the Linotype machine changed tramp printing, too. The pre-machine printer needed few tools to practice his craft. All that was needed was a line gauge, composing stick, a makeup rule, and an apron. He could always borrow a line gauge and printshops usually had a few composing sticks lying around. He could use a piece of column rule for his makeup rule and tie an old shirt around his waist in lieu of an apron. The type and other materials were furnished by his employer.

The following entries in this chapter are a sampling of the variety of personalities encountered among traveling printers of the hand-set era who, as we will argue later, were not so different from those who were still tramping when computers demolished their craft and their traditions.

Stories of traveling printers are legion. They come from all segments of society, and vary from poetic to starkly graphic. Below are a few stories and recollections of tramp printers and of times long past. The words from their mouths and from their contemporaries tell us more than can ever be found in writings of others about tramp printers.

Memories of "Journeymen" Printers
from Harry S. New, an old-time reporter from Indianapolis

"Those were the great days ... The 'jour' printer of my early association was as distinctive an American character as could be found. Neither the cowboy of the West, nor the lumberjack of the

---

[1] adapted from the *Typographical Journal*, May 1, 18%

North, was more certainly a type of American development than was the itinerant printer. There were so many of them that the appearance of the crew in the composing room in any of the larger offices changed with kaleidoscopic frequency. They came from everywhere and nowhere—wafted out one after another after a brief sojourn as a sub. They were known from Boston to San Francisco; from St. Paul to New Orleans. Any town was home. The only ties that were recognized were those that bound them to the trade, and the only certain and indispensable possession was the ITU journeyman's card. I can remember many of them who made their appearance from time to time at irregular periods, coming from nowhere and headed for the same place. Carefree and careless, prone to make too equal a division of time between the cases and the Dutchman's. They were days of camaraderie and good fellowship."

The following is a speech given at the annual banquet of Schenectady Typographical Union, May 20, 1911. The tramp printer's words of 85 years ago sound familiar. If one substitutes the word "computer" for the word "Linotype" his speech would be contemporary. It would appear, however, that his lament for the vanished tramp printer was somewhat premature. At the time, the economy was wallowing in the doldrums. But two more eras of plenty were yet in store for tramp printers: the 1920's and post World War II.

The Box Car Typographer

"There are only a few of us left. And we old-timers must acknowledge with a mournful sigh that the craft and its craftsmen have undergone wonderful evolutions. We charge it up to the Linotype, but we must confess that there are some other causes. Alas, the world is changing, or rather has changed. To turn back thirty years puts us in another world completely. The telephone was a struggling infant, the typewriter an upper case monstrosity, the arc light a coming possibility, the touring car a weird unknown, wireless telegraphy a dream, and aerial navigation worse than three unknown quantities.

"But what need had we for any such creations? For had we not the companionship of the peregrinating printer, the typographical tourist or the box car 'bo, whichever appellation his fancy seemed best suited with? And he was truly a rich and rare old gem. How every lad in his time envied him. How admiringly the galley-boy gazed upon his wrinkled visage and what draughts of inspiration were drawn in from his tales.

"And the young man just out of his time and holding down cases on the first rag upon which he had ever worked. What envy, what resolves to equal and excel the touring record of the last arrival permeated his breast. Just as soon as parental objections could be removed so as to allow of seeking fortune at a distance, that young man vowed to be out on the road. And sometimes the objections didn't count, and the cases were jumped. And the boys who had already hit the road a clip or two! How gladly they extended the hand of fellowship. How easily they stood for the panhandle, for they had been on the other end of that game too. A two-bit piece got a bracer and a shave, and then one of the boys calmly took a half day off and handed over six bits to the tourist to throw in his case, or rather left it where it could be secured when the throwing in operation had been concluded. Did he want a night's work? Half a dozen men were ready to lay off just to accommodate him.

"And then how he could stick type! And how his conversation enlivened the alley he was located in! And what an argument he put up to the proof-reader about the galley that should have been passed to Slug Seven on one alleged thin-spaced line.

"A near-poet once sized him up and poured forth these lines along with some others:

> *What paper hasn't he worked on? Whose manuscript hasn't he set? What story worthy of remembrance was he ever known to forget? What topics rise for discussion, in science, letters or art, That the genuine old tramp-printer cannot grapple and play his part? It is true that much grime he gathers*

in the course of each trip he takes, Inasmuch as he boards all freight trains between the gulf and the lakes. Yet his knowledge grows more abundant than many much titled men Who travel as scholarly tourists and are classed with the upper tens; And few are the contributions these scholarly ones have penned That the seediest, shabbiest tramper couldn't readily cut and mend.

"But, now, alas, those days are gone beyond recall. And when once in a while some of those old ghosts drift in on a freight train, the young men of today, manning the machines, know them not. The panhandle game is played, there are no cases to throw in, there is no room for a 'sub' unless in special cases of emergency, and the day of the old-time hand setter is past.

"But while we live, they cannot beat us out of the memories of the past. Your printer of today is matter-of-fact, unimaginative, and his memory is not cultivated as a store-house of erudition. But the old-timer, what an imagination, what a memory he possessed. And the greatest enjoyment in this world is the possession of a memory which can delve into the past and bring bubbling forth the many pleasantries of bygone days. And to the mind clothed with the genius of poetic imagination all of the things which seemed to be hardships in the olden time have drifted into the pleasantry class. Of all the talents we are endowed with, we can be most thankful for memory and imagination.

"There are many memories swirling back to me to-night out of the vast depths of the clamoring years agone, but one of the sweetest is that I carried a card of membership in the International Typographical Union, and another is a jumble of various means of free transportation, 'side door Pullmans,' baggage car fronts, mail car vestibules, upper decks, bumpers, tenders and 91 engine pilots. I must omit for truth's sake, 'riding the rods,' as I always considered that beneath the dignity of an artisan whose work was to preserve all other arts, and in this most of our great craft agree.

"And let me tell you that all that the schools, law offices and Courts were ever able to do for me in the line of education was but secondary to that secured in a few months of box car touring. That was why when you picked up the old-time newspaper, it proved a joy to the eyes and a delight to the soul. Most of the men employed in its make-up had 'toured' in primitive fashion. They had imbibed their knowledge by hard knocks, and they knew all the styles prevalent in newspaper work throughout the land. To be able to catch on at a moment's notice and make good, one had to set some errorless matter, and oft times edit it as well while he worked. And the proof-reader too was generally one of the same brand—a man with 'an eye like an eagle.' You could read page after page understanding then on almost any rag in the country and the most of it was like Dana's best. But in this day and generation of rapidity run riot, you cannot read over four lines in any paper without stopping to ruminate over what in the world could have been written in the copy that the Linotype man gazed upon, when he clicked off that meaningless rot which now confronts you. Of course you of the newer cycle will say that we are old fogies and too hanged particular. We had to know how to spell, but you fellows can blame it on the Linotype. We had to emit a cuss word now and then, but you gently tinkle your fingers down the keyboard and wind up the line with those wonderful modern cabalisms: ETAOIN and SHRDLU.

"Of course the old-timer chewed tobacco, but it was a gentlemanly looking fine cut usually, and not the alfalfa now handed out. And he was not averse to a drop of red liquor now and then, but the liquor of that day is just as scarce now as is the old-time tramp-printer. No, he didn't bother the churches much, but his word was generally as good as the preacher man's. And he gambled in a quiet way, too. Who hasn't jephed with the quads, when there wasn't a nickel in the bunch, to see who should make the attempt for credit at the corner dispensary? And then among the roadsters, when no quads were handy, who hasn't played 'crum or no-crum' to determine which should make the next back door invasion and procure the breakfast hand-out?

"Oh! When the leaves bud and the balmy zephyrs blow in the springtime, how the old memories will cling and cluster, and how the oldtime roadster will wish to cast off his respectability and glide back upon the road. It is well for him that he does not attempt it, for the rudeness of the shock he would receive therefrom might bring a quickened wakefulness that would forever disgust him with the pleasures of memory and imagination.

"The old-time tramp-printer is for the most part filling some unmarked grave. The scattered remnants of the tribe remind one of the disappearing American Indian. But the world was better that he had his being and lived and breathed. Many was the bit of sunshine he scattered. Many the smile he brought to faces usually wreathed in clouds—his last dinner he always divided. When he had two shirts or two collars, the one not then in use was always at the service of his neighbor, and the whole world was his neighborhood.

"He is gone or fast going. Peace be to his ashes and memory. God bless that type of humanity. We will shed no tears, for tears were things he shunned. But drink he loved, and so in keeping with that love which distinguished him, let us drink to the memory of the old tramp-printer."

. . . and a Battered Suitcase in Hand
Franklin M. White, condensed from the ITU Journal Dec. 1969

The story of that inimitable master craftsman of yesteryear, the "tramp printer" or roadster, is an American legend. His shirttail full of type, battered suitcase in hand and a grin that spanned the globe, this wandering, freewheeling individual sprinkled knowledge and literacy as enthusiastically as Johnny spread his Appleseed. Syracuse was a real "print town." "Cincy" was the place to be. Frisco was "the spot." But the landscape lover, the connoisseur of scenery, the tourist printer, needed no reason to move on.

Who was the Number One Traveler? No one knows or ever will. The title would have to be decided on the basis of mileage, number of traveling cards drawn, states worked in or most locals or chapels visited. No one kept score.

I have drawn few travelers, myself, having done most of my printing in the southern part of the United States. But I have known or seen nearly all the tourists of the past 50 years. Some traveled for a time, then got "off the road." The roster is endless because it is unwritten. "Weary Willie" Waterhouse, Nate Bergman, the "Gadget,"

"Shack" [or Shanty] House, "Muskogee Red," "Bull" Kelly, "Fuzzy" Chapman, "Sentimental Sam" Ball, "Gulf Coast" Foley, "Poor" Bill O. Bundick, Gene Hadley, "Dixie" (I've Been Every) Ware. And I can't forget "Rabbit" Ormond, "Harry the Huff," Ed Bates, "Cactus Jack" Crawford, "Horrible Harrigan"—the list includes many, many others. The real travelers and subs have done more to enlarge and protect our union since its beginning than any class. They toured the continent preaching unionism and solidarity.

I remember working in my father's country weekly when I met my first tramp. This was around 1919. He had just been discharged at Fort Sam Houston after overseas service in the battlefields of France, and he stopped at our shop, seeking a day's work. He hadn't reached a town where he could deposit his old traveler, drawn before the war's interlude. So my dad hired him to do some "distribution."

He pitched in and cleaned up the dead-type dump. He unerringly picked the correct cases after sizing up the layout, and distributed the type fast and accurately. He amazed me with his dexterity at the case. The gentleman was a competent printer. There were about 40 cases, and the mixture was awful. Two or three sizes of DeVine, odd single cases comprised of one size of Livermore and other unpopular or obsolete faces. We had a lot of miscellaneous type families seldom seen. A veritable hodgepodge.

Dad gave him four or five dollars: country wages then. The fellow shouldered his bundle and asked me to accompany him to a restaurant where he told me a few tantalizing tales of the open road. We parted ways at the local railroad station. I saw him climb under a boxcar and position himself on the rods and I waved him on as the freight highballed.

The next year dad accepted a legal brief of about 72 pages, agreeing to print and bind it by a certain deadline. Hand spiking all through my teens, I had practiced about six months on the shop's Model 15 Linotype (the old "junior" machine with only 14 mats to a full channel), and could grind out the equivalent of three quarters of a galley of single-column type for the paper. But this was an overwhelming job.

Luckily, a tourist with a heavy beard and wooden leg blew in and dad put him at the old B-point cases, which type matched that on the Linotype. I don't recall the oldster's name or much of anything except that he was a whiz—as long as he was supplied with paregoric. Paregoric, or "PG" as it was called, was a mild, legal narcotic, and created many addicts back in those days. The old hand comp set plenty of type for the brief, but dad had to keep sending out for PG. With me at the Model 15 and the roadster almost keeping pace, we got the job out on time. As the old PG with the peg leg set type he kept telling tales of his travels. I remember him telling of setting type under a fig tree in the Mojave Desert.

I believe I knew the champion job jumper of all time. The poor guy jumped almost every time he was hired over a period of 30 years. Just about every time he came to my town of Shreveport, he jumped both papers in the same day[2]. However, on his last visit, he surprised everyone by working a full month without jumping once. But he still left town deep in hock. He was known as "Poor Bill O. Bundick," as he signed his name on his ITU travelers. His career ended when he died in a boxcar in Memphis, partially from exposure to weather.

I have met tramp printers who could recite Shakespeare, Wilde, Chaucer, Gibbon, the Rubiayat, Mohammed, Uncle Remus, Flavius Josephus, Isaiah, and Daniel Webster. They could edit and correct copy, spell, punctuate, parse, conjugate, and occasionally, knew Latin, French, and Kant. They took competency for granted.

On the other hand, there were plenty of exceptions. Ignorance never has engendered bliss in printing. As editor of a weekly on the gulf coast during the depression, I once had a Cajun printer working for me who could neither read nor write English. He set guts for display ads from the cases and worked at distribution. There were many others who were elbow benders, imbibers, roadsters who hoisted the cup or jigger that cheers. I will not go into that other than to mention the old rumors about alcohol being an antidote for lead poisoning, and its use to eradicate incipient tubercle bacillus. Good excuse, and anyway, the stuff made waiting for trains tolerable.

---

[2] To "jump" a job was a serious offense for which one was almost invariably fired. "Jumping the job" means accepting a hire from a regular or for the office, and then not coming to work and not notifying the chairman in time to hire another substitute. Other subs considered this exceptionally unethical conduct, since it allowed a job to go "dark" (not covered) when another sub could have earned a day's pay

Every old-time printer you talk with has a favorite tramp printer story. The same names keep coming up time after time. Occasionally we find a narrative about less-famous travelers. Below is one of them:

The Duke Who Came to Dinner
from Thomas W. Holson, of Bakersfield

Back in the mid 1920s, I worked in Texas down around the Mexican border, a popular place during prohibition because of the availability of liquor across the Rio Grande. A tramp printer used to frequent West Texas composing rooms in those days, a typesetter we knew as "Duke" Wellington.

A big, well-built fellow with a charming British accent, Duke was ruggedly handsome and about 40 years old. We all assumed that "Duke" was his nickname. We thought it a coincidence that at the time, there was a flurry of publicity over a lost heir to the title and estate of the British Duke of Wellington who was last heard of in Arizona. But for some reason, Duke kept a low profile.

Then one day, when Duke Wellington was working as a sub at the *News-Globe* in Amarillo, his cover was reluctantly blown. Turns out he actually *was* the missing heir! In Detroit, the British consulate arranged for his passage to England. The *News-Globe* capitalized on the story far and wide, printing his photo with the caption: "From Type to Title." The Duke said goodbye to us, leaving for England and his estates—without much enthusiasm, oddly enough.

In the meantime, the Great Depression descended like a pall across the land. I ended up taking a job in Borger, Texas—an oil boom town about 50 miles from Amarillo. My wife Clarice lost her job and my wages were cut to a pittance. We were forced to surrender the equity in our lovely home and rented a modest house in a very modest neighborhood. Our first child was due. Oh, how we envied the Duke and his vast estates in Great Britain! Living the life of luxury.

The *Borger Herald* hired only half a dozen printers, all members of the Amarillo Union. Work was scarce, and situation holders were in no mood to hire subs. (In those days there were no paid vacations, no unemployment benefits, and very few office hires.) One winter afternoon—cold as only a Texas Panhandle day can be when a norther sweeps from the Rockies and across the plains—a vaguely familiar figure ambled into the *Herald* composing room. It was the Duke!

He wore heavy work clothes of solid, dark color, and sturdy boots laced over the ankles with clasp fasteners half way up to the calf. He had a toothache and grumbled about having to spend 50 cents for toothache medicine. There was no extra work, and I didn't feel prosperous enough to hire him. But I did invite him home to dinner. Clarice went on a hasty shopping trip for pork chops and extra food. At the dinner table, Duke told his story.

It seems that he was the younger son of a younger son in the Wellington family, ordinarily a position without the least prospect of inheriting a title. His father had been given an obscure government position and was sent to far-off Arizona. Mike learned the printing trade there, never dreaming he would someday inherit the title of "Duke of Wellington." His father returned to England where he died, as did all others in the line of succession. Thus, the inheritance came down to "Duke".

When he arrived at the Wellington estate (actually in Ireland), just as he expected, he found it so heavily in debt that it had no prospect of ever becoming solvent. Each succeeding title holder had borrowed heavily against the estate. Poorly managed over the years, there was no possible way the estate's revenues could begin to cover the debts, much less support the Duke of Wellington, not even in the style of a tramp printer! The only assets were a quantity of peat to be spaded from the earth to be sold as fuel, and several full decanters of Irish whiskey the Duke found in the mansion. "No one seemed to bother them—except me," he said.

Finding no joy in becoming a peer of title realm—particularly when he couldn't afford it—he decided to renounce the title to return home to America. Somehow, he managed to arrange another loan against the estate to cover his passage and he sailed happily away, headed once more for Texas and the Mexican border.

After thanking us for his dinner, the Duke said goodbye again and walked away into the night, his boots scuffing gravel. Somewhere he would find work as a printer. He was sure of that. We never heard of him again.

The King of the Tramps
from John Edward Hicks

Peter Bartlett Lee, was known throughout the craft as "king of the tramp printers." He was a fine figure of a man, usually wearing a spike-tailed coat and a wide-brimmed hat, though at times he sported a silk hat. He wore an unusually heavy watch chain and never was without it. He came and went in a quiet sort of way and little was said of his coming or going, how he arrived or what mode of travel would take him away. Sometimes he walked, at other times he rode the freight trains, and again he would ride the cushions. He always carried a number of newspapers which he had picked up off the exchange desk of the last newspaper office visited and he handed these out in the homes of farmers where he often was an overnight visitor. The papers were welcome because reading matter was scarce; and Lee was welcome because of his entertaining conversation, his courteous demeanor and gentlemanly bearing.

He was one of the best-read of the many well-read printers who roamed the country in those days. He would sit at the foreman's desk for a while with a sheaf of papers and when he handed the result over it would be an editorial that for breadth and depth exceeded anything the regular editorial force might devise. It was a genuine tribute to his ability to observe and put the result of his observations cogently on paper that his editorials invariably were printed and welcome.

He was an effortless typesetter, and his product was remarkably free from errors. What is more, when he dumped a take, it would lift. And that, as all printers in the handset days knew, was a desirable accomplishment. He was always, in my opinion, at least, a sort of prince-ambassador between the journeymen and the employers. The latter recognized him as an unusually capable workman and respected his learning as equal to if not superior to their own. I am sure that many of us lesser lights of traveling printers were many times hospitably received in our travels because there was the hope, though unvoiced and perhaps only subconsciously entertained, that we would turn out to have some of the qualities that so highly recommended Peter Bartlett Lee, the king of the tramps.

SUBSTITUTE SYSTEM

THROUGHOUT THE CENTURIES, printing jobs have always conferred higher social status on its workers than most other occupations of manual labor.[1] Consequently, the printing trade was continually deluged by learners, newcomers, and job applicants, encouraged by proprietors with a desire to maintain a generous labor pool from which to draw workers. This over-supply of printers tended to keep wages low in relation to the skills needed to become a printer. It also guaranteed a certain number of unemployed printers at any given time, with a number always seeking work while others were changing jobs to better their position. Since printing skills were interchangeable from printshop to printshop, quitting one job and going to another presented little challenge.

Another characteristic of printing is that work tends to be seasonal. Work loads fluctuate on different days of the week and at different seasons of the year; a major slack period falls in the summer and another after Christmas. Since more printers were available for employment than there were steady jobs, proprietors were able to hire enough extra help for the busy days or busy seasons, without paying overtime wages. Then, when business dropped off, the workforce could be trimmed with confidence that printers would be available when needed for the next rush. This led to a condition of "permanent" part-time employees. A regular staff of printers would be maintained—enough to handle the work during slow periods—and surplus work would be handled by a pool of day-to-day or week-

---

[1] See *Union Democracy*, Lipset, et al, pp 109-111

to-week employees. In this manner, labor costs rose and fell in tandem with income and profits.

This system of continual unemployment was a major factor in printers' appreciation for the Typographical Union. At least in a union shop, a worker received a certain amount of job protection. Those with longer service (called priority rather than seniority), were guaranteed they would be the last to be laid off. Those with lower priority received fair treatment when it came to handing out extra work. A complex system of rules, laws and customs evolved to ensure order in the workplace.

This system of underemployment created a remarkable sense of brotherhood, loyalty to the union and militancy among the rank-and-file ITU members. They were acutely aware that without strict enforcement of the union contract, union laws and chapel rules, they would be at the mercy of profit-minded employers, their jobs and livelihood at the whim of business cycles. This was the basis for the traditional militancy of the ITU.

Even in small composing rooms with half a dozen workers, union rules were rigidly enforced, not by the local union officers or representatives of the International, but by the workers themselves. In most other unions, small groups of workers are reluctant to stand up to management; they depend on the union business representative to make an employer observe contract conditions. They tend to shrug off minor contract violations as unimportant. But printers were acutely aware that their jobs depended on strict contract enforcement. They used custom, solidarity and loyalty to the union as a means of self-defense. Since the ITU's General Laws were incorporated into every union contract, printers in small shops used these laws as a shield. Fines for minor infractions could be imposed by the chapel on an individual who didn't observe the contract, and the local union could fine the chapel for not enforcing the contract. If the local union didn't impose a fine, the ITU could fine the local, the chapel and the individual union member. Therefore, pressure from "above" became the defense of a timid worker when the proprietor asked him to break the rules. "Gee, I'd like to do that, but I'd get into trouble with the Union." The more militant printer would simply tell the boss to "go pound sand." The worst that could happen would be that the boss would fire him and he would have to go across the street to work for another print shop.

Non-union printing plants experienced the same business cycles. They tried to resolve the problem by paying lower wages to fewer workers, working overtime during rush periods, and then laying off fewer regular workers during slack times. Non-union printers rarely were paid for overtime hours; they were expected to stay at work until the tasks were completed, and occasionally were given compensating time off during slack times. Frequently, they never got the time off.[2]

Non-union workers were always acutely aware of the higher wages, better benefits and fair working conditions awarded to union members. Often, as soon as they were good enough to qualify as journeymen and had the required six years experience, non-union printers would make a bee-line for the nearest union office to make application for union membership. They felt satisfied that working part-time for good wages and conditions was better than insecurity, unfairness, and abuse so common in non-union printing plants. This continual drain of competent printers cut into the low-wage advantage of non-union employers and leveled the playing field somewhat between them and union employers.

Evolution of the Slipboard

Because of this chronic condition of underemployment, a complicated system of rules and customs evolved for hiring substitutes in union-controlled plants. The mechanism was called a "slipboard," or a "sub-board." A slipboard was essentially a place for substitutes to place their names to indicate that they were available for work (usually on a slip of paper, hence the name "slipboard"). A new sub placed his name at the bottom of the list, thus acquiring a priority standing in the chapel. Once or twice a day there was a "show-up time" when the sub was expected to appear and wait to see

---

[2] This notion of non.paid overtime accounts for the Typographical Union's preoccupation with overtime, insisting that all overtime be paid at least time.and-a-half, and that the hours each individual worked be posted by the slipboard so everyone knew exactly how many hours were worked. The union also evolved a system whereby overtime was discouraged and even penalized.

if he were going to be hired.

When an extra printer was needed, the foreman had to hire the available substitute with the highest priority standing. When a regular situation-holder needed a day off from work, he or she could hire a substitute as well.[3]

An extremely important point is: all that was required to be available for work was to place one's name on the slipboard. There was no need to apply to management for a job, or to even talk with the foreman. The traveling printer simply presented his union card to the chapel chairman and waited for someone to hire him at show-up time.

The system was designed to distribute extra work .in a fair manner and to smooth over the ups and downs of business cycles. Two more innovations accomplished this by "storing up" work during busy periods and handing it out during slack times. Storing work was done by overtime cancellation and by resetting "bogus" ads.

Overtime cancellation worked this way: when a union member worked the number of hours to equal a shift's work (usually 7-1/2 or 8 hours) he was obligated to hire the first available substitute to "cancel" this overtime. Thus, during rush times, when everybody worked overtime to keep up with the work flow, the hours were stored up, ready to be given to printers who were laid off during slow periods. Instead of overtime being looked upon as a bonanza, as in most trades, printers regarded overtime as burdensome. Regular situation holders often grumbled about having to cancel their overtime, and referred to it as being "bumped," but most realized the overtime law's place in the scheme of union rules and regulations. Although employers occasionally complained when some of their key men were "bumped" they realized a benefit in that overtime was considered a necessary evil by employees, who they often worked hard to get the paper out *without* overtime. Furthermore, this system allowed the foreman to reduce the workforce without running the risk of subs leaving because of lack of work.

---

[3] Whereas the foreman always had to hire the high-priority substitute, situation-holders could often hire whomever they pleased; this was up to the local union's rules. Sometimes personal hires were made though drawing numbers, or "jeffing" to see who would get the day's work

The other method of storing up work was the "reproduction law" which was mandated to be included in all ITU contracts. This clause required the office to reproduce, or reset, all advertising matter which was exchanged from one newspaper to another. This practice originated back in the days when most cities had several competing newspapers, and was instituted by newspaper publishers themselves. The idea was to prevent competing newspapers from exchanging typeset advertisements to cut labor costs to the disadvantage of another competitor. In later years, particularly with the trend toward one-newspaper towns, publishers strenuously fought this rule. But the ITU held onto reproduction with stubbornness, and with some success, until the advent of "cold type" advertising. Reproduction came to be known by various semi-depreciatory terms, such as *bogus* or *deadhorse,* but was usually called "repro."

At first glance, this system of employment might seem somewhat overbearing, taking hiring options away from management (usually referred to as the "office" by composing room workers). But in practice it was beneficial to the office in several ways. Because the advertising work load varies widely in most newspapers—typically with large advertising volume on Wednesday, Thursday, and Sunday—it was to the composing room foreman's great advantage to have extra workers he could hire on busy days, and not be obligated to them on days when workloads were light. There was no need to hire extra Linotype operators for regular positions when only needed two or three days a week. Overtime was kept to a minimum and a sufficient number of employees ensured a smooth flow of work to meet deadlines. Another benefit: when someone became ill or unable to work for any reason, the absent employee had to hire a competent substitute to work in his place. This meant the foreman could count on a stable workforce. Finally, the foreman could cut payroll expenses when advertising volume slowed by laying off workers, with the assurance that most would remain in the shop as substitutes until work became abundant once more and they could be put on full-time jobs, or "situations" as they were called. Employees scheduled to work five days every week were known as "situation holders."

This right of an employee to hire a substitute without approval of the foreman was the key to worker mobility in the printing industry. Regular employees could decide at the last moment to go fishing and simply instruct the chapel chairman to hire a substitute for him. An unpaid vacation could last several months if the situation holder so desired. The slipboard not only provided unheard of flexibility for regular employees, but instilled a marvelous feeling of independence to all printers. They didn't *have* to go to work unless they damned well pleased! Few other tradesmen ever had this option.

Traveling Cards and Itchy Feet

Competent printers had little difficulty transferring their skills from one printshop to another. A new job was pretty much like the last one. Moving from place to place was often necessary, given the seasonal fluctuations in newspaper advertising and commercial printing as well as economic ups and downs. Losing a job wasn't particularly traumatic, since layoffs in one plant or town were often matched by labor shortages in other places. So, printers commonly changed employers, transferring from shop to shop or from town to town as necessary.

To make mobility even easier, the Typographical Union developed a system of "Traveling Cards" which certified that the bearer was a union member in good standing and "entitled to the good benefits" of membership. A printer could draw a "traveler" from one local and go to work in another town simply by handing his traveler to a chapel chairman and requesting that his name be placed on the slipboard. If a tramp printer timed it right, at show-up time, he could go to work immediately, and rent a hotel room after the shift was over. He needed no approval from the foreman to work, no application blanks to fill out, no physical examinations. Just a yellow piece of paper with the seal of the International Typographical Union.

Slipboards in the 1890s

The following excerpt from John Edward Hicks' book illustrates the employment situation in the 1890s:

"The Cincinnati *Commercial-Gazette,* I found, was a morning seven-day paper with sixty-two regulars and perhaps thirty to thirty-five subs. The building was at Fourth and Race streets with a stairway at the rear of the Race Street side, up which compositors toiled to the composing room which was located on the fifth floor. It was necessary for the printers to climb these stairs twice a day—at noon to throw in their cases for the night's work and in the evening when the actual composition was begun. The regulars drifted in around one o'clock in the afternoon and the subs waited to be hired."[4]

❄❄❄

As can be seen, the slipboard had one substitute for every two regular employees. This probably meant that subs had to show up for every shift to catch work. During slack periods, hiring would get worse, and those with the least priority would be tempted to move on.

Slipboards in the 1960s

This daily practice of showing up for work brought substitutes into close social contact, reinforcing a feeling of brotherhood and solidarity. This contributed to what sociologists call an "occupational community" among the substitutes. Rules of conduct and etiquette evolved which were separate from the formal chapel rules. Substitutes abided by their own code of honor, helped each other when possible, and shared information about where work could be found. The process bonded subs with friendship and brotherhood much stronger than that found among regular situation holders.

The following extract from the book *Union Democracy* shows that in New York City, in the 1950s and 1960s, the substitute system was intact and of great importance:

"[In New York City] substitutes are hired day by day. Every printer working in a print shop, regularly or as a substitute, has a priority number within that shop, assigned according to the length of

---

[4] *Adventures of a Tramp Printer,* John Edward Hicks, MidAmerica Press, Kansas City, MO, 1950

time he has been in the shop. However, the company's daily hiring of *substitutes* is not carried out in accordance with priority. Instead, the chapel chairman holds a lottery in which each sub draws a numbered ball. Those men with the highest numbers get the positions for the day while those with lower numbers are out of luck for that shift.

"The first consequence of this procedure is that every man feels constrained to show up every day. Those subs who do not get work find themselves downtown with nothing to do for the rest of the day. (Subs are permitted to show up on all three shifts if they like.) Many men who do not get work in the morning will often show up for the evening shift as well. If a man needs money badly, he may show up for all three shifts, trying his luck each time."[5]

---

[5] *Union Democracy,* by Lipset, Trow, and Coleman. Macmillian, New York, 1956

JOHN BARLEYCORN

THE OLDTIME PRINTER was a product of his environment and time, which were not exactly conducive to producing angelic characters. Nearly all papers were published in the morning, which, of course, meant night work. The hours were long and the work exacting and nerve-wracking. The composing room too frequently was a space not useable for any other purpose; it was poorly lighted, ill ventilated and subject to extremes of summer and winter temperatures. Printers worked while others slept, slept while others worked. They became in a certain sense social outcasts, nomads, their habitat the North American continent.

Under a system where work was uncertain and irregular at best, substitutes spent a great deal of time socializing with other substitutes. Those who failed to "catch" work, had several hours before the next shift, and naturally passed the time with other subs who also missed out. A natural tendency was to head for the nearest bar, to start a card game, or engage in other activities with their companions. In this way the subs socialized with one another throughout their entire substitute period. When they "went on the road," they traveled together, had many mutual sub friends, and took care of each other wherever they might go. Their paths crisscrossed often during their careers as itinerant printers.

Substitutes also found it necessary to ingratiate themselves with regular situation-holders, because regulars could usually choose who they wanted to work for them when they took a day off from work. Therefore, a sub's work opportunities were enhanced to some extent by an ability to make friends among other printers in the shop. This accounts for the winning personalities of many tramp printers; being liked and trusted by situation holders and foremen alike made it much easier to pick up work any time the traveler drifted into town. A likable character would be welcomed back as an old friend, with everyone going out of their way to make him feel at home again. Someone with a bad personality, poor work habits, or an extreme alcohol problem found it more difficult to catch plentiful hires. That's not to say some misfits didn't travel anyway. In fact, an inability to get along probably accounted for some traveling patterns.

Given the nature of the work system, it shouldn't be surprising that substitutes in general, and tramp printer substitutes in particular, spent a good deal of their spare time drinking. The saloon across from a newspaper served as a tramp printer's social club—the printers leaning against the bar substituted for the tramp's family. When substitutes drank, it almost always would be in the company of other printers, either regulars or substitutes. Of the stories presented to the *Tramp Printers' Newsletter* the vast majority involved drinking or took place in bars or saloons.

Jim White (died in El Paso about five years ago) said, "Tramp printers did have their share of good times, mostly centered around saloons of one kind or another. There was always at least one hangout near the newspapers in every town. In Juarez everyone remembers Fred's Rainbow (Fred Mendez died some time ago) and Don Felix's on Juarez Ave. In El Paso it was the Stag Bar, also known as the Stagger Inn, a block from the Times Building. In Washington it was Randy's near the *Post*, and another Randy's near the P-I in Seattle. In Chicago, many bars seemed to be "downstairs", the Grand Rush, Ohio Inn, Radio Grill, and of course St. Louis Browns Fan Club. In St. Louis it was the Press Box and Typo Grill. Most tourists stayed at the McKinley Hotel. In Cleveland the Headliner and Pat Joyce's and the Eagles, where you could get a drink on Sundays. There was the New York Bar and the Jackson Bar in Toledo, and "anonymous" joints everywhere. Frisco had Breen's by the *Examiner* and the Oaken Bucket across from the *Chronicle*.

"At the Washington *Post* a floorman on the lobster shift had the booze concession, with an apron full of miniature bottles of whiskey. Old Crow went for 50 cents . . . they were easier to hide and dispose of than half-pints. In Albuquerque, Sundays were dry, so we brought coolers of beer and had some good parties on the parking lot. In Fairbanks, Pete Peterman kept his Early Times in a Listerine bottle, going to the john to gargle several times a night.

"This is not to say that *all* tramp printers drank. But all the ones I knew did!"

❄❄❄

The following stories illustrate the sense of camaraderie and socialization which involved alcohol. The tales come from tramp printers, and are typical of the stories they used to relate when they would come in "off the road", and slip up at a newspaper or printing plant.

Salty Boardman
John Edward Hicks, early 1900s

"Salty" Boardman, printer, was in appearance the typical bad man of the West, with his high-crowned black hat angling on his head and wearing a long flowing necktie. He had a coal-black mustache and a cocked eye that was so badly off the beam it was impossible to tell where he was looking. He wasn't really tough, but had all the appearances. One night when he was laying off and drinking, he tried his luck at faro and won several hundred dollars. He came up to the composing room to tell us of his luck and invited the entire force to have dinner as his guest when time was called in the morning. He had made all arrangements with a fancy and high-priced cafe. But when we showed up for the eats, "Salty's" luck had changed and he was flat broke, with the caterer swearing vengeance. Oh, well, the chili down at the corner wasn't bad.

Brownies Bar
Don Cleary, 1960s

Brownie's Bar has been a printers' hangout in Ft. Lauderdale for as long as it has been there. It's the oldest bar in town. Paul Newman filmed a movie here once and some scenes took place in Brownie's. It's a shot-draft type saloon, where if you pile up peanut shells in the ashtray, the bartender (Frank or Ernie) comes along, picks up the ashtray, and throws the shells at the floor behind you.

On lunch breaks we'd all pile into the chairman's car and head for Brownies; Frank and Ernie would have the beer poured and sandwiches half made by the time we got there. Ed Wernike was chairman in those days. Of course we were always late getting back to work because the drawbridge would usually be up to allow the "Jungle Queen" cruise ship to pass. If it wasn't, we told the boss it was and gave him a bag of peanuts. That always pacified him, just like any monkey.

Federal Bar, Albuquerque
Jack Renter and Frank Graham, 1940s

In mentioning printers' bars, don't forget the Federal Bar (now gone) in Albuquerque where many a printer's wristwatch adorned the bottles on the back bar as security for bar bill. Then in Cleveland, there was: Mickey's Radio Grill, Billy Goat, Grand Rush, Bob & Junes, Bowl Mich, Trotter's Ohio Inn, Queen's Paradise and the King's Palace, etc., etc. And don't forget the Texas Ranch.

It was in Cleveland when a tramp printer went out to lunch one night, got to enjoying himself too much to go back to work. Assuming that he'd been fired, he returned three nights later to collect pay for the half-day's work. When he came into the composing room, the foreman jumped him, screaming, "Where the hell have you been? You're late! Get to work!" Things were so confusing, with new tramps, one-town tramps and all that overtime, that the foreman didn't know who was working where or on what shift. The guy got paid for the week!

Another time a tramp named Rigsby was slugged up on the Chicago *Tribune*. After belting away a few drinks at lunch he forgot where he was working. He entered the *Sun-Times* composing room and was pounding away on the keyboard for about half an hour before the foreman (Koerner, I believe) told him that he was working on the wrong rag.

Gilmore's Zoo, Indianapolis
John Edward Hicks, 1890s

"When I was in Indianapolis, Gilmore's Zoo was in North Mississippi Street, across from the State House. It was a burlesque house with a bar attachment—something on the free and easy order ... one of the better class saloons was the House of Lords on West Washington. Then there was Pat Welsh's bar on the south side of Washington Street between Illinois and Meridian; and Bird's Point at Illinois Street and Indiana Avenue, which were frequented by the typographers. There were other places, too, that arrested the attention of those who juggled the silent little messengers of thought, such as the Corn Exchange and the saloons of Henry Smith, Charley Lauer ... to say nothing of Doc Zapf's Washington Hall where a thirsty printer could get a drink and play a game of cocked hat.

Frisco Birthday Party
Don Cleary, 1950s

In San Francisco, the printers had a private club a few blocks from the newspaper where Bob Brice and I used to go to play cards 'til dawn. The fridge was usually stocked with beer and a cigar box for contributions. One day Pappy Hilton, a well-liked makeup man showed up in town. We found out his birthday was coming up soon. So his big-hearted printer buddies got him a birthday cake and took it to the club on the night of his birthday.

Pappy didn't show up right away, and we found that no one thought to bring any candles. But someone found a box of big wooden matches, so we stuck them upside down in the cake instead of candles. We played more cards and drank Lucky Lager. Towards dawn Pappy came out of the rickety elevator, feeling no pain, giving no explanation as to why he was late for his birthday party. The card game broke up and we all sang "happy birthday." Then someone lit the "candles." Pappy leaned over to blow out the candles while all gathered around telling him to "make a wish.

But someone had stuck a two-inch salute firecracker into the cake, fuse up, and it was lit along with the matches. When the salute went off, it didn't leave a bit of cake on the plate; it was all over the walls and ceiling. A few days later Pappy told us: "That was the best damn birthday cake I ever had."

St Louis Printers' Saloons
Lou Brueske, 1950s, 1960s

The bars near the St. Louis *Globe* were: the Typo Bar (at one time a swinging place); the Chili Bowl and Bar (later the Press Box). These were the hangouts for drinking your lunch. On 12th Street, was the Missouri Mule (now Missouri Grill) where printers from all three papers ate. Next door was Pete's Bar and Grill, a small place, but where most tramps first hitting town went. It was owned by Pete Catanazaro and his wife Gert. They liked the tramp printers and granted them credit for food, a few drinks and maybe a few dollars for room rent until payday. Pete would even call in sick for you if you were too sloshed to go to work. He would call the cash-in man for you, and if he okayed a loan, Pete would give you the money and the cash-in man would pay him. Pete and Gert died several years ago, then it became Larry's 711 Club. A retired *Post-Dispatch* proofreader ran it for a while, but today (1972) it is called The Front Page; the younger travelers of the 60s and 70s probably know it by this name.

Jakle's Chapel
John Edward Hicks, 1890s

"When I arrived in Terre Haute, I went immediately to the saloon of John Jakle at Fourth and Ohio streets, where it was only necessary to lay a printer's rule on the bar to get a drink. This jovial old German, known to the printers as Jake, would stake a traveler to a meal ticket and a room until work could be found. He told me he never lost a cent on a tramp printer, for as soon as they got work, they would come to him on their first pay day and repay the money advanced and in many cases pay the bill of some pal who had failed to get work. His place was known to the touring fraternity throughout the country as Jakle Chapel."

Christmas Party 1953
Lou Brueske, 1950s

I enjoyed my many years on the road, meeting hundreds of

printers in all parts of the Great ITU-USA and the satisfaction of working in many different composing rooms . . . commercial, news, trade shops, etc. Most of the time it was exciting, but it could get rather lonesome in a new town, especially around the Christmas holidays. One exception I remember was Christmas 1953.

Several of us tramps were staying at the York Hotel at Geary and Jones in San Francisco and we decided to have a Christmas party. We all chipped in to rent an extra room, buy food, booze, etc. It lasted several days. WHAT A PARTY! Those attending were: William G. (Bill) Smith, Albert (Al) Kusch, (Big) Bill Kerschoff, Gene Hodges, Dick (Little Richard) Guthrie, Rolla (Bob) Roberts, Clarence Brohoff, Byron (Jake) Jacobs, Hubert (Frenchie) Desaulniers ... all coast-to-coast tramp printers; and a fellow named Gus from Detroit (either a pressman or stereotyper), and a proofreader known as Shanghai Lil.

All of the above have gone West long ago and no doubt are slipped up on that Great Print Shop in the Sky — God rest their souls. As far as I know, John Burt, Martin Tunnel and myself are the only ones still kicking of those who attended the party. It was like a Christmas family get-together, for in those IT we all looked after one another just as fraternal brothers should.[1]

Christmas Eve at the L.A. Examiner
from Don Cleary, 1950s

It was 1956, on Christmas Eve—a group of editors came trooping through the composing room, accompanied by a bunch of Disneyland characters in full costume, (Mickey Mouse and friends). They sang Christmas carols and brought bottles of liquid cheer for their printer friends. The Disney cast would sing a joyous carol, then pull out a bottle and hand it to an editor. He would crack it open, take a swig and hand it to a nearby printer who would take a swallow and pass it on.

The composing room was huge, having at one time been the

---

[1] This was written 15 years ago, and I'm sure almost all of the party celebrants have passed away. Lou Brueske died ten years ago.

pressroom (so I was told), so the merry troop sang quite a few carols and handed out quite a few bottles. The Managing Editor became quite a popular guy that night, and also became quite mellow, as you can imagine!

San Mateo Celebrations
John Howells, 1950s

To those who traveled out to the West Coast, the San Mateo *Times* was known as a good place to catch some overtime and get "well" for the next leg of your journey. The foreman, a feisty rooster by the name of "Tex" Mobley, enjoyed a battle more than anything. He loved to try and browbeat the help and terrorize the chairman. His main frustration was that not many took him seriously. His favorite stunt was to fire someone by yelling for the chairman and pointing at his enemy screaming in his West Texas accent: "That there man is farred and barred!"[2]

As far as I can remember, Tex seldom made a discharge stick, but that didn't deter him. He fired men right and left, fast and furious, and the chapel voted the discharged members back to work just as fast. Sometimes a fired printer would simply ignore him and keep on working. On one occasion, Tex fired the chapel chairman three times in one night and finally called the police to try and get them to remove the contemptuous chairman from the premises. That didn't work either. Firing a printer who was in the process of quitting anyway was Tex's way of making himself feel important. Those who worked there in Tex Mobley's day could fill several issues of the *Tramp Printer's Newsletter* with amusing incidents.

My story: most of the "sporting men" on the night shift acquired the habit of going to the Linotype machinist's apartment for beer and cards after work, especially on payday. The bars were closed after we finished our shift plus overtime. Since none of us got home much

---

[2] When a printer was fired, the foreman could bar him from being employed in the plant for up to six months. However, the fired employee could demand a chapel meeting, and the chapel could vote to overrule the foreman and reinstate the discharged printer. Surprisingly enough, the chapel usually upheld the foreman's decision unless the discharge was obviously unfair or unjust.

before daylight, we were understandably lethargic on the next shift. One payday, Tex warned us that if we didn't go home and get a good night's rest, he would "farr and barr" the kit and kaboodle of us guts, feathers and all! He especially warned his machinist to stop "keepin' my boys up all night 'til they ain't worth a damn the next day."

Of course, we went to the machinist's apartment as usual and stayed until dawn. A few of the crew couldn't make the next shift. Tex was furious. He charged up to where the machinist was working on the Intertype G-4 "bomber." Quadder and saw parts lay strewn about the floor as if a tornado had struck. There were only two ad mills in the place, so half of the "ad row" was down at that time.

"Smitty, you is farred and barred!" Tex screamed hysterically. He bounced about like a bantam rooster, waiting for his victim to plead for his job. But when the machinist simply shrugged his shoulders and headed for the door, Tex's eyes grew big as ping-pong balls. "Wait, now! You come back here right now, and fix this here machine! You hear me?" But Smitty had a cool drink on his mind and had little intention of returning before he had one.

Tex ran along behind shouting, "Smitty, if you don't come back here and put this machine back together, you is *really* farred and barred!" Tex had to follow the machinist to the Captain's Cabin bar and buy two double Jack Daniels and promise to behave before the machinist would consider returning to put the ad mill back together.

LEGENDS IN THEIR TIME

[A] man's work is one of the most important parts of his social identity, of his self; of his fate in the one life he has to live, for there is something almost as irrevocable about choice of occupation as there is about choice of mate.[1] Work is so fundamental to the life of man, that we cannot understand the human condition unless we can make some sense of the ways in which man comes to terms with his work; these terms provide clues to the ways in which men live out their lives and see their destinies. Indeed, for many, work becomes a "central life interest" in which the concerns of the workplace intrude on and inform nonwork relationships.[2]

IN COMPOSING ROOMS throughout North America, whenever the conversation touched on Tramp Printers, certain characters were sure to be discussed. These were true celebrities in their own circles, legends in their own time.

At the end of this chapter are listed the names of well-known travelers who either have been mentioned to this book's authors, or who were personally known by us. Surely some readers will recall other names to add to the list. Feel free to contact us and fill us in. There will surely be revises of this book before long. As we scan this list in late 1995, we notice that many of these are truly past history.

---

[1] Everett C. Hughes, "Work and the Self," in John H. Rofhrer and Muzafer Sherif, eds. Social Psychology at the Crossroads (Harper, New York, 1951, pp. 313-23).

[2] Hughes, p. 127. Work and Workers: a Sociological Analysis (2nd. ed.) Lee Braude. Robert E. Krieger Pub. Co., Malabar, Fla. 1983.

The 1920s created some famous tramp printers, but those who could, settled down during the Depression. Some, however, became so used to the life of a vagabond, and so enjoyed traveling that they continued tramping until the end of their lives, bridging the lush 20s, the tough 30s and into the once-again easy 40s and 50s. One example of this is Nate Bergman.

Nate Bergman, the Wandering Jew

Nate Bergman, the self-styled "Wandering Jew," was a tramp printer who truly enjoyed and exploited his status as a celebrity. He made a point of contacting news reporters on the papers wherever he worked, and enjoyed the publicity. He always carried a stack of news clippings. Reporters loved the human interest angle of a Jewish "hobo" gentleman printer. No doubt, during the Depression days, Nate hitchhiked and occasionally caught rides on boxcars, but I suspect he exaggerated some when interviewed by newswriters. As far as we can tell, he never drank, was always neatly-dressed (always wore a tie), and in later years traveled in a late-model car, not the boxcars that he bragged about to reporters.

Because he didn't get along with his father, Nate took to the road rather early in life. He learned to set type in Evanston, Wyoming, and left for Ellensburg, Washington, as soon as he felt himself proficient. That was the first of many, many moves. Nate was proud of his Russian-Jewish heritage, and always introduced himself saying, "I'm Nate Bergman, the Wandering Jew." But, apparently, he never practiced the religion. He once told of attending his wealthy father's funeral in Cheyenne, Wyoming. The relatives wanted him to say a Jewish "kaddish," and since he knew nothing of Jewish prayer and ritual, they had to teach him what to do. But when Nate discovered that his father left his estate to his young wife, Nate told them, "Go ahead and pray—but without me. You got the money."

Below are stories collected about Nate Bergman.

❅ ❅ ❅

from Chris Frishe

The first time I met Nate Bergman, "The Wandering Jew," was in July 1919 at the Walgreen Printing Co., in Denver, Colorado. I was in the second week of my apprenticeship, and had learned to sort leads and slugs and put them in the racks, using the wooden line gauge given to me the first day I worked. I had advanced to the point where I had started to learn the case, and was trying to do so, when I glanced up and saw a group of journeymen gathered around a well-dressed man. They were looking at me, so I ducked my head and studied the case.

A few minutes later, I noticed the well-dressed gentleman approaching. He stopped at my side and asked, "How are things going, young man?"

"I think all right," I answered nervously. "I'm beginning to learn the case."

"That's good. I am Mr. Walgreen, the owner of this plant, which is part of a chain, all over the country. I'm making my yearly visit to this branch. The journeymen here tell me you are catching on rapidly. I'm certain you'll make a good printer." Then he shook my hand and said, "If you ever come to Chicago in the future, be sure to visit me."

I was proud as a peacock that a big shot like Mr. Walgreen had treated me so royally. I noticed that the journeymen appeared to be amused at this, but I could hardly wait to tell my father, who was a Linotype operator on the *Times*. As I related the story to him later, he listened attentively, and then smiled broadly when I finished.

"Son, you were the victim of a trick they play on all apprentices there at Walgreen's. That Mr. Walgreen you described is a famous tramp printer, Nate Bergman, who calls himself the 'Wandering Jew'."

from Lou Brueske

The first real tramp printer I can remember meeting was Nate Bergman (the Wandering Jew). It was about 1931-32 while I was still going to high school and working in a country weekly. I was about 15 years old. During the summer vacation I went to work at 8 a.m. and finished up at 6 p.m., Monday through Saturday. But

Wednesday, we usually worked until 8 or 9 p.m. and Thursday sometimes until midnight — until the paper was printed and ready to mail. For this the owner paid me $3 a week. One day Nate Bergman dropped off a freight train and stopped into the printshop. Turns out that boss knew Nate Bergman quite well.

The boss told me, "Son, you watch this *real* printer and you might learn something." Nate made up an ad, hand set it all. What with the time he spent shooting the bull with the boss, I guess it took him an hour or so. By this time it was time for lunch, and the boss took Bergman to his home for a noon meal. When they returned, Nate said he didn't want to work any more, because he wanted to catch the next freight.

The boss said that was fine, and he paid Nate Bergman five bucks for what little time he worked. I wasn't happy about this, since I was getting only three dollars for the whole week! Anyhow, on Thursday night, as the boss made up the back page for the final press run, he picked up that ad, it fell apart.

When he started to raise hell with me, I pointed out that his tramp printer buddy was the one who made it up. He cooled down, remade the ad and we finally got the paper out about 2 a.m.

One good thing came out of that: on payday that next Saturday, the boss raised my pay to $4 a week. Many years later I met and worked with the "Wandering Jew" in many places, but always west of the Mississippi River. I don't think he ever traveled East.

from Chet Pyle

I was ITU - Chairman of the Oregon Journal, Portland, Oregon 1956-1957. During that time I was fortunate to have Nathan Bergman (the original Wandering Jew) on the extra board for about six months. He told me how he had worked on most of the major newspapers in all the major cities in the country.

He told me that being a tramp printer was not a good idea, if one is married. Which prompted me to query him about his physical and female contact needs. His reply was that there was a nice, clean brothel at The Dalles, Oregon, which he visited occasionally—about 60 miles East of Portland.

I found him to be a clean and well-dressed man. He told me that earlier in his life, he had "ridden the rails," but at the time I met him, he traveled in a late-model car. I guessed his age at about 55-60 years. The last that I read about Nathan was that he had retired in New Mexico. (I am now almost 85 years old myself.)

❈❈❈

from Leo Baker

The last time I saw Nate, he was on pension, but needed money, so he slipped up and tried to work. He didn't do very well, could hardly see. I remember he got a rough correction that needed some close sawing. I did the sawing for him, and he made the shift. Nate had his faults and wasn't the neatest printer I ever worked with, but he was a hard worker, even after he got older. If I remember correctly, he passed away at the Printers Home a few years back.

❈❈❈

John Henry Curtin

John Curtin was another Depression era tramp printer who continued traveling after the war into the "good times." John was an intellectual, the epitome of a "gentleman" tramp. He didn't drink, he was always well dressed (always in a suit and tie), and had the vocabulary of a college professor. It wouldn't come as a surprise if we discovered that Curtin had an extensive university education, but if not, he was clearly one of the more successful of the self-educated tramp printers. He finally settled down in Davenport, California, a little town up the coast from Santa Cruz. He called his new home "The Garden of I Love You, Newtown-by-the-Sea." He deposited his union card with San Jose ITU Local 231, and faithfully drove across the mountains for every union meeting, always with constructive ideas and suggestions to contribute to the assembly.

John Curtin loved to write letters and enclose interesting news clippings and always included some of his poetry with his letters. Those who corresponded with John will remember that he liked to write his messages with different colored pens, sometimes making each word a different color. He spent his last years writing poetry and working for worth-while causes, not the least of which was a public relations campaign for labor unions. He was a true gentleman.

❋❋❋

from Don Cleary

When I was at the *LA. Examiner,* I met John Henry Curtin and Bunny Bunce. We made a pact to meet the following winter in West Palm Beach at the *Post-Times.* (Bunny Bunce told me that as a young man he had posed for a statue in Rockefeller Park in New York City. He still had a good build and I think he was beyond 65 at that time.) That following year I walked into the Palm Beach *Post-Times* and there, sitting at a machine was John Henry Curtin. Bunny didn't make it. John said Bunny had died, and that this would be John's "last trip around this great country." He said he was going back to California to settle down. He was proud that he had a son that was a college professor out there.

John Curtin was also a poet and he self-published several volumes of his work. Here is one he wrote when he was in his 80s, living in Davenport, California.

For All My Familiar Friends ...

With clocks and calendars, we make our own recording of Time.
If we had no Time, would we have Age?
Would we all live in Eternity?
I wish to live in Eternity now. Each year, I welcome Spring.
So I shall try to welcome— Death.
Each is a part of life. Both are familiar friends!
Being Eighty and a little bit, these words are my will:

To Sundry Survivors

When I shall die, without much fame nor shame,
Just plant a tree and, near it, plant my frame.
For folks will come to rest there in the shade
And they will still amuse me, I'm afraid!

Let none feel sorry! Spare me tawdry tears!
I'll have the kind of rest I've missed for years!
I'll just stretch out and yawn and wait and see
How well the world gets on . . . without much me!
There may be Time enough to comprehend
The love of Enemy and hate of Friend.
There may be Time to learn the reasons why
No goods have worth . . . That Goodness will not buy.
But, if there isn't then these thoughts shall pass
While I remain . . . to fertilize the grass!

—JOHN HENRY CURTIN

❄❄❄

Jumpin' Joe Owens
from John Howells

An operator with a slight drinking problem, Jumpin' Joe earned his name not because he failed to show up for work occasionally—known as *jumping the job*— but because of his proclivity for jumping from city to city. He was an example of a tramp printer who bridged the Depression area through the "golden years" of tramp printing, from the end of the war to the 1970s.

Although he drank every day, and often a goodly amount, this writer never remembered Jumpin' Joe ever fail to turn in a good day's work at the Linotype. I can't remember ever seeing him not able to handle his liquor. He always dressed neatly, and wore a suit and a tie to work, like most Depression-era printers. The following is my favorite story about Jumpin' Joe:

One time, the foreman at the San Jose *Mercury News* fired a proofreader for coming to work intoxicated. Back in those days we customarily called chapel meetings to determine whether the discharge was acceptable to the chapel or not. During the chapel meeting, the head proofreader—a pompous office man whom everyone, detested—testified against the unfortunate member. There was sufficient evidence that the proofreader was probably drunk, but the head proofreader's arrogance influenced chapel members to vote against the foreman and reinstate the discharged printer.

But Jumpin' Joe wasn't satisfied. He was sitting in Duffy's Tavern (across from the newspaper) nursing a drink when in came the head proofreader. Joe stood up, glared at the "homeguard officeman" for a moment. Then he belted him with a roundhouse right. The next day the proofreader came charging up to the local president and demanded that he do something. A crowd of printers gathered around, enjoying the scene. Jumpin' Joe stood by the slipboard and glowered threateningly.

The president answered that there was nothing he could do since the attack occurred off company premises and not on company time. "But," he added, "If had I been at Duffy's at the time, I might have been able to do something."

"What would you have done?"

"I would have held you, so Joe could take another shot before you could run away." (I happened to be president of ITU 231 at that time.)

Gulf Coast Guy Foley

Many claim that "Gulf Coast" Guy Foley was the champion traveler of the later-day tramp printers. Every printer, when asked to list tramp printers they've known or heard of placed Gulf Coast Guy Foley toward the top of the list. Guy claimed to have had more than 900 traveling cards. He was another who worked during the last two golden years of tramping, bridged by the Depression years.

Reprinted from ITU REVIEW Oct. 3, 1974

When Frank J. Graham wrote to ITU Headquarters to express his regrets over the death of Guy C. Foley, the ITU Review contacted several locals to find a picture of the well-known traveling printer. The search has proven fruitless. Even Guy's sister, Mrs. Mary E. Oeakle, in Biloxi, Miss., could not help. "Guy traveled too much," she said "I guess he didn't hold still long enough to have his picture taken."

Guy Foley learned the printing trade in his hometown in Mobile, and was initiated by Sheffield-Florence #802 in 1925. One week later Guy hit the road to Birmingham and from then on his life was one of travel. He went from Birmingham to Mobile, to Atlanta, to Key West, to Okmulgee, to Memphis, to Little Rock. By the time he deposited his last traveling card in his hometown, Mobile, on June 9,1973, Guy Foley had had a total of 918 cards. Most of his traveling time was spent in the south. He returned to Mobile a total of 55 times, to Shreveport 45 times, to Austin 40 times, Atlanta 37 times, Montgomery 34 times, Houston 30 times. Other cities he liked were Baton Rouge, Chattanooga, Birmingham, San Antonio, Macon, Memphis, Temple, Dallas and scores of others.

Rarely did this famous traveler go west. In 1945 he spent one day each in Denver, Colorado Springs and Pueblo. In 1947 he was in Glendale, Fresno, San Francisco and Los Angeles, San Diego and Bakersfield saw him briefly in 1961.

Several times Guy entered the hospital at the Union Printers Home. Twice he left after successful treatment. Then there were times when he tangled with Rule 27-B and lost.[3]

G. C. Foley died in the Mobile General Hospital on May 10, 1974, in the city where he was born seventy years earlier, and was laid to rest in the Magnolia Cemetery. "I will miss him," says Frank Graham, "We were long-time friends." Now that he is gone, Guy would want it known that the initials 'G. C did not stand for 'Gulf Coast,' or 'Good Conduct' or Good Credit,' as many of his pals had kiddingly told him: it was Guy Christopher Foley.

from Franklin M. White

A few bits of "Foleyana": I believe Guy circulated in the East occasionally. I seem to recall his story about proofreading on one of the big Boston papers and "getting away with it" although some of

---

[3] Rule 27-B was a rule against getting drunk on the Home property. Because so many of the home residents were drinkers, the rule was enforced rather loosely. (Behavior necessary for expulsion had to be somewhat outrageous.) Gulf Coast Guy became an ITU pensioner in 1966. Still, he liked to travel. From April 1966 to June 1973, he took 57 more traveling cards.

the readers were Harvard graduates. He was quite literate, excellent on proofs. Although a "hand-man," Guy told me of working a shift as an operator. I think it was on the Pueblo *Chieftain*.

His disarming smile and sly humor were appreciated by all and everybody joined his smiles when they heard Foley indicate he wanted to quit the road. Perhaps he held a few situations, but moving on seemed inexorable or inevitable. He complained little. He opposed injustice, disapproved of incompetence, despised hypocrisy, frowned on 'cardholders" disloyal to working class, and despised selfishness in general. But he rather accepted things as they were and "let it go at that." Guy was well-read and a keen observer, he was difficult to describe but easy to anticipate. He frequented libraries until later when he became virtually bed-ridden. He kept in close contact with his mother and sister, visiting them often.

I suppose my brother-in-law, "Italics" Whitaker was his best friend for about 20 years. Whit said Foley was beaten up by a cop in Chattanooga or Nashville, which hastened his passing. Being badly handicapped after that, he didn't venture to North, Northeast or West in his last few years. He had been bounced from the Printers' Home a number of times for "imbibing too many bubbles" and was unable to spend his last days there.

❈❈❈

from Lou Breuske, another Foley tale

Ran into Guy (Gulf Coast) Foley several times and places over the years. One of those times recalled was either in February 1952 or '53. I had just hit New Orleans and was looking at the slipboard on the New Orleans *Item* (The *Item* was union in those days). I heard someone holler "Put that man to work, put that man to work!" I looked up and saw the chairman and foreman with Guy, each holding Guy's arms, trying to get him out of the composing room — drunk. A couple nights later, the chairman asked me to go with him to get Guy out of jail. It cost five bucks; we split the deal.

After work ran out on the *Item*, I took a traveler and went to Mobile and slipped up on the *Register*. Guy was there along with Guy Hatcher, Little Eddie O'Donnell and wife Mary, Felton Legge and

Carl Fikes. Gulf Coast got on another one and ended up in the pokey. Fikes and I went and got him out. Guy left town.

About a week later, Fikes and I pulled our slips and went to Pensacola, on the *Journal*. Foley was there, and buddying with Dick Sieber. Guy was on another one, and ended up in jail there. Again Fikes and I got him out. Guy was broke, so he passed his card at the shop to leave town and got a good haul. A couple of nights later he is back at the shop, panhandling. The chapel took up another collection, but this time the chairman took Foley down to the bus station and bought a ticket. But he made the mistake of giving Guy the ticket. As soon as the chairman left the depot, Guy cashed the ticket in. A night or so later, here he comes again, passing his card. By that time the homeguards wouldn't give a thing and passed the word not to give him a cent. After he went through the shop, he came back to me with such a pitiful look and clicking teeth with his thumb (you oldtimers remember that habit?). I felt sorry for him and reached in my pocket and pulled out four bucks, and told him that was all I had, but would split it with him. I gave him the two and asked what he was going to do with it. He replied, "Going to get a bottle, what do you think?" Everybody in the composing room was mad at me.

After Fikes and I got off *work*, we went to the bus depot to get something to eat and ran into Foley on the street. He said he wanted to go to Macon, Georgia if he could get a ticket. Fikes and I took him in and bought him a ticket, but wouldn't give it to him until the bus was ready to pull out. We gave it to the driver and told him not to let Guy off until he got to Macon, and gave Guy a quarter for spending money after he got there.

In February 1963, I was in San Antonio and had an operator sit on the Express, and Guy had a proofreader sit on the *Light* (yes, even with OT). We had the sits about three weeks, and ate lunch at the same time. One night I said to Guy, "You know, if any of those tramps found out that you and I were home guarding San Antonio, they'd expel us from the Tramp Printer Benevolent Society." The next night he doesn't show for lunch. I asked one of the printers that usually came with him to the cafe; he told me that all the way back to the shop, Guy kept saying, "I don't want to get kicked out of that society." He went up and pulled his slip.

I don't know how many times he was in the Union Printers Home after that, but I remember I saw him in Pete's Bar in St. Louis and he had just left the home "completely cured." The next month's Journal showed he'd been cured by Rule 27-B. (A violation of "rule 27-B" of course, meant excessive drinking, cause for expulsion.)

"Gulf Coast" Guy Foley was one of the most likeable printers I ever met. Every time I'd see him it cheered me. God rest his soul!

Sam Ball

Another famous tramp from the 1930s and early 1940s was Sam Ball. He and Gulf Coast Guy Foley often traveled about together. Sam Ball may have wandered fartherafield than Guy, but he was better known in the South.

source unknown, written about 1974

The last I heard Sam Ball was still moving now and then. It was a good idea, because the older he became the more ornery and rambunctious he got. I believe he was married, and perhaps had kids. Until he reached his middle 30s, Sam was a nice fellow, always agreeable and sociable. About 1935 he became a part-time rough character, gained about 40 or 50 pounds. A few drinks and became a belligerent cuss. Last time I saw him, he came to the *Times* composing room and tried to bully several people, including me. At lunch time, several of us were eating at the cafe next door. Sam came in and argued with the cashier about something and threatened to wreck the joint. A waitress called the cops. Sam rushed outside bellering, "She called the law!" and lumbered toward the bus station. Another story about "Sentimental Sam" was when he worked a shift at the Mobile paper and wanted to cash-in. The foreman refused to cash him in, so "Sentimental Sam" grabbed the form for page one, which was ready for the mat roller and held it hostage. He brandished a mallet as a weapon, refusing to release the page until he was paid off.

Stutterin' Walker

from Ed (Bing Bang) Burr

It warms my heart to think back about all the people I knew, both as a homeguard and as a traveler. I knew Stutterin' Walker pretty well. We first met in Newark, N.J. back in 1928. Walker came in from Texas driving a Gardner touring car, Continental motor and all. He knew a place in New York City where he could get way over the scale for about three months work. But the Gardner didn't fit New York living, so I offered him $60 for it. He stayed around Newark, working some, until I had it all paid for. I didn't know how to drive very well—you should have been riding with me up busy Broad Street on Saturday night with quite a few ounces under my belt. Didn't dent a fender, but they sure did some ducking! The last time I saw Walker was in 1960. My wife and I had him over to our house for dinner.

from Lou Brueske

Believe it or not, my wife Del thinks Stutterin' Walker is the best. He was the only one to give us a wedding present; he brought a bottle of champagne to our apartment in Chicago, the first and only time I ever saw him dressed up in a new suit, white shirt and tie!

from John Howells

One of my favorite stories happened in San Jose at the *Mercury*. "Stutterin'" Walker slipped up one day and the foreman knew that Walker had a reputation for doing a little nipping on the job, so he resolved to watch him very closely. Every time Stutterin' Walker would go to the locker room, the foreman followed. He saw nothing out of line. Yet it was obvious that Walker would begin the shift sad and sober, and finish with gay hilarity, suggesting that he had been getting something from somewhere. Yet the only thing the foreman saw him drink was a carton of milk on his copy table next to the machine.

The foreman was fit to be tied. He couldn't complain about Stutterin' Walker's work, because the man could set more type and cleaner type than any operator in the place, no matter what his condition. Then someone tipped the foreman off: Walker's scam was to empty out the milk, fill the carton with muscatel and place it beside his machine!

The next shift that Walker was hired, a wiser foreman decided to pounce upon the unsuspecting tramp printer. As he walked past Walker's machine, he inadvertently knocked over the milk carton. Expecting to see booze pour from the carton and a satisfying opportunity to fire his adversary, the foreman saw a splashing of milk all over the floor. Walker hadn't had time to empty out the milk and refill it with something more healthful.

With furious indignation and a lot of stammering and arm waving, Walker called for the chairman. He demanded that the foreman buy him another carton of milk. Defeated and sullen, the foreman relented and ordered an apprentice to go out and buy a "fifth of milk" and then called for a janitor to clean up the mess.

Col. Claggett
from Ed Burr

Another favorite printer of mine was Colonel Clagget. He was a Spanish-American War vet, staying in a Vet's home. I knew him in 1926 and he was quite elderly, but feisty. The veteran's home would let him take a leave about once a year. He would work here and there and have a good time traveling about the country. He was the exact size, same features and all, of Harry Morgan the actor, and he always wore a heavy winter overcoat and a well-worn derby hat, even in the summer time. One July day, he showed up on the Wheeling *Register* and caught a hire. He had on his usual heavy clothes. He parked his overcoat and derby hat in a corner and went to work. When quitting time came around, the Colonel couldn't remember where he had put his coat. You should have heard the racket he made! According to Col. Claggett, the chairman should have known where a person put his coat. And if the chairman didn't find his coat and hat right now, the Colonel was going to bring him up on charges for neglecting his duty. Col. Claggett was only about 5'4", which made it all the more comical. The chairman was Paul Curran, long since deceased.

Tom Quinn
from Don Cleary

Somebody claims "Gulf Coast" Guy Foley as champ with over 900 traveling cards. Although an impressive number, I doubt he is champ. I'll nominate Tom Quinn (also known as Tom Kelly). I worked several times with him in different places in the 60's. He slipped up here (Fort Lauderdale *News*) about seven years ago, and then again two years ago. The last I heard, Tom was still traveling, because he can also work as a baker or an electrician.

Sunshine Wilson

Jesse "Sunshine" Wilson died a few years ago in the Union Printers' Home with number three priority of longest residents. He contributed to the *Tramp Printers Newsletter,* sending reminisces of the "good times where a man could get all the overtime and over-scale jobs he wanted, particularly if he knew monotype." Sunshine was a hand man and worked lots of job shops where he worked with mono composition and ran monotype casters as well. He related how he learned the printing trade:

"Kokomo Phillips taught me to set ads. I ran away from home when my mother moved from Russellville, Arkansas to Little Rock. I didn't want to go to Little Rock, so I got on a freight train and got into Kokomo, Indiana late one night and I was sittin' in a cafe there by myself, and a man came in and said, 'Boy, what are you doin' out this hour?' 'Lookin' for a job in a print shop,' says I. He picked up a local newspaper, looked through it, and found a want-ad for a boy wanted at the Kokomo *Dispatch*.

"They hired me as an apprentice boy, and I hopped galleys about a week. Then a machinist-operator came in and said he wouldn't take a sit unless they gave his son an apprenticeship, too. So they moved me to the ad room and Kokomo Phillips taught me how to set ads. He was about the craziest guy I ever knew. He loved to whistle and sing and carry on around the composing room! He worked most of the year at printing, but in the summertime he would always be out with some vaudeville show."

In the Printers' Home, Sunshine kept himself busy with a 5x8 press and some handset type, printing business cards for his friends and staff at the Home. He talked ITU headquarters into cutting a special union label logo for him, and he was proud to have the only union label in Colorado Springs (ironically a non-union city, despite the presence of the ITU Printers' Home).

❦❦❦

from Marion Dearman

I first met Jessie Lyde "Sunshine" Wilson in Memphis, January 1952. I had just come in from Little Rock, where there was no work for me and found plenty of work in Memphis. Even though I was really fond of the city and enjoyed catching five days pay a week, I only stayed three weeks. The reason was that Sunshine already had itchy feet and easily talked me into going with him to Nashville to work on the Bankers' Directory, which was just beginning its annual production at Benson Printing Company. The same company also printed a wide line of fundamentalist Christian gospel songbooks (bankers and the Bible belt seemed to go together). Joining us for the trip was Oscar "O.T." Banks, newly divorced in Birmingham and still hurting. I sold my elderly Oldsmobile to one of the Memphis homeguards and we all rode in style in Sunshine's late-model Frazier (remember the cars that Henry Kaiser built: The Kaiser, the Frazier, and the Henry J.?).

Tall, lanky, redheaded, with a ready smile and pleasing Arkansas drawl, Sunshine was a delight to work and travel with. He had seemingly endless supplies of travel tales as well as an abundance of dirty jokes and great skill at telling them. He had also spent some time working various scams on carnivals—but I had the feeling that he exaggerated this part of his biography (isn't exaggeration a proper prerogative of legends?). When his hands were not otherwise occupied (as when he was printing or driving his car), he would constantly roll a silver dollar back and forth across the top of his hand—I don't know what that was all about.

O.T. Banks was actively treating his divorce trauma pains with Early Times and Johnny Walker, but nevertheless was a good travel companion: witty, good natured, intelligent, and a competent all-around printer.

Sunshine's information regarding work in Nashville was reliable: the three of us went to work as floormen on the directory pages. The work, Sunshine liked to say, was like "picking fly shit out of black pepper." We stayed with it for two weeks. Sunshine generously loaned me his Frazier so I could visit my cousins in Old Hickory and Cookeville, Tennessee. These were relatives on my mother's side—the Ferrells. Although my mother had left Tennessee in 1907, they still treated me like visiting royalty—that's Tennesseans for you! Before leaving Nashville, we took in the sights, like the Grand Ole Opry, the Maxwell House Hotel, for which the coffee was named, and paid a courtesy visit to the Nashville newspapers—the *Banner* and the *Tennessean*—where everybody seemed to know and love Sunshine. I got the feeling that I was traveling with a noted dignitary and that a lot of high status was rubbing off on me simply by virtue of being his travel partner.

Through the tramp printer's information pipeline, we heard that work was booming in Detroit. So we three drew travelers and headed for Motown, cracking jokes and singing songs all the way and, of course, pausing occasionally for libations. We deposited our travelers February 26 1952 (less than a week before my 25th birthday) and got rooms at the Detroit YMCA—not so compatible with a tramp printer's lifestyle, but we were thinspacing by this time, despite having worked five days a week in Memphis and Nashville—good living is the best revenge!

We slipped up on the Detroit *News,* an afternoon daily which was Detroit's dominant paper (TV has since destroyed any possibility of that recurring—few afternoon papers have survived). The economy was sizzling, work was booming, but the weather, being Detroit in February, was icy. Instead of doing the sensible thing of putting on warmer clothes, Sunshine stood around on street corners shivering and cursing the climate; as expected, he was soon on his way to warmer pastures. O.T. and I stayed in Detroit.

The next time I saw Sunshine was 22 years later when I was doing some research at the Union Printer's Home in Colorado Springs for an article which John Howells and I later published. Sunshine was a resident of the home and—pardon the expression—

very much at home. He showed me around so proudly that you would think he owned the place! When I drove back to Los Angeles, Sunshine rode with me as far as Las Vegas, where I put him on a plane to San Jose to visit his daughter. I never saw Sunshine again, but I will never forget his joy of living and his love for the trade and for his countless tramp and homeguard friends. He truly brought a lot of sunshine into our lives.

Jack Crawford
from Leo Baker and Jack Renter

Jack Crawford, sometimes known as 'WindyJack,' 'Cactus Jack,' or 'the Dirty Old Man,' has been mentioned in some of these newsletters. Jack did a lot of traveling, but most of it seemed to have been in Texas. He was born in Houston, and his father was a mailer on the Houston *Chronicle*. I remember one day, some of the Mexican-American printers went to Juarez on a Mexican holiday and took Jack Crawford along. Someone fired a cannon or something and it hit the back of the car. Jack was in the back seat; he didn't get hurt, but it sure shook him up.

One day when I was walking down a street in Evansville, Ind., heading for the newspaper, and who did I see leaning against a lamp post but "Mr. Jack." He had been in Evansville about a week. He grinned at me and asked, "Yuh broke?"

"Nope, but bent," I replied.

Jack took me to the Sontag Hotel and told the clerk he'd vouch for me. Then he took me to the shop and introduced me around. Everybody liked Jack Crawford.

Cactus Jack had a theory — if he borrowed any money from you, he'd wait to pay you back until he met you in a bar or when the gang went to Juarez after work. He figured by paying you in a bar he'd have his debt paid and you'd probably spend some of it back on him during the night. He was usually right.

Jack came to a sad ending. He keeled over on the street in El Paso one day. They took him to the County Hospital and he lay there with a stroke for a long time; no one knew where he was, or could help him any before he died. He has been gone several years now and we all miss him.

Gadget Reeves
from Al Chandler

The most outstanding traveling printer I can remember was a man by the name of Gadget Reeves. I first met him in Peoria. He finally got sick in Chillicothe, Ohio, and since he never had any money, the local union spent a lot on doctor bills for him before he died. The undertaker who knew the local printers agreed to take the mortuary benefit to bury Gadget Reeves. I was a pallbearer. When we set the casket down over the grave, a corner of the casket started cracking open. Everyone concerned breathed a deep sigh of relief when the casket was finally lowered into the ground. A short time later, my wife and I and another printer were out riding, and I was going to show them Gadget's grave in the printers' plot in a small town cemetery in Chillicothe. I looked, but couldn't locate the grave. I said, "Oh, well, Gadget never stayed anyplace very long. He probably put his tombstone on his shoulder and went someplace else to slip up!"

Shorty Comfort
from Ed Burr

Those who knew Shorty Comfort would have a hard time forgetting him, all 7-feet 2-inches of him! He and a brother Harry lived in a "printers' hotel" in Newark. Harry was a tabular whiz and worked on the *Wall Street Journal* six hours a night, always making over scale. Shorty had a sit on the Newark *Star-Eagle,* but had a sub on half the time. I worked for him quite a few months. I had a scrap book with a clipping of him and a dwarf who was appearing in a local show. My scrap book has been lost somewhere.

It was a picture of execution to see Shorty wind his long legs up and get them under the keyboard and start to work. Short takes were not for him. Shorty got to feeling bad about 1931 and went back home to Columbus, Ohio, where his sister lived. He got sick and was put in a hospital and just didn't want to live any more, so he jumped out of a window and died. I can see him in my mind still, rolling a cigarette with a sack of Bull Durham hanging from his hand. Harry left soon after Shorty, and I never heard what happened to him. He was about 6-ft. 6 himself.

Circus Tramp

The year was about 1938 when a somewhat small but athletically built adman slugged up on the Memphis *Commercial Appeal* and caught. Several of the situation holders knew him and told this story:

Years before he had been a tight rope walker in the circus but fell, was badly injured, and had never regained his nerve to walk the rope again. For years he had tramped, always going where the circus was showing in the hopes that he would regain his nerve and join the circus again. When the circus was in winter quarters in Florida he would work at the trade nearby, and from there follow them on the road.

During all the time I spent at the *Commercial Appeal* he regularly came in seeking work when the circus was in town. He would tell his friends each time that he was there to join the circus. To my knowledge he never regained his nerve.

Another sad character I observed was a very distinguished looking man whom I guessed about sixty or so. One day he showed up as a proofreader. Not only did he look like a gentleman but he was nicely dressed and spoke in a polished manner. After a few days, wanderlust got the better of him and he moved on. I was told by older workers who knew him that he had been a professor of English at a California university but after several times being intoxicated in the classroom they were forced to let him go. His bad habit had exhausted his other teaching possibilities at other colleges and he then had been reduced to a tramp proofreader because he couldn't hold a steady job.

❊❊❊

Lou Brueske was not only one of the better known travelers in the 40s to the 60s, but he was famous for "keeping in touch." He seemed to have written letters to everyone he'd ever befriended, and kept in touch by telephone or through the grapevine. After he retired, he continued his mission, even having a friend take dictation when a stroke paralyzed his hand. Lou died in the late 70s.

Old Days in St. Louis
from Lou Brueske

When I first showed up in St. Louis, there were three daily papers with separate composing rooms: *Star-Times* (folded in 1951), at 12th and Delmar, directly across the street from the McKinley Hotel; the *Post-Dispatch,* located at 12th and Olive, a block or so east of the Park Hotel; and the *Globe-Democrat*, at 12th and Franklin (now the *Post* building, where they also print the *Globe-Democrat).* The *Post* was a block north of the old McKinley. There were several large commercial shops, plus the *Daily Record* (legal paper), the *Sporting News,* and across the Mississippi, the *East St. Louis Journal.*

Most of the travelers I knew stayed at the McKinley or the Park hotels. I remember paying $9 a week at the McKinley, it was a dollar or so cheaper at the Park. Towards downtown from the *Star-Times* was the Bon-Del Hotel. A room there was about a buck a night. Actually it was a whore house, but if one came into town broke, he could stay a night or two until he had a shift on the hook so he could hit the cash-in man and move to a better hotel.

There were several bars around the old *Post:* McIntyre's was one that most of the *Post* printers hit. You could go down the backstairs from the *Post* right into the bar. There were also three or four small night clubs close.

The travelers who worked on the *Star-Times* and the *Globe* usually stayed at the McKinley, some ventured out to the Milner, others with dough might stay at the Warwick on 15th and Locust. Mr. Abrams, owner of the McKinley, told me once that I'd stayed in every room in the hotel during my travels in and out of town. The McKinley was torn down in the early 1970s, the Park and Bon-Del went in the 1950s.

After about 16 travelers into St. Louis, I decided to homeguard it on the *Post* in 1964, and retired in 1977. During that time, I met many of the younger travelers who are still at the trade one place or another across the country. One thing I can say for St. Louis is that I never had to walk a shift, although others have; it seemed like I always hit it when business was good. The scale was $96 a week my first trip there, working seven days a week and all the O.T. you could take.

Joe Wertz
from Tom Holson

The first time I saw Joe Wertz, I was a Linotype operator at Sims Printing Co. in Tucson. It was 1926; I was working nights and attending classes at the University of Arizona in the day time. Joe came in looking for work, and I decided to take a night off and hired him.

The boss was doubtful because Joe walked with two canes; he'd lost both feet. He wore prostheses consisting of false feet and boot-like extensions which reached to the upper part of his legs. Once Joe demonstrated his ability to do the job, including dumping type and starting the distributor, he got along very well.

He was in his 20s, well built, and blond, befitting his German name. He had a brother who was also a printer. Starting out on a road tour, he had attempted to board a moving freight train and fell. Both feet were severed above the ankle. At the hospital they fitted him with the substitute feet and canes. Then he resumed his tour. He said that while working in Detroit he found winter coming on. He priced an overcoat, but discovered he could buy a ticket for Florida for the same amount, so it was Florida for that winter.

In 1930 I was working in Borger, Texas, and was planning on getting married. I needed a sub to cover my sit for a six-week stretch while my wife and I honeymooned in California. Just at that time, Joe Wertz walked in looking for work. When I returned, Joe had become one of the boys. He hated to leave, saying, "Give me a call next time you get married."

Twenty-two years later, I was working on the daily paper in Bakersfield, California, and was elected delegate to the 100th ITU Convention in Cincinnati from Bakersfield, in 1959. To my surprise I again ran into Joe Wertz, who was a delegate representing Detroit. A little older, of course, but he looked very much the same except that he managed to shed his canes and walked about like anyone else.

He told me that he never expected to marry, but he'd found a fine, understanding woman and they had a couple of children. Although, as a member of the Detroit delegation he was a dedicated Inde, and, I a lifetime Prog,[4] that didn't prevent us from having a memorable reunion. I often wonder what became of him.

Tramps and Semitramps I Remember
from Marion Dearman

This is a very brief mention of tramps I have worked with and where I worked with them. I don't remember the names of all of them, but their faces and personalities are indelibly etched on my memory.

Okemah, Oklahoma: this was during WWII, so tramp printers tended to be old or 4-F—these were both. Both were proud to be printers and told many interesting travel stories. I remember how they could make the sloppiest page of combined handset type and Linotype straight matter lift with the application of copious amounts of wadded up pieces of wet newsprint and toilet paper and pieces of toothpicks wedged between the handset letters. I don't remember their names.

Flagstaff, Arizona: Perhaps Mary and Wayne Shields—he was the foreman and she the makeup person—should be included; they finished up their ITU careers in Alaska, after walking the picket line in a losing strike. Also Slim Slaymaker (from West Virginia), the chairman, Lonnie Cagle, the machinist, and Arnulfo Luna, my colleague in the ad alley. But the true tramp I remember most was Snuffy Bryant. His moustache was always stained a tobacco-juice brown—whence the nickname. Snuffy filled my head full of stories about traveling as a printer and that, along with a broken heart received from an ill-fated summertime romance, got my feet to itching.

San Francisco: Jimmy Doolittle—about jockey size and an incurable horse player. He always thought he would eventually make a killing at Golden Gate Fields, Tanforan, or Bay Meadows. He never

---

[4] Two political parties of the ITU : The Independents and the Progressives.

did so far as I know. Eddie O'Donnell: sharp, bright, witty, a caring human being and dedicated union man, well-read and intelligent. Guy Cannon: suave, erudite Texan (is this an oxymoron?), who always wore bow ties. At the end of the swing shift would often spend the rest of the night discussing the finer points of Shakespeare, Chaucer, and Cervantes with Eddie O'Donnell. Martin Tunnell—quiet, well-dressed, his horned-rimmed glasses gave him a professorial look, and from Bristol, Tennessee.

Kansas City, Missouri: Tex something or other. I don't remember his name, but he was the easiest man I ever saw to talk into falling off the wagon.

Dallas: Rabbit Orman. I fell victim to one of Rabbit's favorite scams: the old "I broke my glasses and could you loan me the money to buy a new pair so I can work tonight?" I loaned him the money out of my meager funds and never saw him again. I'm sure that Rabbit helped some other tramp out somewhere down the line, however.

Detroit: Joe Wertz. An ex-tramp who had become a Detroit homeguard. Joe always greeted and welcomed newly arrived tramps. He came over to me to chat about traveling and to see if I needed anything. Joe had a prosthesis for one of his legs, which he had lost riding the rails during his tramping days.

Cleveland: Johnny Hatfield. One of the first to greet me on the Cleveland *Plain-Dealer*. He gave me all the scoop about the assistant foremen to watch out for (the general foreman, Deo Padgett, was a prince of a person). Johnny and I exchanged notes about places we had worked for several hours after work (see section on Hatfield by John Howells elsewhere in this book).

Memphis: Sunshine Wilson (mentioned earlier). Walter Herod—besides extensive traveling as a printer, Walter had been working in circuses for years as a tightwire walker. I met him again in Las Vegas, where he tried to get me to let him train me to take over his circus act (that was when I was thin, wiry, and at least semi-athletic)—no way, Walter! He took me to the Clyde Beatty Circus and introduced me to Clyde (who was the lion tamer—I didn't volunteer for an apprenticeship at that craft, either!). Simeon Wood Crabtree, Jr. (Sim): always took a half-pint of vodka and a pack of

Picayunes (the world's vilest cigarettes) to work each shift; he reasoned that the foreman couldn't smell vodka and even if some of the odor escaped, the Picayunes would blot it out—too true! Sim liked to make jokes out of each person's name: Herod was He Rod; I was Dear Boy and after my daughter was born, Dear Girl. Needless to say, Sim's little jokes went over like a lead balloon.

Jack Ware, son of Dixie Ware, an ex-tramp. Jack served his apprenticeship on the Memphis papers; he got fired and barred by Dizzy McGowan, the *Commercial-Appeal* foreman (Daffy, his brother, was the makeup foreman) for you know what, then showed up the next day bumping overtime on the *Press-Scimitar*. He went back to work on the same ad and the man he bumped off had six kids.[5] Eddie Wood: another Memphis apprentice graduate, had beautiful wavy blond hair and piercing blue eyes—he would have been a real lady-killer if he could have made it through a date sober enough. Eddie, Jack, and Sim all wound up in San Francisco years later—I wonder if I had something to do with that?

The most unforgettable tramp printer stories from Memphis were the adventures of Henry Lazarus. One trip, Henry recalled, he got on a Greyhound bus, bound, he thought, for Houston. After sleeping away the miles, he got off the bus and went into the terminal's news-stand and asked for a Houston paper. The newsstand operator informed Henry that if he wanted a Houston paper he would have to go to Houston: this was St. Louis! Another anecdote about Henry concerned our watering hole across the street from the shop. One morning, after a few hours of drinking at the end of the lobster shift, Henry called a cab to take him to his hotel. One of the companies had black and white taxis; hence, when a black and white car pulled up in front of the bistro a few minutes later, Henry, assuming it was a cab, clambered into the back seat and said "take me to the hotel." The driver said "Yeah, sure. I'll take you to the hotel—the crossbar hotel!" Poor Henry had gotten into a black and white police car and soon found himself in jail.

Sometimes we would get a couple of cases of beer and perhaps

---

[5] Memphis had two chapels, but only one composing room. The foreman of one of the two Scripps-Howard sister papers could not bar a sub from work on the other paper. A real anomaly in the ITU

something stronger after work and go to my apartment in South Memphis (where I'd moved after becoming an affluent semihomeguard). On one such occasion, I had a tape recorder running on the floor behind the living room couch. Eddie Wood had brought his girlfriend to the party and, when Eddie had to go take a leak, Henry made a move on Eddie's girl. When I later played this back for Henry, he couldn't believe he did what he was hearing. He kept saying: "that's not Henry Lazarus talking; that's the whiskey." I could really identify with Henry—the booze often got blamed for my behavior, too.

Las Vegas: Johnny Burt: when he was sober, which he was for long periods of time, he was one of the best Linotype operators I'd ever seen. I remember Marc Wilkinson, our employer who was definitely not in the habit of complimenting printers, saying to me after Johnny's first shift: "Boy, can that fellow set type!" Johnny would save several thousand dollars, then go on a binge for days during which he was the most generous, amiable person in Las Vegas, often buying drinks for whole roomsful of total strangers.

Bob Howells: brother of John Howells. Bob often worked on the Las Vegas *Sun*, the paper that Unitypo founded and sold (for $1.00) to Hank Greenspun. I worked on the *Sun* in 1954 (I don't believe that Bob was there at that time). I met Bob several times later in Las Vegas, Shoshone, and Death Valley. Bob, like Johnny Burt, had many talents—he was somewhat of a geologist, among other things. Bob, Johnny Burt, and a Las Vegas bartender discovered a silver and lead mine in Death Valley. The mine was a resounding success, with $2 million worth of ore extracted from the first 85 feet of ground. For 16 years Bob and Johnny had steady royalty checks coming in. Unfortunately, since both were compulsive gamblers as well as drinkers, most of the money stayed in Las Vegas.

❋❋❋

Following is a list of well-known tramp printers. The list is far from complete, and the authors would appreciate readers' additions to our inventory. The majority of those listed are dead.

Tex Ables	Pegleg Adams	Leo Aldrige

TRAMP PRINTERS

Greer Allen
Bill Avery
Doug Bancroft
The Red Baron
Nate Bergman (The Wandering Jew)

Shorty Boardman
Big Ben Brooks
Glen Britt
Lou Brueske
Sam Burch
Dan Burns

Charles Carter
Walter Caswell
Paul Cheda
John Canahan
Bob (Shotgun) Chuttijan
Chuck Connors
Ben Crump
Chuck Cremins
(Windy) Jack Crawford
Frenchie Desaulniers
Harry Droege
Ralph (Onion) Eunson
Big Marie Emory
Dinty Finn
Chris Frishe
Lindy Floyd
Mel Franz
Chris Frisch
"Goofy" Gibbs
Little Richard Guthrie
Joe Hale
Guy Hardy
John Hatfield
Virgil Hatfield
John Edward Hicks
Tommy Holmes
Cliff Hewitt
"Wild" Bill Harolson
Bob Johnson
"Jingling" Johnson
Whitey Kline
Lloyd Lamprecht
Ray Lemire
Big Ben "the Arab"
Dave Marcus
Marvin Manning
Alex Mathieson

Paul Aller
Leo Baker
O.T. Banks
Danny Bass (Indian Joe)
Joe Bonior

Don Bosworth
Bob Brice
Clay Brownhill
Bunny Bunce
Gene Burke
Edgar L "Bing Bang" Burr
Roy Carter
Leon Couture
Bob Campbell
Andy Carroll
Lonnie Coleman
Clift Cos
Don Cleary
Simon Wood Crabtree
John Henry Curtin
Marion Dearman
Ed Dudek
George Dwyer
Jimmy Fancher
Charles Fisher
Jack Finch
Gulf Coast Foley
Johnny Foley
Newell Frizzell
DeVere Grover
Frank Graham
Red Haloran
Jim Harmon
Johnny Head
Pappy Hilton
Harry Holabird
Thomas W. Holson
Edgar (Goofy) Howard
Byron (Jake) Jacobs
John Kelly
Mert Kelly
Frank Krutch
Henry Lazarus
Henry Lipschitz
Craig Lewis
two Jimmy MitchelJs
Charles Marcom
Maurice Maubrey

Jack Allison
Sam Ball
J.S. Barton
Dave Bates
Russ Bonneau

Lou Boyer
Teny Brennen
Snuffy Bryant
Poor Bill Bundick
John Burt
Guy Cannon

James Caswell
Al Chandler
Charles Cartwright
John Carey
Shorty Comfort
Ezra Cox
Jeff Crass
Bernie Crites
Charlie Crutcher
James O'Shane
Johnny Dunn
Scotty Dunn
Ed Ferguson
Dick Flemming
Larry Fleming
Bill Fowler
Bob Fladd
Neal Fuller
Cliff Gallant
Otto Hammock Jr.
Roy Hamprey
Horrible Harrigan
Erwin Helmick
Walter Herrod
Gene Hodges
Bob Howells
Dorothy Howells
John Howells
John Kemic
Kerschoff
Al Kusch
Peter Bartlett Lee
Eddie Little
Irish Little
Stanley Madley
Carl Moore
Paul Melvin

99

TRAMP PRINTERS

Paul A. (Chips) Morgan
Bob McNamara
Jimmy Mitchell
Dolores Moser
Chris McEwen
Ray McGearry
Bill Monahan
"Jumping" Joe Owens
Horace Norville
Eddie and Mary O'Donnell
Larry (Catman) McCowan
two Pete Petersons
Frank Porter
Bob Rhynicker
Blaine Schaeffer
Ralph Shoals
Warren "Rocky" Stemming
Easy Pickin' Stewart
Charlie Talbott
John Thompson
Bill Trickey
Bill Upton
M. L. (Tex) Vineyard
Bob (900 Lines) Whalen
Joe Wertz
Scotty Wilburn
Jesse (Sunshine) Wilson
Eddie (Wisenjamer) Wassmer
Joe Zika

"Ace" Murphy
Toad Milbauer
Jack Morgan
Ted Morse
"Dirty Shirt" McKnight
Lzzie Missler
Harry Nobel
Rabbit Orman
Ray Ohms
Junior O'Malley
R. M. Oschenbein
Kokomo Phillips
Tom Quinn
Lou Aider
Lester Schwartz
Homer Smith
Walter Smith
"Soapy" George Story
Bobby Taylor
William Tilet
Jim Turley
Al Vallance
Cliff (Stutterin') Walker
Weary Willie Waterhouse
Franklin White
Jimmy Williams
Zack Wooten
Bob Yagel

Vernon Murphy
Bonnie Mills
Ralph Morgan
Bernard Mehrley
Jimmy Mitchel
Earl Norris
Louise Olson
Michael O'Hearn
Bill O'Keefe Sr.
Jack Parham
Ralph Parks
Ken and Jan Price
Gadget Reeves
Ben Satterfield
Arnold Sears
Red Smith
Jim Stokes
Tom Studdart
Cliff Taylor
John Totsy
Martin Tunnell
Ed Vanderver
Dixie Ware
Duke Wellington
Bobbie Who
Joe Williams
Carl Wright
Lyle Zelis

THE TOURIST'S SOLILOQUY

(work in prospect)

By LeRoy B. Ruggles
To work or not to work... that is the question;
Whether 'tis better in the mind to suffer
The "outs" and "wrong fonts" of a strenuous life,
Or these more courageous comps to panhandle
And thus win out a stake? To brace, to strike,

To beg; and by this means to say we end
all heartache and the thousand frightful things
That work is heir to; 'tis a consummation
Devoutly to be wished. To win, to gain,
To gain we know not how. Aye, there's the rub;
For on that book who knows what troubles lurk—
Pica solid; perchance manuscript unreadable—
Must give us pause. There's the respect
That makes calamity of working life;
For who would bear the heat and dust and dirt,
The leads to piece, the lack of "sorts" much needed,
The cluttered alleys, the foul smells of the gloomy room,
The insolence of devils, and other things
The patient printer while at work must stand,
When he himself might his quick rescue make
By a change of scene? Who would burdens bear,
To rune and sweat under a weary life,
But that the dread of something worse than this,
The unexplored places within whose walls
To tourists are welcomed, puzzles the will
And makes us rather bear the ills we have
Than fly to others that we know not of?
Thus labor doth make cowards of us all,
And thus our inborn spirit of resolution
Is unseated by the pale cast of thought.

—Inland Printer, Vol.29, 1902, page 901
(C)Poetic Printshop Past-Times, Graphic Crafts, Inc.
Lancaster, PA

WOMEN PRINTERS

THROUGHOUT HISTORY, working women have often been the targets of animosity, jealousy, and suspicion from their male counterparts in the labor market. A good deal of this rancor arises because employers traditionally pay women less than men. When it comes to typesetting, brute strength confers little advantage to men. Furthermore, the feminine reputation for manual dexterity, sobriety, and willingness to accept lower working standards clearly appealed to proprietors. There was no reason why female typesetters couldn't match production standards expected of male workers. Although some may blame this on male chauvinism, the truth is in economics. Low wages for women are neither the will of working men, nor devious competitive schemes of working women, but rather a condition imposed upon both by profit-conscious employers.

Women typesetters in North America were around from the very beginning. Two of Ben Franklin's nieces set type in his print shop and many wives and daughters of printers regularly worked in the family business. But women typesetters on a larger scale didn't become a "problem" for male printers until the mid-1800s. Employers at that time began encouraging women to learn typesetting, partly as a way to counter the threat of growing unionism among printers, and partly as a way of cutting composing room costs. Wages for women, in any endeavor, were traditionally lower than for men, and women were more vulnerable, less militant and not likely to agitate for fair wages as men were.

At first, male printers expressed considerable resistance to allowing women to join the union. But when they realized they had no choice, typographical union members grudgingly agreed to the concept of a *separate* union local for women. However, it soon became apparent that this was no solution. Women's local unions had no power. Women members were forced to work under whatever conditions employers could get away with. The biggest danger to men printers, however, was the possibility of women printers being used to replace striking male printers. Like it or not, women typesetters were being installed in composing rooms all over the country. Male printers referred to them as "twin-nicks."[1] Therefore, in 1869, the Typographical Union finally agreed that women should be admitted as full-fledged members. They made one more stipulation—one quite advanced for its time—that is: women printers must be paid the same as men, and there could be no discrimination against them. In fact, since 1869, ITU membership applications contained no reference to the sex or race of the applicant. Thus, male printers shrewdly protected themselves against traditionally low-paid competition. This liberal approach to sexual equality didn't come easy but union locals rigidly enforced the equal pay rules from the very beginning of the legislation.

A humorous example of prejudice against women is examined below. It comes from a speech given at a banquet by a management figure from the *New York World* explaining a failed effort to use non-union women printers to replace union printers in the composing room:

"The *New York World* undertook the experiment of employing women as compositors because it was willing to be at some trouble and expense for the sake of giving practical aid to women and enlarge their sphere of work.

"From the beginning to the end of our experiment, perhaps 100 girls were employed at the type case. Of these, less than half a dozen could set type when they were first received. Some became tolerable compositors, and are now making fair wages at bookwork [elsewhere]. However the majority of them, with every opportunity

---

[1] "Nicks" on the front of foundry type helped identify sizes and fonts. Experienced printers could verify wrong-fonts by feel, with their eyes closed. It should then be obvious why the female printers in old-time printshops were universally called "two-nicks" or "twin-nicks". (This bit of male chauvinism came from Ted Morse).

to learn, never reached an equal skill, nor earned as much as men typesetters. The moment they were tried by the simple test of so much pay for so much composition (which all male compositors undergo), their earnings fell far below the average of the earnings of the men. They worked as many days in the week as men, but could none of them work as many hours a day. Seven or eight hours were more than sufficient to tax their strength.

"Clean composition was next to an impossibility with all of them, and the correction of their 'straight matter' they shirked when possible, and did badly when it could not be shirked. Women seemed to be utterly incapable of deciphering illegible manuscript. Punctuation also somehow seemed to elude them, and their justification must have been by faith since they never justified by spacing well. Such was the incapacity of the four or five-score women we have employed as typesetters, and such its kind and degree. Their hands traveled tolerably well and swiftly from the case to the stick, but not so well from the stick to the case when it came to distributing type. It remains only to add that they were all faithful to the extent of their abilities, neat and decent in their dress, and well-behaved, and that most of them had an ordinary common school education. Such are the facts; whoever pleases may preach the sermon." [To the authors, it seems rather presumptuous on the part of management to expect that after a short training period a woman could produce as much as a man with six years apprenticeship and years of journeyman's experience!]

Women Tramp Printers

Throughout our research, we ran across relatively few women who could easily be categorized as tramp printers. For one thing, there were far fewer women printers than men. And, back in the earlier days of printing, it would be unthinkable for a woman to ride boxcars or put up with the rigors of the open road. Things like that just weren't done. Furthermore, even though union locals insisted on equal pay, individuals undoubtedly discriminated against women printers in hiring subs. Since personal hires were controlled by the individuals, many printers would not hire a woman and allow a man substitute to "walk," particularly not if the man had a family to support. So when a woman gained a regular situation by way of her priority, she was more likely to hold on to that job for life.

This didn't mean that women didn't travel; they were just more likely to make sure a job was waiting for them before making the move. Below is a story of a woman printer and her travels before settling down. She makes no claim to being a "tramp" printer, but she did enjoy the freedom of working where and when she chose. This is an interesting study of not only a woman traveling printer, but of traveling through country weekly print shops.

A Woman Tourist Printer
from Mary McCarthy, Bakersfield

I got married right out of high school, but after six years, my husband traded me for another 16-year-old. So, I needed a job. A friend sent me to the local weekly in Jasonville, Indiana, a coalmining town. I'd never been inside a newspaper before. The girl running it was trying to keep the paper going until her uncle (the owner) got back from World War II. She hated the Linotype, and I liked keyboards—so she hired me to run it at $10 a week. I paid half of that to my dad for room and board.

My two brothers told me I was crazy to work for such a salary, but I felt I was learning a trade. By the end of the week I was setting all the news matter. I really liked it.

A friend of the owner worked nights on the Terre Haute paper, and as a favor to the absent owner, he came every Thursday to run the press for us. He watched me work for a while and said I evidently had a knack for the Linotype. He told me if I stuck with it, I would be able to work almost anyplace in the country. That made me feel good.

One day he was running the press when the rollers melted and ran all over the type. He forgot to change to summer rollers. He used kerosene, gasoline, and carbon tet, but nothing would touch that mess. He worked all night and said he would check with the pressmen at the big paper when he went to work. After he left, we tried about the same things he did. Then I said, "Wait a minute... Lava soap takes it off your hands." So we made a big pan of Lava soap suds and it came off.

Eventually he taught me how to feed the press. I was scared half to death and ruined the first 15 or 20 copies, but finally got the hang of it. My pay was raised to $12 a week. Of course, for that I also had to melt pigs for the Linotype and cast the stereotype cuts. After the press runs, it took both June and I to lift off the forms. Sometimes I fed the foot-powered job press.

$12 a week still wasn't much money, since I had to pay room and board out of that $12, so I looked for another job. After a trial working for Western Union as a telegrapher, I decided to go back to printing, and found a job on a weekly in Linton, Indiana, about 10 miles from home. Before long, I was making $25 a week.

The newspaper owner also owned two funeral homes. The print shop was located in the back of the funeral home in Linton. If a funeral was scheduled on press day, we had to wait till after the funeral. The owner's son worked with me and sometimes he had to take off work to pick up a body. The worst part was, we had to wash up in the embalming room. Once a body was draining when I went to wash up for lunch. (Wasn't able to eat). One day I was helping stamp the papers, when I looked up and saw a gurney with a body parked across the doorway. I insisted they put it away before finishing the press run.

There was a daily paper in that same town that was union. I started going down there at lunch time, and got acquainted with some of the guys. (Only eight worked there.) They asked my why I didn't work there with them. I talked to the owner and he hired me as a union apprentice at $35 a week. I worked the night shift by myself, except when someone was sick or if anyone quit, and then I'd work days until a card holder came in. The first night I worked, one of the two local cops pulled a gun on me, thinking I was a burglar. After that, he looked in every night, and made sure my car would start before I went home.

The second week I was there, the owner called me into his office. It seems somebody put oil in the Lino magazine, and I was accused. I managed to convince him that I didn't do it, so I wasn't fired. Finally one of the day operators admitted putting the oil in the magazine. He said he did it because he was afraid I would get his job. The owner said, "She just did. You're fired!" I worked days three weeks 'til another card holder showed up.

I was doing fine at the paper, and really liked my job. I had only three years experience on the Linotype, but was setting cleaner type than the other two operators. Then my mother and father started having problems, and she felt she had to get away from him. I sure didn't want to leave my job, but the guys I worked with knew my dad, and they didn't blame me for leaving. So I took on the responsibility of taking care of mother and the four kids. I answered 16 ads in the Publishers Auxiliary and received 15 answers, one a proposal of marriage—seems the man's wife was his Linotype operator and she died. (Probably worked her to death, so I passed on that one.)

We decided on the job offer from Hobbs, New Mexico. My mother made a down payment on a 22-foot house trailer and I agreed to make the monthly payments. I never did learn to back that thing up. We were on the road before 4 a.m. I'm sure the air was blue when my father found out we were gone! This was in 1948, and it happened to be the year of the big blizzard. We were stranded for three days in Munster, Texas, parked between a gas station and a garage, cold, almost freezing, huddled under comforters to stay alive.

When we finally got to Hobbs, I asked a neighbor in the trailer park to back my rig in, and I went to the paper to make arrangements to go to work. When I returned, we heard music coming from the trailer park's recreation room. Turns out that the Carter Family were staying in the park, and they were practicing for a gig down the road. This was 1948; Johnny Cash wasn't with them yet.

The newspaper was owned by a Mrs. Head, a woman who knew nothing about newspapers. This was just a hobby for her, and she was hard to deal with. In the back shop, me and an 80-year old Lino operator (called out of retirement) had to set all the type for the daily. A nice man named Scotty worked the floor. My machine kept squirting lead. When I heard it coming, I would kick my chair away so as not to get burned. I tried to tell Mrs. Head that the machine had a faulty lockup. She wouldn't listen.

It took a lot of hours for such a short crew to put out that daily paper. I went to work at 6:30 a.m and got off at 2 p.m. for two hours rest. Then I went back at 4 p.m. and worked 'til midnight. Printers would come through Hobbs looking for work, but the publisher would find fault with all of them, so we had to put in the overtime.

One night, I was overly tired and didn't hear the squirt coming. It went all over both hands and the keyboard. I went into her office and showed her the damage, and told her I was going home to doctor myself and gave her two weeks notice. She tried to make things better around the shop, fixed the lockup on the machines, but I quit anyway. Scotty quit with me and he said he found us a job on a weekly at Seminole, Texas.

The Seminole paper's owner, Pappy Weston, had an apartment in the back of the shop. He also knew nothing about printing, and at times acted a little "off." After a few weeks he started overloading me with copy from another weekly he owned in a nearby town. One day we were almost ready to go to press. Scotty was making up the last page. Pappy came in with a large ad to run in that edition. Scotty asked if there wasn't a deadline. Pappy replied that he promised a friend to run the ad and insisted on putting it in the paper.

Scotty pulled a page off the press, marked up the ad, and I was setting it when they started having words. Scotty called him a name, and Pappy pulled out a switchblade and told Scotty he was fired. "I quit the moment you pulled that knife," Scotty said.

I went ahead and set the ad, made it up and locked it up in the page. I showed Pappy how to fold and stamp the subscription list on the papers. We actually made it by the post office deadline. But when I went home for lunch, Scotty was there and said he had jobs for us at Levelland, Texas. So I returned to the paper and told Pappy that I couldn't do all that work by myself, and that I was afraid of that knife, so I quit.

The Levelland newspaper published three times a week. It was run by a retired Navy veteran, and had a new building and all new equipment. He needed help badly because a Rodeo Edition was coming up, which would mean considerable overtime. So I sat down and started working while the publisher watched me like a hawk. When I went into his office for my check, he welcomed me to the job, but said he didn't want to hire Scotty. He said he checked with Mrs. Head, who told him I was a good worker, but that Scotty was a troublemaker. I never did see Scotty again.

This was a good job, but Mom started getting restless. She

wanted to go to California. So I wrote to Bakersfield about work at a union shop called the *Bakersfield Press*. I went to work there in 1948 on the night shift. The first night, the safe was robbed, and the police suspected me. But later on, a cleanup boy admitted taking the money.

After two years, I finally got my ITU journeyman's card, but then the paper folded. I wanted to move on, but Mom said she was where she wanted to be. So I decided to stay in Bakersfield and slipped up at the *Californian* It took me three years to get a full time job, since the paper had absorbed most of the printers from the *Press*. I worked for the *Californian* for 38 years and retired seven years ago. Toward the end of my career, I was a technician on the new electronics equipment, making $20 over scale. The printing trade has been good to me.

Mary McGowan

When shop talk got around to famous women printers, usually only a few names would surface. One was Mary McGowan who worked many newspapers around the country. She had been married to Dizzy McGowan, a well-known foreman on the Memphis *Press-Scimitar*. Although Mary traveled, it might be difficult to categorize her as a "tramp" printer. Certainly, she wasn't a flamboyant character as most tramps tended to be. As we understand it, she dressed neatly, was clean, and was a very competent Linotype operator. She didn't bounce around—catching a shift or two here and there as many men tramps did—Mary usually went places where there was plenty of work and held down a steady job until she decided to move on.

Lydia Avery

Another woman who qualified as a tramp printer was Lydia Avery, but her name wasn't well-known among those of the authors' generation; she did her traveling earlier in the century and then settled down in New York to spend 40 years working in one city. Lydia was well-liked and respected by all. We received the following story when she was almost 100 years old.

❊❊❊

I've worked everywhere: worked north, east, south, and west. In my time, I had some 30+ travelers and met many old-time tramp printers. I started when I was less than 20 years old and I've had an ITU journeyman's card for 75 years. I'm sure I got an earlier start on the road than most, although at that time there were plenty like me, before and during the first World War, who joined the union long before age 20.

I did piece work on the San Antonio *Express,* the Atlanta *Constitution,* in Galveston, and all through the South. My travels also took me west to Frisco, where I worked on the *Ex* and the *Chron*. I also held a sit on the Sacramento *Bee* for a time. In the north, I worked various places in Michigan, Indiana, Ohio, etc. I finally stopped traveling in No. 6, when I took a sit on the Brooklyn *Eagle* for 20+ years, and then on the New York *Times* for another 20 years. I retired eight years ago to Minnesota.

In those days, we took no nonsense from any foreman; we developed an independence that remained until the end. In Terre Haute (The Hat), when a regular laid off to put on a sub to kill OT, the regular was forced to keep you on till he killed *all his* OT. They gave me a sit so the OT operator could go back to work. I only kept it for a short while, and left for the next town!

One stay in a little town in Michigan on a morning paper comes to my memory. Shorty Comfort (R.I.P.) hired me to work for him, and he indicated the round pigs that were being used, admonishing: "When you set two of these, you know your string is up." Then before lunch he reappeared to ask if I had lunch money. I told him I had with a gracious thank you. I left that morning for the next town, so never again did I see Shorty. He had made many towns himself in his day.

Stella Maxim

Although admittedly not an exceptionally itinerant Lino operator, Stella Maxim married a tramp printer, A.L. (Tex) Wilie and joined him in his travels for a while. When they finally settled in Seattle, they became active in ITU affairs, with Tex serving as local vice-president, ITU delegate, scale committee member, as Allied secretary and local Labor Councils. Eventually he was appointed by the governor of Washington State to serve as Director of Industrial Insurance and later as head of the Department of Labor and Industries. Several years before her death, Stella wrote:

❊ ❊ ❊

While I am a 56 year ITU member, I never considered myself a "tramp" printer, but I was married to one of the best: A.L. (Tex) Wilie, for 26 years, until his death in 1966.

While at the trade as Lino operator and printer, as well being the daughter of an ITU member, I had opportunity many times to see what benefits the "tramps" brought to locals where the homeguard was unable or unwilling to take risks to see that rules were enforced. Only those who have had close personal contact with these bulwarks of our Union can, I feel, fully appreciate the many lasting contributions these men—and a few women—have made to our organization.

When I was a Lino operator at the Grand Rapids (Mich.) *Herald* in 1940, I was appointed keeper of the Tramp Fund, for those travelers who needed a few extra dollars to tide them over 'til payday. We didn't have a cash-in man. As I was young and the only single woman in the chapel, I was often teased about marrying a tramp printer. One day I replied, "Yes, and he'll be from Texas," and of course, he was!

When a regular didn't show up, we "jeffed" for the night's work. One old fellow often called in on Monday, asking for a sub, as he lived many miles out of town and winters were often stormy. Since we were all hungry for even one night's work, it usually came out that everyone had a chance for the night about two or three times a month. One night he called in, we jeffed and one of the other subs and I tied for it, then tried again. When he finally got it, it turned out to be a stretch of several weeks, as the old fellow was seriously ill. Since I was supporting my parents and younger brother at that time, I really missed getting "the luck of the draw."

❊ ❊ ❊

Big Marie Emory

The one name which invariably comes to mind when talking about women printers is Marie Emory. And if any woman could qualify as a tramp printer, it would be "Big Marie." Stories about her are legend, and like many legends, they tend to gather embellishments until it's difficult to know which details are true and which have been exaggerated beyond reality. Big Marie herself is partially responsible for these exaggerations, because she was a loud, brash individual who enjoyed bragging about her exploits and making them sound bigger than life.

One example of this was related to us by a printer, who said: "One Sunday, some of us were sitting on the steps before attending a Union meeting when Marie drove up in a big Chrysler Imperial. One man asked her where she got the money to buy such a big car. Her reply was, "Running a whorehouse in Chicago. Where do you think?" (One respondent claims that Marie stuck the credit union in Memphis for the Chrysler.)

Herewith are additional stories about Marie Emory, which the reader is advised to take with the proverbial grain of salt. However, if she were alive, she'd be delighted at even the most preposterous tale and would probably try to make it even more outrageous. Marie enjoyed her notoriety and celebrity status as one of the very few, authentic, women tramp printers.

Jack Reuter wrote: "Big Marie Emory passed away—in San Antonio—but her memory lives on. She liked working in El Paso, and we frequently crossed paths there. When Don Siebert was chairman at the *El Paso Times,* he and Marie had some classic 'cuss fights,' for she was hell on chairmen as well as foremen. One time, when I checked into El Paso, Don Siebert pleaded with me to take the chairman's job, 'just for a couple of weeks so I can get a rest from Big Marie.' Reluctantly I agreed. He appointed me temporary chairman, and I spent the entire two weeks trying to out-shout and out-cuss Big Marie. It was sure a relief to give the job back to Don.

"Another time I checked into El Paso, and Marie was there. She came up and said, 'Hi, little fella; it's been a long time. Where did I see you last?' I reminded her that it was in Cleveland, the morning you heaved the beer mug at Walter the bartender.

"She said, 'Let's not talk about that.' It seems that Marie had been trying to get Walter's attention; her beer mug was empty. She grew louder and louder and Walter was trying to ignore her. She leaned back and heaved a beer mug at him. Somebody yelled; Walter ducked; and the beer mug sailed through the stained glass window onto 9th street. The police took a dim view of her action and carted her away."

Another story from an anonymous source: "Back before the war, when our Marine outfit was being shipped to the Philippines on a freighter. When pulling anchor in Honolulu, two of the women passengers returned to the ship after too much celebrating in town; they missed the landing platform and fell into the drink. They were mother (Marie) and daughter on their way to the Philippines to join Marie's husband who was a First Class Petty Officer on one of the ships out of Cavite. Marie was in her late 30's and the daughter in her late teens.

"It was rumored that the Captain found out that mother and daughter had been selling their bodies for $5.00 a session. The Captain confined them to their quarters and posted a sentry outside their door. The troops joked about it and said that a sentry should be posted to watch the other sentry. I don't think there was truth to the rumor, but anything can happen on a ship like that.

"After I left the Marine Corps, I pursued my trade as a printer. In 1962, I was the Union Chairman or Shop Steward at the *Evening Star* in Washington, D.C. One night, before the evening shift started a large woman came into the composing room and handed me her union traveling card and requested that I slip her up on the hand side of the extra board for employment that evening. I overheard a couple of tramp printers refer to her as Big Mama, or Big Marie. I was trying to remember where I had seen that face before.

"The foreman came to me and asked, 'What can she do?' Marie overheard the foreman so went over to him and poked him a couple of times on the shoulder, and said, 'I can do anything a Goddamn man can do except piss in a bottle.' She was assigned to the proof room. Her working card showed her to be 'Marie something or other,' but I still could not place the face. No one seemed to know her background, except that she was a tramp printer.

"I still couldn't remember the face. Then in 1967, I too hit the road as a tramp printer. As I worked on different newspapers over the country I often heard the men talk about 'big mama.' She seemed to be known all over the country.

"In 1970 I came to El Paso, Texas, and went to work on the local paper. On the second night in walks 'Big Marie'; she was already working there. Both of us were assigned to the proof room. I was reading news matter and she was teamed up with another printer reading classified ads. She was then 72 years of age.

"During a coffee break she began telling her partner about going to the Philippines to be with her husband who was in the Navy. That rang a bell. I asked, 'Marie, when did you go to the Philippines?' She said, 'My daughter and I left San Diego on July 5, 1930 on the Navy Transport Chaumont.' I said, 'You know Marie, I too left San Diego on the Navy Transport Chaumont on July 5, 1930 as a young Marine headed for China. And Marie, it wasn't worth no five bucks.' She grinned broadly, as if she knew exactly what I meant.

"She later got in trouble with the Union and had charges preferred against her for 'conduct unbecoming a Union member.' She managed to get a traveling card and leave El Paso before the charges went to trial. About two weeks later, the FBI came looking for her. The story that we got was that her Navy husband had gone down on one of the ships during the bombing of Pearl Harbor. She was drawing a Navy pension from him. She married an old printer in Chicago who soon died and she was drawing Social Security under his name and number. She married another old printer who passed away and she was also getting Social Security under his name and number. Being over 70 she was drawing full Social Security under her own name and number, and at the same time being paid union wages as a proofreader. Was living in a small 15-foot trailer and getting food stamps and giving them to an illegal alien to keep her trailer clean. She knew all the angles. She passed away in San Antonio."

Le Hanesworth

Although she changed jobs often, Le Hanesworth is another lady printer who doesn't rank herself as a true "tramp printer." But she was very helpful and supportive of this project, and we believe her experiences are typical of women who moved from job to job—not from a sense of adventure, but as a normal course of "settling down."

Actually I was unlike most traveling printers in many ways. First off, no one in my family had been in printing; and I sort of fell into it because of World War II. And I've been forever grateful to Mr. Hesla, the principal of our high school, in Orange City, Iowa, who urged my friend Millie and me to go to work on the weekly Sioux County *Capital* after school and Saturdays—for $2.00 a week.

There I learned the printing trade, and I stuck it out for six years. I left for the *Daily Iowan* in Iowa City, Iowa, intending to work my way through college and get a journalism degree. The *Daily Iowan* also had a job shop, where a Literary Quarterly was published, so I had to learn small caps. Not all operators could set them—on the rail, as I recall. And once I set 1 1/2 galleys, 25 picas wide, in French. Job shops were always a challenge: different equipment, tabwork, etc. Just followed the copy!

I came within a semester of a journalism degree, but I'd saved some money, and opted for a trip to Europe in 1952. There I bicycled 1,500 miles, stayed in Youth Hostels, looked up relatives and even found a sixth cousin who remembered the day my two uncles walked from the village in North Holland to catch the boat to America in the late 1800s.

When I finally returned to Iowa City, I got my job back on the *Iowan* and worked to save money for my second trip to Europe. In 1954 I wandered as far north as Norway and south as Turkey (but not on a bicycle this time). I did my first skiing at Zermatt in Switzerland, loved it, and decided to look for work in Colorado when I returned. But first I had to do another stretch on the *Iowan* to get the wherewithall.

In Colorado, I met my future husband. Don was a reporter/photographer, and we quit our jobs to get married, and to ski—which we did at Aspen until the money ran out. No jobs were available, so we returned to Iowa and worked on the weekly Tipton *Conservative* and then to the Fairfield *Ledger* until Don decided to get his M.A. in journalism at SUI. We went to Iowa City and my old job on the *Iowan* for the third time. When Don received his degree, we headed back to Colorado.

I found a job at the Littleton *Independent,* a small daily outside of Denver Tiring of commuting, I looked for work closer to home, and found a job in a synagogue converted to a job shop: Golden Bell Press. That's where I got my International Typographical Union card, some 35 years ago. I really liked that job: a good foreman, interesting people, and as one of four operators, once I got a whole history of the State of Colorado to set in type—copy 3 or 4 inches high!

In 1961 we decided to leave Colorado, to "buy into" a California weekly newspaper, the Sebastopol *Times.* We worked seven days a week, but in the end, we were both "fired." First and only time. It wasn't because we were incompetent. The partnership arrangement just couldn't work with a "partner" who drank like a fish. It took an attorney to get back the money we had put into the paper.

After three years as a sub at the Santa Rosa *Press Democrat,* and working in two job shops as needed, I landed a situation as a Linotype operator. During my 30 years at the P.D., I ended my printing career well versed in three or four computer systems, which one by one themselves became obsolete. I also did proofreading in every shop I worked in, and did a stint as night chairman. I retired in 1991, just three months short of 50 years as a working printer.

I had a unique style of setting type. Because I taught myself the keyboard, I used my right forefinger mostly, all over the right side of the keyboard. My left forefinger "set" the e t a o i n row only. At the Press Democrat, I was known for setting type with stub pencil in my right hand to circle errors the proofreader missed. Between the TTS punchers and errors on the "automatics," there were as many as 3 to 4 inches of corrections slugs per galley. It made work for me on the 'ring' machines.[2] One machine was for straight matter corrections only, one for headlines, and the third for cutlines. I was pretty good at this, faster than the men operators back and forth on those three Linotypes.

---

[2] Linotypes used exclusively for corrections were called *ring machines* because galley corrections were circled or ringed with a pencil to draw attention to them.

The thing I especially liked about working in union shops was that women's wages were the same as men's wages, not always true in non-union places. Although women were not always welcome at first, once you proved yourself as a worker, you'll quickly earn the respect of all, including the foremen!

From a Tramp Printer's Wife
from Greta Cleary

We traveled with two young children. We started in 1956, when our oldest girl, Naomi, was 7-1/2 years old. Our baby, Colleen, was not quite a year old.

We began our travels in a small camper trailer, a replica of an old overland stage coach. We traversed the United States, from New York State to California, back to Florida, up to New York State and then back to Florida again. For over ten years we traveled. From Florida to West Virginia, Ohio, Michigan, Illinois, Tennessee, Arkansas, and back to New York from time to time. We customarily wintered in Florida.

We had friends and good times wherever we went. We visited all the national parks in the area, visited museums and art galleries, as well as parks and playgrounds for the children. It was a hands-on education for the whole family. Our children were in and out of schools two or three times a year. Teachers used to comment on the well-rounded education they had.

Sundays were always family days. The four us always did something together: picnic with friends, go to the zoo or a beach, or just visit with our new-found friends and our old established friends.

Twice in West Memphis, Arkansas, we rented the same house; it was unfurnished. It had a stove, refrigerator and dishwasher, but that's all. We bought a kitchen table and chairs plus a rocking chair at a second hand store. For chairs we used beer cases and we slept on the floor. Most of the time, though we could find a furnished place!

Traveling was fun, educational and interesting for the 14 years it lasted. But I'm glad it's over. I'm happy to be settled down. I no longer have the wanderlust. I have to say, that if I had my life to live over, I would do it again, the same way.

Twin-Nick Printers
from Ted Morse #35932, ITU 59-yr. member

Old-time handset compositors with sharp eyes and sensitive fingers, hand-picking stickfuls of small type, were taught to recognize wrong fonts by "feel." The righthand forefinger touching the nicks of foundry type being assembled into lines in the stick was part of the skill of hand-setting for 500 years. The "feel" acquired by astute journeymen in hand-setting extended to nicknaming female printers "two-nicks."

Gutenberg's wonderful printing trade offered sheltered employment, year-round paydays, and semiprofessional jobs to generations of proofreaders, press-feeders, typesetters, folders, and platen-and-roller washers, and did not require brute strength. Cleaning ink-fountains DID discolor dainty fingernails, but "twonick" printers persisted.

In the early 1900s a flood of magical monsters made more room for "twin-nicks" or "two-nicks." Unitype and Simplex typesetting machines came into being, quickly replaced by Mergenthaler's Linotype, Harris Intertype and (best of all) the modernistic Davenport, Iowa Linograph (15 magazines straight up-and-down with type-face 5 points above the shoulder of the slug, and 81-size mats and 6-mold discs).

"Dummy" keyboards for all of them were widely distributed. Linotype schools with dummy keyboards were found in every town. Institutes for the deaf promised fabulous careers to graduates. "Two-nicks" became ITU members by hundreds; mostly in genteel roles, sitting in comfortable booths reading proofs or "tickling keyboards" with a man to attend to the occasional rude distributor stop or other mysterious machine problem.

As a "journeyman" touring the country in search of an ideal situation, I predicted the end of the Gutenberg era when confronted with "homeguard" two-nicks in Beatrice, Neb.; Van Wert, Ohio; Huntington and Fort Wayne, Ind.; Enid, Okla.; Leavenworth, Kan.; El Paso, Tex.; and even Chicago.

Whistling in the Composing Room

Whistling has been a taboo since the earliest days of printing in the 15th century. It was universally against chapel rules in the old shops in England, and probably even earlier, when the scribes labored at calligraphy on sheepskin parchment. The common comment about such a violation of composing room ethics was: "Anyone who would whistle in a print shop would play with himself in church."

One night shift, just as a markup man was making this caustic accusation against a particularly annoying whistler, Erma Wesson, a sometimes tramp proofreader on the San Jose *Mercury News* happened to be passing by and obviously heard the comment. Everyone was momentarily embarrassed. She took a long look at the whistler and said, "Hell, I bet he whistles in church, too. We all know what he does in the Goddamn composing room!"

❈❈❈

from Marion Dearman

I didn't know about the taboo regarding whistling until I had been a journeyman about five years. I was working on the paper in Enid, Oklahoma, happily whistling at my work, whereupon a woman Linotype operator let me know in no uncertain terms that my whistling annoyed her, and that it violated a taboo, and that I was to cease and desist my imitation of a canary bird.

Wail of the Discomfited

I'm thinking today
Of those days now passed away,
When work was plenty and subs were in demand;
Of those good old days of yore,
Now gone for evermore,
When everything in type was set by hand.
Of work there was abundant
All pockets filled redundant,
In those good old happy days gone by;
When everything was blooming,
The business it was booming,

And the sub he had a "twinkle in his eye."
Old memories now crowd o'er me,
And like pictures pass before me,
like a ship now stranded on the rocks;
How I'd like to hear once more,
As I often did before,
The "rattle of the balls within the box."
Those days now gone forever,
Associations old they did sever,
And what a change came o'er that happy scene;
They have left us all sad-hearted,
From old friends we are all parted,
Through the advent of the deadly "machine."
May the devil keep a corner,
Hot as Hades —even warmer—
In fact, the hottest corner ever seen;
And tack up sign to be observed,
"That this corner is reserved
For inventors of the type-setting machine."

by John Henry Curtin, tramp printer

CIVIL WAR TO WWI

ALTHOUGH PRINTERS traveled ever since the invention of moveable type, the American tramp printer was a unique breed. The constant, rapid expansion of the frontier made the tramp lifestyle possible and the industrial revolution increased his numbers, dictated the direction of his wanderings, and the skills required of him. The tobacco-chewing, hard drinking, but proud craftsman, who was also far more literate than most residents of the towns he visited, was a worthy role model for young printers and apprentices who had not been on the road. On the positive side, the role model included pride of craft, freedom of work and employment, sense of solidarity with fellow printers, especially for International Typographical Union members.

The beginning of true "tramp printing" in North America got under way during the California Gold Rush, and increased in magnitude after the Civil War. The years from the Revolution to the outbreak of hostilities between North and South marked a time of expansion and proliferation of newspapers and commercial printers. Printing's move West accelerated with the flow of emigrants to Oregon and California. Wagon trains often included ox-drawn vehicles loaded with type cases and Washington hand presses. One or two wagons could carry everything needed to establish a tent-shelter newspaper office. Within days of making camp, the first editions of a hand-set newspaper would be circulating through the new community. While these pioneer publishers and editors were journeyman printers, they couldn't exactly be called "tramp printers." They traveled not because of necessity, or for adventure, but rather for the specific purpose of starting a publishing business. They sought to plant roots in the first fertile economic soil they encountered. But once established in towns, villages and cities, printing offices flourished and provided jobs for traveling printers who followed the call of the road and the romance of working in the developing West.

After the Civil War

The War Between the States slowed expansion of newspapers and print shops. This was a time of consolidation. Then, when hostilities finally ceased, the westward migration resumed in earnest. This post-war expansion was the first of a series of boom-and-bust cycles. The post-Civil War era was characterized by happy and carefree days for tramp printers, unmatched until the post-WW2 era. Names of these early tramp printers were well-known at the time, but most have faded away today, just as today's names will someday only be found in obscure publications like the one you are now reading. Nineteenth-century tramp printers moved between mining camps, boom towns, cattle settlements and port cities. Many alternated between a miner's pan and a type stick, usually to find a bonanza with neither tool. Some, like Mark Twain and Bret Harte, failed to find fame and fortune in gold and silver mines, returned to their trade as typesetters and eventually moved on to other writing, rather than hand-pegging pursuits. Alaska beckoned, Hawaii lured. Some tramp printers, frustrated by the Pacific's limiting shoreline, hopped aboard ships and headed for even more distant, western climes.

One of my favorite tramp printing tales is of the establishment of the first newspaper in the Oklahoma Territory. The protagonists were George Price—who retired from the San Jose *Mercury-News* at about age 80—and his father who was an old-time newspaper publisher who was also proficient at hand-setting type and pulling copies of a double tabloid layout on his hand-operated Washington press. The two of them took their place at the starting line on the day of the "Land Rush." Their large wagon was loaded with type, the Washington press, paper, ink, a tent, and everything they needed to go on-line with a newspaper. When they reached their destination, they didn't even wait to pitch a tent before going to work on the paper. They set up their cases and began setting type under the shade of large oak tree. By the next morning, folks were reading copies of the first newspaper in the Oklahoma Territory.

Missouri River Pirates
from John Edward Hicks,

(The years between the Gold Rush and the closing decades of the century marked a glorious period for tramp printers.)

Printers who worked after 1850 had solid sustenance in their 'journeymen" travels. Every little county seat had at least two weeklies. Cities boasted half a dozen dailies and numerous job shops. Everywhere he went, the old-time hand-pegger found employment, card-passing sustenance and friends.

Many stories came to us about a celebrated group of travelers whose names were famous in the latter 1800s. For several decades, an almost legendary crew of itinerant printers—known as the "Missouri River Pirates"—set type and drank whiskey in river towns on the banks of the Missouri and Mississippi. Stories concerning the "Pirates" are steeped in mystery, but enough has been established as fact to substantiate that such an aggregation existed in the mid-Victorian era of the last century.

It's probable that the group formed around 1860 when a Kansas City newspaper went nonunion and fired its typesetters, yet some believe that the Pirates were organized in Omaha in the 1880's. Although they held certain mock ceremonials when a number of the Pirates got together and did a little drinking—which was frequent—it was never a formally organized group. "Pirates" was just a name given those who tramped the Missouri River valley and lived off the country. Over the years many old-timers proudly laid claim to having been a member of the Missouri River Pirates.

For several years the Pirates could be found almost anywhere along the Missouri River from Sioux City to St. Louis, their numbers augmented by drifters from city and small-town print shops alike. They also toured Omaha, Kansas City, St. Joe, Joplin and Memphis, and some would occasionally find their way to towns on the upper Mississippi and in Chicago and even as far north as the Twin Cities.

The Pirates were absolute masters of printing (and card-passing)[1] and knew exactly which print shops to infiltrate for work. Back in those days, every little town had print shops in need of help, the larger towns had daily papers and the cities with publishing plants and large papers. This era was one of the three "golden ages" for tramp printers.

All Pirates may not have been top-notch printers. Many smalltown compositors who joined the Pirates had what the old-timers called "nice fingers," from setting nothing but the larger faces of type, and sometimes had difficulty setting the smaller nonpareil and brevier fonts. Many were eager to join their restless brethren for adventure. A few were exceptional in one way or another, and their names come down to us clear and strong.

"Judge" Grigsby

John Edward Hicks described one of the more colorful Missouri River Pirates the following way: "One of the early-day vintage Pirates was 'Judge' Grigsby. On my way to Sedalia, I ran across him near the little town of Knob Noster. He was dressed in a frock coat, white waistcoat, striped trousers, immaculate linen and patent leather shoes—all topped by a silk hat. He was one of the most picturesque of the old tourist printers, one who never rode in boxcars, but did his traveling either on the velvet cushions or on foot. I believe he preferred the latter mode as being more cognate with his philosophy of a leisurely and gracious manner of spending one's life.

"As we walked along, he told me something of his theory of life: To live fully and richly, to acquire the greatest delight for the mind in the joys of intellectual curiosity. He would study, he said, the text of nature and the book of life, learning from things about him. He quoted Rousseau to the effect that the only way to travel was on foot while one reveled in the freshness and harmony beside the little streams. Railroads and steamboats, he said, had robbed the pilgrimages of journeymen workers of their poetry, thereby

---

[1] When a union compositor couldn't catch a day's work, he could "pass" his union card around the printers who were working. Usually each working printer would put some money on the card and pass it on to another printer to contribute.

shortening the journey through life."

Mining Camps in the 70s
from John Edward Hicks' book

Cheyenne was a disappointment in that it was not as lively as I had expected it would be. When the soldiers came in on pay day from near-by Fort Russell there might be a little heightening of the activities in that district called "Little Chicago," and especially would this be true if there were a liberal admixture of Wyoming cowboys in town to whoop it up.

The two newspapers, the *Sun* and the *Leader,* had hardly enough extra work to keep me going, and, too, there were other subs in town with whom the extra work had to be shared. Therefore much of my time was spent in the saloon of Colonel Luke Murrin on Seventeenth Street or in that of Wes Moyer. The favorite saloon for a tramp printer flying light for dough was Jake Esselborn's Pioneer, where the free lunch was excellent. Here I met and swapped yarns with Cy Houser, sometimes known as "Leadville Cy," and "Kid" George Woods, also a Leadville printer. When they said they were going back to take another look at that rowdy silver camp and invited me to go along, I saw no reason to refuse, for capitalist, criminal, tenderfoot and tramp, all drifted in to the silver camp.

Perched at more than ten thousand feet, opposite Colorado's highest peak, Mount Elbert, on one side of the wide Arkansas River valley, Leadville's was one of the most beautiful settings in America. Next to Elbert, Mount Massive rose to thirteen thousand feet. To the east were the gray cliffs of the Saguache, the Sheridan and the Mosquito. To the north were the Blue Mountains. The town lay in an elevated basin, between the main range of the Rockies and a parallel spur known as the Mosquito Range, with the broad valley of the Arkansas River running mid way between them.

The first newspaper in Leadville had been the *Reveille,* the equipment for which was brought in by R. S. Allen, the proprietor, over rough mountain roads, by wagon and pack animals. At that time, 1878, copies of the paper had been eagerly bought by news-hungry miners at ten cents a copy. At that, the paper lasted only two years. Contributing to its early demise might have been the coming of the *Chronicle*, the *Herald* and the *Democrat*. In the fall of 1879, three enterprising printers, all employed on the Denver *Tribune*, looked to Leadville and decided it offered a rich field for budding journalists. They were James Burnell, C. C. Davis and John Arkins. They started the Leadville *Chronicle* with equipment which they had purchased in St. Louis, shipped by rail to Canon City, thence by team to Leadville, the freight costing more than the equipment.

Soon after, Burnell sold his one-third interest in the newspaper and got rich in mining deals. Arkins went back to the Denver newspapers and acquired a comfortable fortune; while Davis stayed and made his fortune with the newspaper in Leadville.

In 1879, also, the *Herald* was established. This morning newspaper was owned by several of Leadville's capitalists and managed by Billy Bush, manager of the Clarendon Hotel, and right-hand man of H. A. W. Tabor. The following year, John M. Barrett—editor of the *Rocky Mountain News* in Denver—interested the owner of that paper, W. A. H. Loveland, in forming a stock company to launch the Leadville *Democrat*.

Leadville was said to have been founded in 1877, but had its predecessor in California Gulch, sometimes known as "Boughtown," which dated back to 1860, when ten thousand persons flocked to the Arkansas River and washed out more than eight million dollars in gold. "Boughtown" had been one long street with very few houses, the miners living in wickiups, which they abandoned in winter, going back to Denver. Gold dust served for money in that lively settlement, and every merchant, gambler and saloonkeeper had his scale for weighing it. When the pay dirt began to get thin, the population drifted on, not forgetting first to raze the old log gambling hall and pan out two thousand dollars in dust that had sifted through the floor.

The thing that perhaps most of all had discouraged the miners was a heavy sand that interfered with the proper settling of the gold; sand so abundant that it clogged the riffles. This heavy sand was the carbonate of lead upon which the prosperity of Leadville later was built.

When the value of the carbonates was established, a motley crew poured into Leadville, and the joints along State Street catered to drunken miners and a depraved population. The Cyprians were early on the ground, and in the lower part of the town, near California Gulch, established a district where the painted filles in their gaily colored Mother Hubbards were well advertised and are still heard about. This row of little shacks in the lower end of town were called "shotgun" houses, built flush to the sidewalk and with no room between them. The bedizened denizens would all but kidnap any passing male. Early Leadville was rather proud of this district which it called "the row."

In those days Leadville's saloons, restaurants and gambling houses seldom closed, and brass bands and orchestras blared from a score of dance halls. The Grand Union, the Coliseum, the Olympic, the Belle Union, the Canterbury, the Chestnut, the Carbonate, the Little Globe and the Comique, masquerading as theaters, were packed every night.

By the time of my arrival in 1883, Leadville was able to boast of bigger, better, more vicious places and more of them. It then had a district, which in vice and corruption far surpassed the old district. The lower end of Harrison Avenue and State Street and other streets near the gulch, were lined with saloons, gambling houses, dance halls, variety theaters and the cribs of frail sirens.

Fighting, dancing, drinking and general tumult were the accepted thing along State Street. Some of these places were the Texas House, where Mont Duggan, alderman, was shot and killed; the Opera House Club, Louis Mitchell's and the Board of Trade. The uptown parlor houses, such as Mollie May's, Frankie Page's, Mollie Price's and Sallie Purple's, were usually two-story houses, brilliantly lighted at night and catering to the gentlemen who were inclined to be more extravagant than those who visited "the row."

One of the best known and largest places on State was that of Pop Wyman, the activities of which were divided into four classifications; gambling, drinking, dancing, and harlotry. Every game of chance known to the fraternity was going full blast—faro, keno, roulette and stud poker. Every night miners and businessmen, teamsters and tourists, bull whackers and clerks, gathered at the long bar or around the gambling tables. The dance hall girls were in short skirts, with bare arms and shoulders, and busts partly exposed. Dancing never lagged and it was customary always to buy a drink for one's fair partner.

One of the largest dance halls on State, a perfect den of vice, was that of Cole and Alexander, where from five hundred to fifteen hundred men would gather.

Very much to the fore in Leadville was H. A. W. Tabor, known as "Silver Dollar." In the preceding spring he had been appointed United States senator to fill out about thirty days of a vacant senatorial term. He had seized the opportunity to obtain a White House wedding with the "blessings" of President Arthur. For this bride, his second, he had built a mansion in Denver, but still maintained extensive interests in and frequently visited Leadville. One of his interests was the *Herald*, into which he sank $150,000 before tiring of the newspaper game and selling the property to C. C. Davis of the *Chronicle*.

Jugging for Catfish along the Missouri

Some years ago Charley Bishop, one of the Pirates, writing in one of the printing trade magazines, told of the Pirates "jugging" for catfish. He described how the itinerant printers sometimes traveled the river in flatboats with improvised cabins. As they loafed along, they would catch catfish weighing more than 100 pounds. Here is Charley Bishop's story:

"We would take a cord, half an inch thick and almost 125 feet long, with similar cord lines 12 feet long, each with a five-inch hook at the business end, placed 15 feet apart on the main line. A gallon jug, filled with air and tightly corked, was tied to each smaller line, and each hook baited with a piece of beef and liver and covered with a piece of red flannel. A big chunk of wood float was attached to one end of the main line and the other was fastened to the boat. When such an outfit had been rigged and baited, the boat was maneuvered with a rudder to mid-stream and the line was paid out. The wooden float and the jug floated with the current. When the jug went under, the line was pulled in and any fish on it were taken off.

Traveling through Nebraska, Iowa, Kansas, and Missouri, the "Pirates" would tie up at night and go visiting among the farmers and townspeople. Sometimes they'd drift their flatboats beyond St. Louis, down to Memphis, and occasionally as far as New Orleans. Bishop tells of the Catfish Hotel at Jefferson City, where for 15 cents they could buy a six-inch slab of succulent catfish, a quart of potatoes, hunks of cornpone, and all of the buttermilk they could drink.

❄❄❄

The Pirates never stayed long at any one place. The Kansas City *Times* was nearly always good for a half-dozen substitute hires nightly. Sioux City printers were generous in staking their union brothers in their vagrant trips down-river. In Kansas City, after working in shops on both sides of the Missouri-Kansas line they would gather at the Junction, the Arcade, the Red Onion or Miller's Bar to plan new expeditions over nickel beers and the ample free lunches served those days.

Sol Miller, editor of the Troy (Kan.) *Chief,* never rejected a tramp, according to Bishop. Troy is not far from the Missouri River, and the Pirates hazed many a novice by sending him over to see Miller. The editor kept a hogshead of rainwater at the rear of his shop, and whenever an itinerant compositor dropped around for a day or two at the typecase he wasn't permitted to go to work until he'd taken a bath in the barrel, with plentiful use of yellow soap.

Other city and small-town editors who were generous in giving the Pirates a day or two of work when they showed up were: Ed Howe of the Atchison *Globe,* the *Champion* and *Patriot of* the same city, Dan Anthony of the Leavenworth *Times* and several dailies of both Topeka and Lawrence, and their counterparts in Western Missouri.

The travelers knew that in Omaha, Brandeis Week was good for two or three weeks work in the autumn. Des Moines' Younkers Sales meant work. The Kansas State print shop put 40 sits on every April for the legislative session and Chicago Cuneo Press hired 300 hand-men for the Sears catalogs twice a year. Then in the winter time, printers in Montana needed substitutes so they could travel south on vacation. In Phoenix, before the era of air-conditioning, 100+degree temperatures made summer vacations (and subs) popular. A few Missouri River Pirates would temporarily abandon their river haunts and venture after the plentiful work.

❄❄❄

In the days when all newspaper copy was written by hand, and a none too legible hand at that, the story was told that 'Shad' Campbell, well-known tourist printer, had a piece of copy, the hieroglyphics of which, properly deciphered, would read Terre Haute Ind. Shad wrestled with the copy a while, spat a gargantuan stream of amber, swore a mouthfilling oath and set in type, Terrible Hot Indian.

❋❋❋

From the rear windows of the *Gazette,* a fine view could be had of the steamboats which still made regular trips on the Arkansas and the roustabouts could be heard as they chanted their coonjines. An open boxcar or gondola in the freight yards sometimes proved too tempting for the traveling gentry, as in the case of "Shorty Gamble." Shorty had a bottle concealed somewhere in the composing room and from time to time would take 'three drops of the auld craythur," each drink making him firmer in the belief that Little Rock was the least desirable spot in creation, and that wherever those boxcars in the yards below might carry him, the new location, though Hades itself, was bound to be an improvement. The old devil wanderlust kept tickling his feet until at last he made a grand sweep of the hand which held the type he was distributing, with the terse advice, "Go to your respective boxes!" With which parting admonition, he shuffled down the hill, crawled into a gondola and left Arkansas.

❋❋❋

Sam D. Leffingwell was publishing *Our Organette,* the semi-official organ of the International Typographical Union. He was a type of printer not met with every day. He had been a soldier in the Mexican War and a major in the Civil War. He had a vocabulary of cuss words that would have put to shame a river mate or a muleteer. He had been an actor, gaining some prestige in the smaller towns for his rendition of the classics. He was working in New York when Typographical Union No. 6 was organized under the presidency of Horace Greeley and still had in his possession a working card bearing Greeley's signature. He was a delegate from Indianapolis to Terre Haute meeting in 1881 when the groundwork was laid for the organization of the Federation of Trade and Labor Unions, forerunner of the American Federation of Labor.

Anaconda Montana, 1910
from "ol' Uncle Bert" Crampton
(a freelance writer until he died several years ago at age 99)

Before I became a member of Portland Oregon Typographical Union on August 29, 1906, I worked on the Washington *Monitor,* pulling the handle of a Washington Handpress. Lon DeYarmond was Secretary of the Portland ITU local. Wages then? $19.20 per week. I had a room across from the Oregonian building at $1.50 per week. A big platter of beef stew and vegetables at a union restaurant cost 15 cents. A shave in a union barber shop cost 15 *cents, haircut 25 cents. Portland was a nice town, but it wasn't long before I had the urge to travel.*

In the autumn of 1906, just before my 20th birthday, I was foremanizing on the *Rainier Register,* in Rainier, Oregon. Rainier was just a small country town at the time, but the owner and editor of the *Register* had the get-up-and-go of a fire engine, therefore, in addition to producing a twice-a-week paper we also had scads of jobwork, most of it from the Portland area. One of the jobs was a 24-page weekly church paper, 5,400 copies, all hand-set. To face a job like that today would scare me to death! But I had confidence in myself, just knew I could handle any job I tackled, and I still think I was a good printer. I had six union printers working under me and from five to seven girls.

The greatest "Print town" I was ever in was Anaconda, Montana. A sub coming into town in autumn could show up on the *Standard* and work steady all winter. When I put up my slip in the autumn of 1910, Pinky Holderby, a well-known 'boomer", grabbed me and didn't show up again for 17 days. After my first shift, Charlie Houck, another well-known character in those days, came up to me after work and asked how I was fixed for a room and a meal ticket. That was big-hearted Charlie for you . . . everybody's friend. Another time, a proofreader slipped me up, went on a drunk, ended up in a hospital and didn't get back for three months. "Lucky" Hart came through Anaconda that winter. The *Standard* is no more, having been merged with the *Butte Miner,* and is now known as the Montana *Standard.*

One Bill McWhiney, a very good friend of mine, foremanized on the Butte Miner for a time. Now Bill was a good scout, but one drink of 3-star Hennessy or 4 Roses, and Bill was away and running. He told me of one of his escapades: Said he got liquored up, boarded a train and went to sleep. When he awoke he asked the ticket-collector where he was going. Seems he had bought a ticket for a town in Minnesota where his mother lived!

TRAMPING IN THE 1920s

THE SECOND GOLDEN AGE for tramps occurred in the 1920s, between the close of the first World War and the beginning of the 1930s depression. Work was plentiful. Ted Morse said of these times: "All through the 1920s, the traveling journeyman with his make-up rule, pica-pole and favorite type stick rolled up in a well-stained apron was king of the mountain. Every little country village had a weekly paper and most county seats had two papers. Small cities like Wabash, Indiana and Lima, Ohio, often supported four or five flourishing daily newspapers. The 'big time' spots were places like New York City, Philadelphia, Boston and Baltimore, with dozens of nationally-read newspapers. Printing and publishing in the 1920s was the sixth largest U.S. industry. An itinerant printer had only to walk a block or two in any city, anywhere in North America to find a good job."

❄❄❄

(The following is a communication from a 1920s roadster who was well-known in his time. Mose Hartley has been dead for several years now; the following is his story, written in his own words when he was 87 years old, living in a Memphis retirement home.)

Now I'm not a young member and don't know too many of you folks [readers of the *Tramp Printers' Newsletter*]. My first Pine Bluff, Arkansas ITU working card is dated 1918, so you can see I don't know you young kids too well. I did know a few; was a delegate from Oakland, California a few years ago, during the Elmer Brown years. I recall the Oakland trip because it was the first time the ITU had employed a lawyer and the delegate from Chicago asked a question and some young punk on the platform yelled, 'I don't think the delegate has a right to ask that question!'

The old boy from Chicago hit the floor and says, "What the hell are you talking about? My union sent me 6,000 miles to ask that question and get an answer—and that's exactly what I intend to do!" The lawyer answered the question. Those were the days when printers ran the ITU all the way from the bottom to the top, and it was the days of the tramp printers. By the way, I got my nickname (Mose) while working in Little Rock. The baseball team signed a 245+pound Oklahoma Indian named Mose Yellowhorse. We were buddies and they called me "Little Mose" while he was still around.

In the 1920s, traveling printers were always welcome because situation holders worked six days a week then, and appreciated hiring a sub to get a day off once in a while. Fact is, I was chairman on the Arkansas Gazette in Little Rock, and on the first day of the "five-day week,"[1] I got a group of 16 and we all laid off and played golf all day. The foreman, Old W. F. (Wrongfont) McGuire liked to have a fit!

But I wanted to tell you about an incident involving old Conley — I forget his first name—they made him foreman of the *Press Scimitar* in Memphis and he got off to a flying start! One day I was sitting at my machine and somebody from the editorial room stopped to chat with me. Old Conley walked over and told me to stop people from talking to me during work hours. I said: "Conley, if you want them to stop, YOU tell them." I was pretty hot and followed him into his office and said: "Conley, I was here when you got here and I'll be here when you are gone."

A few days later, when they fired him, I couldn't resist the temptation; I walked into his office and said "Well, I'm still here and you are long gone!"

I know the good old days are gone, like when I worked in Little Rock—when such old time printers like Kokomo Phillips used to

---

[1] In 1930, the ITU passed a law requiring every situation holder to hire a sub one day a week during the unemployment emergency. Eventually the union negotiated a five-day week to replace the usual six-day situations.

show up, along with Sunshine Wilson, and others. On Fridays we got paid at 4 p.m. and we would take off until 6 so we could go have a shot of whiskey and eat supper. I was chairman, and one night when we went back to work, McGuire walked over to my machine and asked, "Where is Kokomo?"

"I don't know; he was over at the cafe . . . I'll see if I can find out." I walked over to the slipboard and there was a note for me, it said: "I hear they are selling whiskey for 50 cents a pint in Tulsa. You know where my slug is!"[2] Kokomo was long gone. The foreman just laughed. You think one of them would do that now? Ah, those were the days!—*H.J. (Mose) Hartley, HUReg. #87072*

❉❉❉

Working in the 1920s
from Ted G. Morse

Tramp printers in the 1920s had wonderful access to employment. Printing burgeoned in every town and village in the nation. Printing and publishing was the sixth largest U.S. industry. Frequent job changes were induced by local laws preventing newly-graduated apprentices from working in their home towns for a year; and also by hundreds of opportunities for employment in the help wanted columns of the *Publishers Auxiliary,* printed by Western Newspaper Union, available in every print shop. If you had an apron, a makeup rule and a pica-pole (and knew how to use them), your future was assured.

Every country village had a paper, and most county seats had two. Small cities like Wabash, Indiana and Lima, Ohio each had *four* flourishing dailies. The "big time" spots were New York City, Philadelphia, Boston and Baltimore, with dozens of nationally-read newspapers. An itinerant printer had only to walk a block or two in any city, anywhere in North America to find a good job. The Publishers Auxiliary offered jobs on steamships, in the Fiji Islands,

---

[2] Sometimes, instead of putting a sub's name on a slip of paper, it was set in type, either on the Linotype or the Ludlow machine, and hung on the slipboard. Therefore, a slipboard was often called a *slug-board.*

Guam, Cuba, Puerto Rico, the Philippines and South Africa. "Country" printers were eagerly sought because of their expertise in stone-work, make-ready on Gordon presses, sheet-feeding the drum presses, paper cutting, flat-casting on Dr. Miles' equipment, doing the mailing with hand-operated mailers, and the like.

I remember being hired by Tom Cook, foreman of the Bristol, Va.-Tenn. *Herald Courier* as an ad-man. The $36 weekly for 48 hours work seemed like financial heaven after the $5 a day stints in Omaha and Beatrice, Nebraska, Pana, and Springfield, Illinois, Napanee, Indiana, Westchester, Kentucky and towns in between.

In the early 1920s, I found myself hired before election-time to duplicate Illinois State printing forms at the Springfield *Register* job shop. Towering racks of pre-Civil War type fonts in wood cases were stacked ceiling-high in a 12-foot high basement room. Dusty fonts of long-forgotten, un-nameable and un-describable type faces in curious sizes like small-pica, brevier, brilliant and burgoise, reached almost to the ceiling like boxes in a shoe store.

Climbing ladders with stick in hand, we hand-set worn-out lines of 8-1/2 point Maximillian, 45 picas wide. The type often had been distributed by careless apprentices. This caused many corrections, so to correct the proof meant once more climbing to dizzy heights. An old man in his 70's, named Mr. Hoyle, directed all new journeymen to the proper ladder. I often wonder about the fate of Illinois State printing in the 1980's, with Mr. Hoyle not around. Needless to say, things must be different.

I worked in 33 cities and 20 states as a journeyman, but I never saw such a confused set-up as the Springfield, Ill. State Register job-shop. Although I worked on handset weeklies, the Springfield *Register* deserves first prize.

Riding the Freights
from Horace B. Norvill

Freight trains always stopped at "division" points, about every 100 miles, where there would be a roundhouse and shops. There they would change engines and crew before proceeding. When riding a freight it was necessary to alight before entering the freight yards at a division point because there would be railroad "dicks" patrolling the freight yards, looking for riders

We alighted before entering the first division point at Butler, Pennsylvania, walked around the yards and positioned ourselves for boarding the train just outside the yards northbound. When the train reached us it was proceeding at a pretty good clip. I grabbed it and waited for Cody to do the same. He grabbed and missed and was thrown onto the roadbed, cinders and gravel. By that time the train was rolling so fast that I couldn't jump off. So I waited for Cody at the next division point, and there we connected and hopped the next freight northbound.

During the trip through the Pennsylvania mountains, we had to travel through several tunnels. Two coal-burning locomotives pulling and two in the rear pushing created quite a tunnel full of coal smoke. It was so acrid that it became very difficult to breathe. Also, we were riding on the coupling between two cars, the one in front of us was loaded with lumber stacked on a flat car and fastened in a not too secure manner. It was subject to sliding. A very dangerous situation, but we made it to Buffalo without mishap.

At the *Buffalo News,* a perusal of the slipboard indicated poor prospects for floor work but excellent for Linotype operators. As the saying goes, that's where the work is, that's where I show. Cody slipped up on the ad floor, but didn't catch a hire.

I was assigned to a machine, and the copy cutter pointed to a copy box containing stock tables. I didn't even know how to align tabular matter; I'd never had to do it before. After struggling for about 20 minutes and not aligning even the first two lines, it became evident to the foreman that I could not do it. He told me to work off the straight-matter work.

I finished the night, and since nobody said anything about being fired, I showed up the next day. While waiting for show up time, the foreman told me there was no use showing up any more, that I would not be hired. So Cody and I went to the hotel, checked out and took a trolley car to the freight yards. The Buffalo yards were quite large and we had went out to the fringe where we could wait for trains, beyond the range of railroad cops who patrol the yards. I carried a freight time table and tried to pick out a train and destination. But the freight yards were so big that by the time the trains reached us, they were rolling along too fast to catch. At least they were too fast for Cody, who was scared of them after the spill he took in Pennsylvania. It was a moonlight night and even though it was midsummer, it got quite cold. We spent the whole night there trying to catch a train. Finally, as day was breaking, I was getting impatient. I was determined to catch the next train, no matter what it was or where it was going. I just wanted to get out of these yards. I could find my destination later. We didn't have to wait long before a likely train rumbled past. I urged Cody to grab it. He was afraid. Finally, I decided that if I grabbed it, it might give him the courage to do so. I did but he just stood there, hands raised.

As I saw the caboose pass him, I jumped off. Just then I saw a railroad cop run from behind the caboose and grab Cody by the arm. I couldn't do him any good and I certainly didn't want to be picked up there. So I ducked into the bushes. Just the day before, we had been loitering around in Buffalo, in the wrong part of town, and I had been questioned quite mercilessly by a plainclothes cop. Accused of everything from wife desertion to bank robbery. That told me that Buffalo was no place to be arrested.

I waited a short time until another train came along. I caught an empty flat car, which was careless, because it provided no protection from view or from the cold. Not far out of Buffalo the train stopped at what must have been a division point. I hopped off and started walking along the tracks looking for an empty box car. I encountered a man walking in my direction. He addressed me, "Where do you think you are going?"

"I'm looking for an empty box car, what do you think?"

"Where are you headed?"

I had somewhere heard that if you are picked up by a railroad dick you could be charged passenger fare to your destination. I had been studying the freight schedule and knew the towns along the way, so I told him the next little town.

A typestick which was the essential tool for handsetting type. some typesetters were so skillful and swift that they rivaled Linotype operators.

The gentleman standing at the Chandler & Price job printing press is supposedly one of the infamous "Missouri River Pirates" who roamed the length of the river between Kansas City and St. Louis. These carefree vagabonds alternated between working and fishing (as well as drinking copiously during both endeav-

From tramp printer to author.
Co-author John Howells worked for numerous newspapers and commercial printing plants before being displaced by computers. He switched to a successful career as an author and freelance writer. Pictured below working on a teletypesetter, a transition from the Linotype.

The Authors of *Tramp Printers*

From tramp printer to college professor. Co-author of this book, Dr. Marion Dearman worked all over the United States as a tramp printer before returning to the university to earn a degree in Sociology and a successful career in academia.

The Last Shift.. Expressions of despair ar hopelessness tell this story. The last shift at a Florida printing plant whe telephone books were printed. Composing room printers are "killing out" th pages of type as their job come to an end. The type will be melted and sold fo scrap. Computers will tak over jobs of printers, ending hundreds of years of tradition.

The San Francisco *Picayune* and the San Francisco *Herald*, side by side. These are just two of more than 20 daily newspapers published in San Francisco's heyday of handset type. When the Linotype came upon the scene capital investment increased, and smaller, less successful newspapers began dropping by the wayside. The San Francisco *Chronicle* was the only survivor.

A battery of Linotypes at the Sa Francisco *Examiner*, probably bac in the 1940s. A newspaper of this size might have as many as 50 Linotypes to set news and ads -- a many as 300 printers (sometimes more) working around the clock to produce a daily newspaper.

TRAMP PRINTERS

An early print shop. A woodcut from the 1500s showing the division of labor between typesetters, pressmen, and young "printer devils." Printing was originally done in the church chapel where the scribes worked illuminating manuscripts before they were displaced by the new process called *printing*.

Neckties and white shirts were traditionally worn by newspaper printers until the 1960s (when fashions changed forever, for everyone). But editors were expected to dress even more formally. Here we see the editor wearing his uniform: a coat with tails!

A newspaper from the 1880s. Note the neckties, even on women printers and apprentices. A mark of pride for a tramp printer: work a 10-hour shift in a white shirt and keep it clean enough to wear that night to the local dance hall or saloon.

The stereotype of a tramp printer as he was pictured by other printers, editors, and the townspeople: A rolling stone with a typestick in one hand a bottle of cheap bourbon in the other. Not all tramps drank, but enough did to maintain this image. The saying was: "A tramp printer only knows of two good jobs: the last one he had and the next one he will find."

A tramp printer as he might picture himself: a romantic wanderer who could quote Shakespeare, Mark Twain or Robert Service as easily as he could hop the next freight train, always looking for that next adventure. (Few actually fit this picture in real life.)

Famous tramp printers... from World War I, through the Great Depression, until the end of hot metal technology.

Lydia Avery traveled from the end of the first World War until the the beginning of the Depression. She worked on more than 30 newspapers, from coast to coast. Always dignified and a competent Linotype operator, Lydia enjoyed a welcome wherever she traveled. She settled down in New York City in 1930, retiring from the *New York Times* 40 years later. She was a regular contributor to our *Tramp Printers' Newsletter* until she was almost 100 years old.

Don Cleary Example of post-war tramp printers who traveled because they *enjoyed* traveling rather than looking for find work. As soon as he completed his 6-year apprentice-ship, Don and his wife Greta began an odessy that lasted until new printing processes changed the printing industry.

John Henry Curtin, the "poet laureate" of tramp printers, started traveling during the Depression era and continued traveling long after the war into the "good times." John was an intellectual, the epitome of a "gentleman" tramp. He didn't drink, he was always well dressed in a suit and tie, and had the vocabulary of a college professor. He was famous for posting his poetry on chapel boards and mailing poems to friends.

House trailers were favored homes for many tramp printers. Both of this book's authors traveled this way for several years. Pictured below was one of Don and Greta Cleary's homes on wheels. When staying in a town for a while, they would rent a furnished house. They would usually winter in Florida.

An explosion in technology. The Linotype was one of the earliest examples of automation. An extremely complicated machine, with more than 5,000 moving parts, the Linotype made an enormous impact on the process of printing and the dissemination of information. Within an incredibly short space of time, Linotype machines were in place in all sectors of the country, and all over the world--from big-city daily newspapers to backwater county seat weekly newspapers. One Linotype could easily set all the type a small newspaper needed for a weekly edition, thus making it possible for more pages and better quality, even in isolated country communities.

Skills needed. Because of the high level of skills necessary to operate one of these costly and delicate machines, a competent Linotype operator could find employment in almost any city or town in the country when times were good, and could travel and find work when hard times set in.

(above) **A woman editor,** publisher and printer, setting type for her small town weekly newspaper somewhere in in the Midwest.

(above and below) **Newspaper composing room** in Roseburg, Oregon in the 1890s. Note that most typesetters here are women, a common practice. The Typographical Union insisted that women be paid the same amount as men starting in the mid-1800s. Some printing plants preferred women because they didn't tend to drink as much as men, and women weren't so quick to quit and move on to the next town at the slightest excuse.

Two ancient components of newspaper production: the composing room (above) and the cylinder press (below). Skills were tediously learned, but once acquired were transferable from one printing shop to another, thus making it easy to travel from one job to another. Traditionally the apprenticeship took six years, after which a period of journeying from town to town was required to polish one's skills. This period of travel was the origin of the word "journeyman".

He said, "Get the hell out of here, and don't let me see you again." I did exactly that.

Since I had spent a long, tense, rather cold night in the Buffalo freight yards, I was tired and hungry. I vacated the yards and found myself in a very small village. I came upon a lot where a house was being built. It was framed, with a sub-floor, but that was about all. It was still early in the morning and nobody was around so I lay down on the floor and took a little rest. Actually fell asleep briefly.

I awoke, looked around and noticed a small house, what appeared to be a farm house, on the fringe of the village. While I considered myself a "tramp printer," I had never until now, actually gone to a back door and asked for a handout, like an ordinary tramp. But I packed up my pride and did just that.

I was greeted at the door by a very kind, middle-aged lady, who listened to my story and invited me into the kitchen. She asked me to sit at the kitchen table while she prepared a real breakfast for me: bacon, eggs, toast and coffee. She said it might even be her son in that position some day, and she would hope that he might be treated so well.

After a little rest and that good breakfast, I felt refreshed and ready to take on the world. Consulting my freight time table, I realized that I wasn't too far from Rochester. That would be my next destination. I walked out of town far enough to be clear of the freight yards and hopped the next train to Rochester.

Militancy in the 1920s

As an apprentice, I had extensive exposure to several of the widely known tramp printers on the "central circuit," Ardmore being directly on the circuit, midway between Oklahoma City and Dallas-Fort Worth. I became acquainted with such characters as Weary Willie Waterhouse from Walla Walla, Washington. And there was "Kokomo Phillips," "Santa Claus," and many others. Their standard practice was to show up and make themselves available for work in their work classification. If someone in their work classification wanted a day off, he would hire the drifter for the day. If not, he would give the chairman his card to "pass." They generally came up with the equivalent of a day's pay, and would go on to the next town on the circuit.

One day, while making corrections on a certain galley of society copy, the operator had correction on a line referring to a meeting of a local women's club known as "Ladies of the Leaf." He was in the habit of referring to them as "Ladies of the Fig Leaf." One day, while making corrections, he just automatically, without thinking, set the correction line that way. I was inserting corrections at the correction bank and I did not catch it. Consequently, it went to press and was published thus. When the paper was distributed to the ladies of the club, naturally all hell broke loose. They insisted that the operator responsible for the reference to them as "Ladies of the Fig Leaf" be discharged. And he was. Burt Gaines, chairman of the chapel, called a special chapel meeting and defended the operator, making the point that it was an innocent mistake and that discharge constituted unduly harsh discipline; that it did not justify discharge. He said that if the operator was to be discharged, he, for one, was also through. All members of the chapel concurred and the chairman reported to the publisher that if the operator was discharged, the entire force was through. Naturally, the man was immediately reinstated. This occasion made a very strong impression on me; that the union could bring such pressure to bear, and so quickly.

Carpinteria Herald
from Gerald Bamitz

Back in the old days (1921-1925) Arthur Clark was owner, publisher, editor and printer-pressman of the *Carpinteria Herald*, a weekly printed in Carpinteria, California, located 5 miles south of Santa Barbara on Highway 101. One day, Arthur ran some editorials about local servicemen discharged from service after World War I—regarding the handling of benefits granted them by the government. Some of these ex-servicemen resented the editorials. A group of them appeared at the *Herald* office in Carpinteria. The editorprinter was busy setting type by stick. (The *Herald* was handset in 8 and 10 pt. Standard Clearface.) They asked the editor to accompany them to the local servicemen's post headquarters. There he was escorted to the boxing ring and the veterans horsewhipped him across the shoulders. This story made headlines in daily newspapers throughout the U.S.A.

After this incident Arthur called the local ITU union for help; his back was a mess of black-blue marks and scabs making it tough to sit on a stool and handset type. I answered the call and we worked together nights to get out the sheet. Both of us smoked corn-cob pipes while working. Arthur was kinda dizzy from his ordeal and would get mixed up on the pipes, sometimes smoking my pipe instead of his own. When this happened I would cut off the stem and start smoking again. Soon my pipe was nothing but a corncob bowl.

Old ITU local 394, Santa Barbara, always granted help to the *Herald* when the workload grew too heavy for the one-man newspaper-job shop. Many an old-time ITU member received a day or two of work at this shop. Later, an early model Linotype was installed, bringing the hand-set days to an end. This paper was printed on an old-style flatbed Goss. The first sheet had to be put in position in the grippers, ready to go. Then the operator had to turn on the press from a box on the other side, then run back around to the feeder platform and feed the next sheet without a miss, as there was no offset pedal. This was a four-page weekly, 12-pica column. When short of type to fill, you placed 1-column metal base with a track in the center. Western Newspaper and others sold plate to fit the track which were stories and ads to be used as fillers.

❊❊❊

from Ed Burr

In Cincinnati, back in the 20's, prohibition had made the town pretty dry, but we managed for a while. Then one day we ran low on supplies. Scorcher Burns, a tall, angular dude with bushy black hair volunteered to go to Newport, Ky. for a new supply, even though he had a little trouble walking straight. When he got the gallon of booze his next problem was to get by the bridge guard. His reputation for acting crazy was well known. When the guard asked him what he had in the jug, he said loud and clear: "Whiskey, Goddamnit!" They must have thought he really had kerosene, for they waved him on through. Scorcher died young, but he sure lived a lot while here.

Ralph Warden was a traveling machinist. He had a vicious temper. One night he was fixing a machine on the *Wheeling Intelligencer* when a fellow by the name of Weakley, who had words with him a few days before, said something to him. Worden let a hammer fly that just missed. The next thing I heard of Ralph was that he had killed his girl friend in a jealous rage in Cleveland. He went to prison for life. Next we heard he was a hero when they had a fire in prison. He was about to have his sentence shortened, but his temper flared again and he killed another inmate and got the life sentence back.

THE GREAT DEPRESSION

IT WAS A TIME a lot like the present. It was a golden age of peace and plenty—or so it seemed. Reflecting the optimism of the era, President Herbert Hoover said in a speech given March 4, 1929: "... man is in sight of triumph over poverty." Why not? We had mass production and ways of coaxing the masses to buy; easy credit was encouraged and savings discouraged. Movies, radio, and the print media urged us to consume endlessly and whom to emulate and imitate. The stock market reached new highs almost every week, just like 1996. There seemed to be no end to the good times.

But there was a jolting, abrupt end: on October 24, 1929—Black Tuesday—a stock market crash erased two-thirds the value of all listed securities. Banks closed throughout the country. One-fourth to one-third (estimates vary) of the work force were unemployed and one-fourth of our farmers lost their farms. The products of the remaining farmers sold for less than the cost of production. Industrial production fell to fifty percent of its pre-crash levels. But Henry Ford said that unemployment was due to the fact that "the average man won't really do a day's work unless he is caught and cannot get out of it. There is plenty of work to do if people would do it." Soon afterwards, Ford laid off 75,000 workers. Skilled and unskilled workers alike felt the agony as unemployment spread like a fire storm throughout the economy of the United States of America, the bastion of the free enterprise system.

We changed leaders in 1932. On becoming president, Franklin Delano Roosevelt, a paraplegic pragmatist, assured us that we had "nothing to fear but fear itself." He was willing to try almost anything. He gave us alphabet soup: AAA, CCC, FHA, NRA, TVA, and much more. He gave us Boulder, Grand Coulee, and Bonneville Dams. He gave us the Social Security System and some relief for the hungry and homeless. But he did not give us prosperity; as late as 1938 unemployment was still over twenty percent. We had what appeared to be a permanent paradox of three-fourths of the work force working full time or more and the rest underemployed or unemployed. This could have been fixed by fiat, the way Hitler and Mussolini did. Or it could have been remedied by adoption of the 30-hour week as the standard, as was proposed by Hugo Black of Alabama (later Supreme Court Justice) and seriously considered by Congress. We could have produced everything we needed, received leisure, and solved unemployment with the shorter work week. Instead we opted for the forty-hour week with overtime, which enabled those working to earn more and consume more. We are still paying for this mistake.

Printers, like other craft workers, were hit hard by Depressionera layoffs. However, unlike most other occupational groups, they strove mightily to lessen the pain of the unemployed by sacrifice on the part of those fortunate enough to weather the layoffs. Printers had a long history of volunteer sharing of work, due in part to the erratic nature of the work. What had been voluntary became a necessity during the Depression: de facto became de jure.

The ITU, at its Long Beach convention passed a law limiting its members to 5 days a week. Printers at many locals already had been hiring subs at least one day a week. Others devised a system that some called "the dole" whereby money was made available as a gift to the out-of-work printer (this was not the same as the time-honored system of "passing the card"). Some locals even paid excess printers a set amount to leave town. Kansas City, Missouri, for instance, paid 60 printers fifty dollars each (a goodly sum then) to leave town, with the provision that the money was to be repaid if they returned.

Almost alone among workers' associations, the ITU pursued shorter hours and shared work. San Francisco Local #21 successfully negotiated a 37-1/2 hour week as far back as 1934. For the last several decades of the ITU's existence, the 35-hour week was the standard, with 30 hours or even less for the lobster (graveyard) shift. This model would have been very useful in solving the nation's unemployment problems—then and now. Unfortunately, the nation opted for longer hours and overtime for some and unemployment, underutilization, and poverty for too many of its workers.

Although ITU members attitudes toward the reproduction contracts (sometimes called "deadhorse" or "bogus") were somewhat ambiguous, our respondents were nearly unanimous in their defense of the overtime laws. This was true for all age cohorts as well as for both homeguards and travelers. Even many foremen realized that if printers disliked long hours and didn't profit from it, they would be more likely to try to avoid it by working more efficiently. In any case, as one traveler put it, "the foreman could not reward his pimps by giving them the overtime if it was bumped by a sub." The overtime laws emphasized that the ITU members valued the rest, recreation, education, more time with friends and families, and other leisure activities above and beyond the extra earnings they could have gotten by working long hours for extra earnings. Overtime hogging was antithetical to unionism. "The overtime law," according to one of our respondents, "was one of the most innovative and humanitarian things I had ever seen. What Union men they must have been to pass that law!"

Economic conditions created another mode of itinerant printer. The Depression of 1929-1942 forced a small army of printers "on the road" for reasons other than adventure. Most tramp printers in Depression years had no choice. Moving around in search of work was their only option. Not until World War II created labor shortages, did the problem of work scarcity ease up. Even then, because of paper shortages and war-time restrictions on travel, moving about was difficult and steady jobs were easier to find, so many tramp printers settled down. By the time the war ended, they found themselves as permanent fixtures in their jobs, and to their chagrin, "homeguards."

The following are tales from printers of struggles and success in coping with that terrible trauma in the nation's memory: the Great Depression.

Black Tuesday
from Ted Morse

(Ted Morse was foreman on the Omaha Bee News *during this traumatic period of unemployment, downsizing and cost-cutting. Ted died several years ago in Zanesville, Ohio.)*

Black Tuesday, late in October, 1929, was the beginning of the end for thousands of foot-loose journeymen printers. Hand-set experts and traveling Lino operators suddenly discovered that the next job (a block away) was jealously hung onto by a "homeguard" and no new help was needed.

In Omaha, Hearst's newly-consolidated *Omaha Bee-News* laid off 106 night-side printers. In Des Moines, the *Register Tribune* absorbed the *Capitol,* in Chicago the *Evening Journal* disappeared. In hundreds of other cities in the midwest, composing rooms were linked to print fewer and smaller newspapers. Finding a job (for a traveler) was no longer a matter of walking into the composing room and slipping up.

Many retired ITU newspaper composing-room printers remember the tribulations of the Great Depression. The publishers pulled every trick in the book to keep production up and expenses down.

In Omaha, Hearst's top efficiency man (if I recall right, his name was Mitchelon) was paid $50,000 yearly to cut costs to match time-study schemes by other big employers. Clocks informed the foreman of Linotype production. If you turned in less than 1,600 corrected lines, your slip was pulled. (Some places, like Baton Rouge and Corpus Christi had 2,500-em deadlines.) Ad-men qualified if their tally sheets showed 160 column inches or more. Make-ups had to slap together, plane down, and lock up six pages every edition, four times each shift — or seek employment elsewhere.

Burned-out light globes had to be unscrewed and turned in to be duly booked and registered; otherwise you worked in darkness. Pilfering of light globes, toilet paper or clothes pins (used for holding copy and proofs together) was prevented by forbidding lunch boxes in the composing room. The single water faucet for 106 men was cut to a weak trickle.

In a top-floor, flat-roof composing room, the smothering Omaha summer nights sent the thermometer to its limit -130 degrees - and held it there. Windows open to catch some faint breezes, attracted tons of leafhoppers, moths, midges and other night-flying insects to cover sweaty printers' arms and faces. When the cast-iron turtles were pushed to the stereo steam-table, they made no sound over the hard maple flooring because an inch-deep carpet of dying, sprayed insects acted like a Persian rug silencer.

The efficiency man fixed our washroom, also. He removed the doors from all eight booths and dangled one 15-watt light bulb from the ceiling. That way the foreman could conveniently check on malingerers and see if anyone was attempting to read. The sanitary dispensers of paper towels were replaced by scraps of newsprint from the pressroom, hung on a hook. When pencils wore to a nub, they had to be turned in for replacement. Of course, newspapers were not allowed to be purloined from the plant—if an employee desired, he could subscribe at a 20% discount, or he could be conned into buying Hearst stock.

At a memorable ITU convention in Long Beach, California, the members debated and finally passed the law limiting printers to five days a week. Printers at the *Omaha Bee News,* working six 8-hour shifts for $48 weekly, immediately began hiring subs one day each week, voluntarily reducing their pay to $40 for 40 hours. Newly-organized editorial employees, earning $12-$14 a week suddenly became $34-$36 maharajas! Hearst management modestly has never admitted helping establishment of the Newspaper Guild.

A Case History of Depression Printing

from Bill Taylor

(Bill Taylor died not long after writing these memories; about 15 years ago.)

Traveling? Yes, some folks traveled on the Twentieth Century Limited, Santa Fe Chief, or the North Coast Limited. But we printers seldom could afford luxury travel. We usually went by freight train, slept in barns, and ate dinner from cans.

When I was 13, I took up printing at Lathrop Trade School in Kansas City. At 14, I went to work in a small shop on Missouri Avenue. They had two Pearl presses, foot powered, a few racks of type, etc. The owner was quite old, about 70 or 80. I was honest, and admitted that I knew the case like a monkey recently escaped from the organ grinder. Therefore, he gave me a job feeding the Pearls.

I worked at two other places, one plant that was too large to be good for a printer's devil, and then a smaller one that gave me much experience. But, feeling I should get into a better grade of work, I went to work for Triumph Printing on Fifth and Delaware, where I spent a full five years.

I received my ITU union card April 1930. That meant out, out! Make room for another apprentice and go look for a job.

Kansas City had always been a good town for printing work, but during that hot summer of 1930, I canvassed every shop in town only to hear horror tales of woe and poverty. There was no work to be found anywhere. Newspapers in those days still worked a six-day week; job shops five days and four hours Saturday. But nothing for subs.

By January 1931, my funds were very low. Just in time, the Kansas City local adopted a plan to pay a dole to out-of-work printers and also voted to go to a five-day week. That meant regulars had to hire a sub once a week, even those who had never missed a shift in their lives.

Now, the *Kansas City Times* had at that time, the champion firing foreman of the world: Sammy Hayward. Sammy was 80 years old; everyone felt sure he would live at least another 80 years. With this local five-day law in effect, another newly graduated apprentice slipped up on the *Times* in hopes of catching one of those sixth days. Sammy fired the kid before he could take his hat off. However, according to the union contract, the boy collected a day's pay anyway!

I decided that I had nothing to lose, and that I was going to do the same thing and collect a much-needed day's pay ($9.16). I showed up on the *Times*, fully expecting to be fired. To my surprise, I was hired for two shifts that week; Sammy never seemed to notice me. I worked on the *Times* as much as two or three shifts a week for about four months.

That wonderful work lasted the length of time the five-day proposition had been voted to run. Then back to six days for those poor, poor old regulars! The only chance to catch a shift now was from the few union-minded printers on the *Times*. With about 80 subs, that meant one night a week for the lucky ones.

Then came the summer lay-off! There were so many subs on the clipboard that my slip was tacked way down on the mop-board, almost on the floor. No more work for six months. That was the summer of 1931. I was never so close to starvation. Then a dole was voted in—just a dole, no five-day rule. Soon so many printers were out of work, the dole started to fade away. My last dole was $1.62—and that had to last a whole week. I had walked six months straight. And I do mean *walk!* Carfare was an expensive two tokens for 15 cents, so I walked to the paper to show up and then walked back home.

By the fall of 1931, I began to get the feeling that I just might not be needed on the *Kansas City Times*.

A friend encouraged me to go to the *Journal*. I did a little better there. A shift every month, sometimes two. But unexpectedly, I was put on a situation, due to a death of a regular situation-holder. That was in 1938. I was ecstatic. I now had a real, full-time situation, a *lifetime job!* My future was secure.

As an aside: The Kansas City *Journal-Post* had an interesting history. Originally, the morning *Journal* was at Eighth and McGee Streets and the evening *Post* at Tenth and Main Streets. The *Post* belonged to Fred Bonfils and Harry Tammin. As Fred was closing the deal to sell the *Post* to the Santa Fe Railroad, Harry came into the room with a breathless protest: "I just put two freight carloads of paper into the warehouse. We can't lose that, Fred!"

The Santa Fe was reluctantly hedged into buying two carloads of paper to get on with the purchase. Fred and Harry were long gone to Denver when the buyer found only two rolls of *paper* in the warehouse! The *Journal and Post* were later sold to W.S. Dickey, a tile manufacturer. In 1928, the papers were simmered down to one evening paper, the *Kansas City Journal-Post*.

By the time I joined the *Journal-Post* it had changed hands again; adopted a new dress and dropped the name to just the *Journal*. When the war started, we put out nine editions daily with chasers any time Hitler blew his nose or Mussolini belched. When Hitler marched on Poland, we went to 12 regular editions plus chasers all along. There was plenty of work and I thought I was set for life.

Then, on April first, 1942, I arrived in the composing room for my usual 8:30 a.m. starting time. My mouth fell open when I saw a sign on the copy cutter's desk that said: "This will be the last day of the *Journal*." At first, I smiled; after all, this was April Fools Day! But I suddenly realized that the copy cutter wasn't pulling my leg. The tears in his eyes told me this was the bitter end. On April 1, 1942, the *Kansas City Journal* folded. Three hundred employees, whose families depended upon their paychecks, were dumped into the street at the end of that shift.

All sixty of us out-of-work printers realized we could never find work in Kansas City, not in 1942 with the Depression still very oppressive. The Kansas City local voted to pay each of us $50 if we would leave town forever. That amounted to a week's pay. So much for my lifetime job! The agreement was, if we ever returned to Kansas City we were obligated to repay the $50 to the union (which I did later on.)

That was how I came to leave Kansas City to become a tramp printer. First, I traveled to St. Louis, where fortune smiled unexpectedly on me, to the extent of a shift or two a week.

Two other *Journal* printers also came to the *Post-Dispatch* the same week. They had both spent their working lives on the *Journal;* one 20 years, the other 30. Both slipped up on the P-D, but the next morning, before show-up time, they had me instruct the chairman to pull their slips. They were afraid to try to work in such a strange place! Any printer who spends his entire life in one spot will very likely have a strong feeling he is inadequate and handicapped, simply not able to to work just anywhere.

But work didn't last long in St. Louis, not after paper rationing came on. That cut out editions and advertising on the *Post-Dispatch*, which in turn cut down on the subs' chances for work. The nation was then heavily at war, yet still deep into the Depression. The local secretary sent me down into the Ozarks, to the town of Washington, to work a little print shop called the Miller Press. The job paid $24 a week—low pay, but it sure beat starving. The Model 5 was in perfect condition, like factory new; it had a Bunson Burner, no thermostat. The big hitch was a font of ten point roman with italics and small caps. All I'd ever set on a keyboard was heads and captions. I soon learned why printers were driven to drink: small caps. Unfortunately, the shop was about to close due to the owner being eligible for the draft.

I was looking for a way to survive, when a "help-wanted" ad in the *Publishers' Auxiliary* led me to Bastrop, Louisiana, where a little weekly paper needed a printer. In August! Ohhh! It was hot! There was no decent food in town; the only thing really edible was ice cream. Ned Bolton, the newspaper publisher, was trying to purchase this marginal weekly on a shoestring. He was a fine fellow who worked 14 hours a day, and the help stayed right with him. Not easy, but it still beat starving! Near the end of the week there was always a little overtime; that is, we worked 18 to 20 hours a day! But Ned was a right fine fellow; he'd always send out for pop or beer for the crew. He, his wife and the foreman were from Missouri. Mrs. Bolton worked too, as a Linotype operator. There was also a pressman, a young office girl and a teen-age Negro boy who was janitor, ran errands, etc.

It had always been an accepted custom in the South for Negroes to take a little something now and then: never much, just a little. One day the pressman intended to get a haircut. He had a half dollar coin in his pants pocket when he changed into his overalls, but when he went to pay for the haircut, he found a quarter in his pocket.

In that Turkish bath of a shop, a complete change of clothes daily was a must. The laundry bill was killing me. Then a barnstorming ad promoter came into the shop one day and told me I could catch some work in Monroe, 26 miles away. So I was off to Monroe for some week-end hours. I was hired for a night shift and fired at its end. When I asked why, the foreman said I didn't do enough work. He didn't add, "you Yankee bastard," but it was plain he meant it.

So I made it back to Bastrop in time for another 14 hour shift at the *Enterprise* on Monday. (Had to keep my shoulder to the wheel to send money to my wife and oldest boy who was then nine.) Yet, to my surprise, I did collect a day's pay from the Monroe *World*. About $7.

I was beginning to feel like I was doomed to stay in the hot, steaming South, when a letter arrived from Ed Hand, a Ludlow salesman based in Kansas City, telling me to hurry back to St. Louis.

"Things have changed," he wrote, "the war is outwearing the Depression. The *Post-Dispatch* is short of help!" I could work up North again! The news was just like manna from heaven!

I felt Ned deserved a week's notice. So I agreed to stay until he could run an ad in the *Publishers' Auxiliary* and find a replacement printer. Then, one hot afternoon, an old tramp printer drifted into the back shop. Since Ned was out, the printer talked to me. I must have been affected by the heat, because I should have told him to start work, so I could leave at once. When I did finally think about it, I went running after the old boy. But he was gone before I could catch up with him. When I returned to the shop, dripping with sweat, Ned was there and asked what was the matter. When I told him I'd been chasing a tramp printer, Ned asked in alarm: "Did he steal a numbering machine?"

I didn't find much enjoyment or adventure in traveling—at least not the way I had been doing. It was simply a way of surviving and getting money to the family.

I arrived in St. Louis April 4, 1942, in a downpour of rain, a Missouri cloudburst! In the short block to the nearest hotel I was soaked to the skin. I wore a topcoat but no raincoat. Had only one pair of shoes with me. They were soggy. The clothes slowly dried over the radiator. The shoes were oozie for days. The Ludlow salesman was right about St. Louis. I worked full time on the *Post-Dispatch*.

While I was in St. Louis, the secretary occasionally sent me to a Jewish shop on Easton Avenue for extra work. It was a confusing place because there was much shouting and waving of arms. At times it seemed sure the owners would seize each other by the throat. Then one of them came to me and said, "Don't mind us, Bill. We're Kikes, that's just the way we talk to each other." Each Friday afternoon the proprietors provided beer served in stew pans, like the bootleggers used to do. I always remember the oddity of drinking beer from a saucepan at that place. While most of the composition was in English they also set Yiddish. They never gave me anything to set in Yiddish, but oh my, sometimes I had to distribute some Yiddish! Talk about confusing!

But my wife refused to move to St. Louis. That forced me back to Kansas City, where I had to return the "leave-forever $50." That was early '43; the war had finally rubbed out the Depression (our only thanks to Hitler). I went to work at McWhirter Printers. That was another 12 hour day due to a mass of war work. It was a crowded little shop, but busy, busy, busy. Work, work all the time. But the McWhirters were fine people to work for. The old man took the crew to dinner now and then. But work, work, work. Just sleep and work.

After the war (missed the draft due to war work) I was working at Barrich Publishing. They put out a national weekly. All ad proofs were very carefully read before store proofs were air mailed out. The lady proofreader was very particular. Old Mitch was with us in the ad galley. He was working on an office proof, ninth revise. "There is no way to please that woman," Mitch moaned, "Just no way at all! I moved this two points, that one-point. Now she wants it all moved again!"

I looked at the newsprint proof and said, "Try this, Mitch." I took his ad to the proof press, pulled a good, sharp proof on book paper without any more moves at all.

"Oh, Mr. Mitchell," the gal came running. "You have moved it just right! Exactly what I wanted. Pull the store proofs.

After the war, work was good everywhere. So, in 1947, we left Kansas City forever in search for Utopia. We departed like immigrants, towing a baggage trailer with all our worldly possessions: our clothes, the boy's bicycle, the family dog, and all, to re-establish ourselves in the promised land of the West.

Our first stop was Delta, Colorado. My wife's sister lived there. My brother-in-law had a fine job waiting for me. It was in the shop of Frank Sternes, an old printer from Denver. Frank, his son and daughter-in-law ran the shop. The hours were any time I chose, the conditions of work were perfect. Every one came and went as they pleased. But paydays were far apart. I worked there two weeks and am still waiting for a pay check.

On to the Mormon Utopia. I was put on a sit at the *Salt Lake Tribune before* I took my hat off. After a few days, the local secretary suggested that I see George Brother, a Mormon Bishop who ran a job shop in town. George was in need of a printer so I quit the *Trib*.

This was another family shop; George, his wife, two daughters and one son-in-law. The chapel chairman was a nephew. One morning, I shocked everyone by asking where they kept the coffee can with the numbering machines. (Always kept 'em soaked in kerosene-filled coffee can, remember?) They were aghast: "Bill, you *know* we don't drink coffee!"

Then we were off to Seattle: Utopia on Puget Sound. But during the time we left Kansas City and our arrival in Seattle, the *Seattle* Star folded. In a time of plenty everywhere else, Seattle printers faced woe and poverty. I subbed about a month on the *Post-Intelligencer,* but had to bump overtime to get work, so we left.

We were sad, because Seattle was a fine place. During the month of July we could always wear coats, even at noon. A far cry from the Turkish bath of Kansas City. Fresh sole could be caught in the Sound in abundance. Delicious, not like the embalmed sole they serve in hash houses most places.

Since there wasn't any work, we headed for Portland where I found a situation on the Oregon City *Enterprise*. We put out a 200 page centennial edition on a flatbed press! They had horse drawn street cars in Oregon City during that time, an interesting place, but I could smell the stroke of doom for the *Enterprise*. (It was sold to the *Courier* about a year later.)

That sent us to San Francisco, where there was plenty of work; at that time the city still had four dailies. But it seemed like most San Francisco landlords wanted a month's pay for a week's rent. I worked a few shifts at Porno- Walsh on Market Street and decided to leave. We went back to Salt Lake for a few months, off to Spokane for a few months, down to Denver for a few years. But we never found Utopia.

We had always liked Montana; so off we went to Great Falls. That was a real busy place. Rents were high and food cost double the prices in Denver, but it was nice there. I worked two years on the Great Falls *Tribune*. We even hunted elk; and we got two of 'em!

It seemed like there was always something wrong with every place. We packed up and headed for Calgary, just for a short vacation on our way to Spokane. But it started raining, raining, looked like it would never stop. Trying to get to Spokane would be a mistake since all roads were washed out in British Columbia. To pass the time until the rain stopped, I went to work on Max Bell's *Albertan*. Finest of conditions, nice people to work for, but of course $20 below the Great Falls' scale. Still, it covered expenses until the rains stopped.

Rent was reasonable around Spokane, so I went to work for Hill Printing. We liked Spokane a lot, and decided to settle down. After working for Hill for about two years we made a drastic mistake: we bought our first home. Immediately after buying the house, I was laid off because business was slow. This added my body to Spokane's surplus printing help.

We went to Bozeman, Montana, where I found a situation in a job shop. It was another family place where I would naturally earn the smallest pay check of the crew, and with no security. From there I went to Butte to work on the *Standard* (owned by Anaconda Copper) which was very busy and a good place to work, as well as a place to earn a good pay check. However, Anaconda sold out to the Lee Syndicate, whereupon conditions of work went down, down, down. After working there 15 years I returned to Denver to work on the *Rocky Mountain News* and put my slip on the bottom of the board again. My wife passed away about this time.

If I would have had only myself to look after, my earnings would have been ample to get me out of here years ago. I could be living in a far better place than this. Traveling today? Impossible. The only traveling I ever intend to do this late in life is to return someday to western Montana to get out of this hot, hot climate forever. That will have to be when I can retire. Montana is a poverty state now. No chance to ever work there as a printer again.

Living alone here is only a matter of staying in this room to avoid being robbed, beaten or murdered! It is a risk to go out for meals. There is nothing to do here anyway. Just wait to go back to the office at show-up time to see if there's any work. And to hope to make it there and back alive. My only recreation is to get out of this state twice a year; go somewhere there is still room to go fishing.

(Bill Taylor left the Denver Post after work for substitutes became nonexistent. He managed to escape from Denver's skid row and move to his beloved Montana. There, he eked out an existence on Social Security income, bitter and disillusioned, until he died of a heart attack, alone, in a

cheap hotel in Bozeman, Montana.)

In Mysterious Ways
from W. O. Wildman

Jobs were scarce for college graduates that June of 1936. The Great Depression, a world-wide phenomenon, was at mid-point and the Plains states were still in the grip of drought and dust storms. One of my fraternity brothers who was also a Phi Beta Kappa considered himself lucky to get a job as a shoe salesman in a relative's store at $12 per week. Many young women simply went back to their homes; a few were able to get teaching, secretarial, or clerical jobs.

One young man who was working with a hay baling crew that year summarized the situation when asked why he, a college graduate, was pitching hay for $2.00 a day. "A sheepskin isn't very nourishing, even with salt and pepper," he replied.

Of the journalism graduates at Kansas University a few were sons and daughters of newspaper owners and so had a starting point, but a number went jobless or into other fields. I was luckier than most since I had a degree, Typographical Union card, and work experience dating back to a very early age; also, a wife who was not afraid to work.

Alf Landon was then governor of Kansas and the Republican nominee for President of the United States, running against Franklin Roosevelt. Landon had been an excellent governor and was highly respected by the people of Kansas and the Midwest.

Both Topeka daily papers were busily engaged in promoting Landon's campaign, and upon graduation I was offered a job with the Topeka *Daily Journal* to represent them in 16 counties in the southwest corner of the state. People also worked in all other sections of the state, blanketing it completely. The job offer included Frances' services, also.

The day after my graduation from K.U. we drove over to Topeka and were briefed on our duties, then went to my parents' home at Garnett to establish our base (our furniture was, by now, in storage with various relatives).

We made double-page ad layouts of each of the 16 counties,

contacted the county Republican chairmen to get lists of potential endorsers of Landon, and set out to secure these endorsements along with contributions to pay for the Landon advertising campaign. The purposes for all this effort were: (1) To make money for the newspapers; (2) To produce a huge newspaper issue the day of Landon's acceptance speech showing the overwhelming support of Kansans for their governor.

Once the layouts were made we sallied forth to get names and the dough. Names were easy but money difficult; however most people believed in Landon and contributed—even my father, a life-long Democrat. It was not an easy job. June and July in southeast Kansas can be oppressively hot and humid, and motels were not air-conditioned in those days. Tracking down people in their offices, businesses, farms and ranches took stamina and determination.

When the big day came for Landon's acceptance ceremonies, both the Topeka *Daily Journal* and the Topeka *Daily Capital* came out with huge issues carrying thousands and thousands of endorsements of Landon for President.

In the ensuing election, if memory serves, few others than Kansans supported our Governor, and the first steps toward the huge bureaucratic government and deficit spending which have ever since plagued us were taken with Roosevelt's election.

One of the places we had worked in during the campaign was Coffeyville, and while there I had been offered a job as city editor of a small paper. The job didn't pay much but seemed like a step in the right direction, so after Governor Landon's acceptance ceremonies were over we left the Topeka *Journal* and headed for Coffeyville, a town on the Kansas-Oklahoma line. Its early history included a raid on the bank by the Jesse James gang, and the bullet holes were still there in the bank's doorposts as evidence of that battle.

The paper was struggling for survival, and after a few weeks as "city editor," a job which included everything from actually writing and editing to selling advertising and setting type, I began looking for a more promising job.

The next fair-sized city down the line was Bartlesville, Oklahoma, an oil town that was comparatively prosperous, so we drove down there one weekend to look it over.

Going into the daily newspaper office I inquired about a job on the editorial staff, but was told no vacancies existed. The managing editor to whom I was talking said, "Too bad you're not a printer, because we need one who can handle the ad machine."

"Well, I AM a printer," I told him.

"Go back and see the shop foreman, then," he said, "and maybe he'll hire you."

So I went back and tried to corner the foreman who was rushing madly about trying to get the paper out on time. Following him around the composing room I answered his questions.

"Do you have a card?" referring to the ITU union card.

"Yes, and a college degree."

"I won't hold that against you. Can you run an ad machine?"

"Yes."

"Had experience on Intertypes?"

"Yes." (This was stretching the truth somewhat, as I'd had very little experience on Intertypes, and absolutely none on the big new models they were equipped with.)

"When can you go to work?"

"Two weeks from today."

"O.K. Be here."

"What's the scale?" I ventured.

"Thirty-four dollars a week for 40 hours."

"O.K. See you then."

I left him to his work and thanked the managing editor for his help. So Mickey Ryther's prophesy regarding ITU membership was coming true already. The printing job paid a little more than double what my "position" as city editor had been producing.

On arriving back in Coffeyville I told the publisher there that I had a better job offer and was quitting in two weeks.

"That's fine," he said, "I can get all the college graduates I want for less than I'm paying you. Good luck!"

At the end of the last week there I had an unpleasant surprise. "Sorry," said the owner, "but you'll have to let me mail your check. We just don't have the funds today."

We arrived in Bartlesville with barely enough money to rent a room with cooking privileges and to buy a few groceries. Payday would not occur until a week from Monday—eight days away—but we figured we'd make it.

The job was tough. The paper was running short-handed in every department trying to make ends meet. The composing room was no exception. They expected a lot of production and a lot of quality, which they were getting. The whole crew were top-notch craftsmen who knew all the tricks of the trade.

My first day there the foreman put me on a newssetting machine, which posed no problems, but told me to get acquainted with the ad machine as that was where he wanted me. I later discovered his reason, namely changing 120-pound magazines frequently during the day to obtain the different type faces. Some of the older printers shied away from that sort of thing if possible.

The two standard typesetting machines of the hot-lead era were Linotypes and Intertypes, with Linotypes being far more common. All of my printing experience had been in shops using Linotypes with the exception of the Lawrence *Journal-World* which had five Linotypes and one Intertype, which I had seldom had occasion to use.

Now this job depended on how quickly I could adjust to the differences in equipment and how tolerant the foreman might be. Those big, complex Intertypes with strange keyboard arrangements, different magazine shifting mechanisms, and dozens of other mechanical variations were somewhat intimidating. Errors in operation could result in a molten-metal bath, a damaged Intertype, and—worst of all—fouling up the schedule and missing the deadline. It was obvious that speed and accuracy under pressure were essential to hold this job. but fortunately the other printers were friendly and helpful.

By the end of the first week it appeared that I would make the grade and everything was lovely.

Everything except that by Thursday morning of that first week Frances and I had only enough money and food to last one more day, and payday was still four days away. Here we were in a strange town, broke, and not daring to ask my employer for an advance in wages. That was something that simply was not tolerated by most employers at that time, even for employees who had been with the company for years, and I didn't want to risk it. Had I known it, the union secretary would have advanced the needed money, but this was my first job in a union shop and I didn't realize that fact.

When I got home after work that Thursday, Frances said, "Sorry, but our last money is gone. No breakfast tomorrow."

That was the first and only time we had or ever have been literally down to our last cent. While she was preparing for the last supper I sat on the front porch and scanned the paper for errors I might have been responsible for, meanwhile wondering just what to do in a case of this kind. I could have wired my Dad for money but we didn't have the price of a telegram or phone call. That seemed like the only chance, but it still wouldn't work.

Like most people, I knew of individuals who called on the Lord every time they got the sniffles or a hangnail, but I was not one of those. I figured the Almighty had more important things to worry about, so I muttered, "Lord, we need some help. Show us a way out of this situation," and continued scanning the paper.

About that time Frances came to the door and said, "Supper's ready—what there is of it."

At that instant we heard a crash and looked out to the street where our Model A Ford was parked. It was a quiet thoroughfare and our car was the only one parked in the whole block, but someone had crashed into it.

We ran out to the street where a woman was climbing out of the car which had struck our Ford. It was apparent she had one too many—in fact she could scarcely stand, and seemed rather agitated about having hit our vehicle which was now short one rear fender.

"Don't call the cops—don't call the cops—I'll pay you! I'll pay you!" she gasped.

After a bit of haggling she agreed to go with us to a garage for an estimate of the damages, which the garage man placed at $12.00. She dug the bills out of her purse, handed them to us, and took off with the utmost haste.

The garage man said he could repair the car and have it ready for us the next day, but strangely enough we decided we'd rather eat than have a new fender right then.

As it is written, "God moves in a mysterious way, His wonders to perform."

Christmas, 1936, marked the end of my job on the Bartlesville paper. The usual Christmas rush with all the stores advertising heavily was followed by an almost total lack of business, necessitating a reduction in the work force. The secretary of the Typographical Union suggested I see if any jobs were open in Tulsa.

So at the beginning of 1937 I "slipped up" as a substitute on the Tulsa Tribune and hoped for the best. The Depression was still very real, and people were adjusting the best they could.

The Tulsa union was made up of men and a few women who were very unselfish in sharing work with those on the extra board. If I remember correctly I was number 26 on the list of substitutes, and there were only some 60 or 70 "situations" or regular jobs. It was a sort of unwritten agreement that situation holders would lay off one day a week and hire a sub, thus spreading the work around.

This spirit of brotherhood and sharing was prevalent throughout the union shops of that period, and for some years after the Depression. It came as a severe shock to old-timers, both financially and emotionally, when the later generation of printers in the prosperous 1970's refused to honor their obligations regarding the pension fund to which the veterans had contributed all of their working lives. Needless to say this loss of pension created stress and hardship on many of those who had unselfishly shared the work, carried the load, and trained that later generation.

In those days on the *Tribune* there were three shifts and a sub could show for one, two, or all three if he chose. Since it was a seven-day-a-week paper that could mean showing up 21 times a week, waiting around for an hour or so to see how many hires were made, and, if not hired, returning home.

Again I was fortunate in having learned the trade in a country shop where I had been required to do everything and so had a wider range of skills than many printers. So long as I was on the bottom of the board I could work in other shops, of which there were a number in Tulsa, so for several months while accumulating priority on the *Tribune* I worked for the *Oil and Gas Journal*—a prestigious trade journal—The *Legal News,* a law-brief printing firm, and small shops who would call in for a printer for a day or two's work. In this way I worked almost full time, but often at three or four different shops during a week, sometimes a second shift immediately following the first with no rest in between.

We had been fortunate in finding a small brick home, mostly furnished, which rented for $25 a month. It had a nice garden plot in which we raised much of our food. The owner, Mrs. O'Neill, lived in a small apartment and rented her home, hoping to keep up her mortgage payments.

During the time we were in Tulsa I saw a long procession of "tramp printers" looking for work. They would "ride the rods" or hitchhike from city to city hoping to find jobs. Many were sober, competent men, but a few were boozers who were not interested in working beyond the point of getting enough money for a bottle and a place to sleep. If work was not available the man was allowed to "pass his traveling card," the identification of a union printer, and everyone on the job contributed whatever he felt he could spare. These itinerant printers often brought new ideas and methods that were of real value to the plants they visited.

Among the itinerants were some who were quite famous throughout the newspaper world because of outstanding characteristics or abilities. One of these was Carl Wreidt, a "swift" who a couple of years later came to my rescue during a short stint at a trade plant in Kansas City, Missouri.

A "swift" in printers' parlance, was a person, who, without effort, could set far more type than even an excellent Linotype operator. I do not pretend to know the basis of this ability, but probably it is a super-fast coordination of eye and hand movement, combined with rhythm. I was considered a fast and accurate operator, but Carl Wreidt and the two or three other "swifts" I have known could set more type in six hours than I could in eight.

Billy Swingle was another "swift" who specialized in working for state printing plants during legislative sessions. A good operator could "hang" the first elevator consistently on 12- em lines, but Billy Swingle could do the same on longer material—even on long tabular work. Billy also wrote a little manual on keyboard techniques which was quite helpful. The first system I used in 1929 was by Milo Bennett, if my memory is correct.

The usual requirement in most shops was 1800 lines per shift, or 1600 for tabular matter such as markets, baseball scores, etc. "Swifts" sometimes helped slower operators, placing the latter s name-slug on type the "swift" had set so if the galley proofs were measured the slower ones would show up as O.K.

All the "swifts" I have known and worked with were gregarious types, at home anywhere. They seldom stayed anywhere very long, but were always welcome wherever and whenever they did appear.

Tramping Odyssey
from Franklin M. White, Shreveport

(This was written in 1974 as a first draft of a "soliloquy" on Gulf Coast Guy Foley, and meant for the ITU Journal. Mr. White submitted to us to be published in the Tramp Printers Newsletter. I don't think he ever finished the article, for he died not too much later.)

For those without regular situations, work became very scarce during the Depression. I had lost my job in Monroe local 540 due to a merger late in 1930, and for a while I managed to scrounge a few days and an occasional "stretch" at Temple #688, Long View #742, Baton Rouge #25 and points between. But the Great Depression was deepening.

Then the vital "five-day law" went into effect, whereby members on six-day sit were obligated to hire subs if available, for sixth shifts. The problem was finding shops without too many subs, so one could catch some of those sixth days. I knew I had to go on the road, if I was going to keep bread on the family table.

The time probably was early in 1933. I borrowed an antique Dodge coupe from a cousin, left my wife and baby son at Monroe, and I headed for Baton Rouge, 250 miles Southeast. I may have had a tankful of petrol and $5 in folding money.

I had worked in Baton Rouge several months before, but when I arrived, substitutes were plentiful. There I met Guy Foley, Sam Ball and Johnny Crews; they were bunking at a "floppery," and were in a quandary. It seems that someone found Johnny Crews sleeping, and as a joke proceeded to give him a "hot foot". Johnny woke up and flung his left hand violently against a window pane, and received a severe gash. He severed a tendon, and the wrist was horribly damaged. Johnny was undergoing surgery when I arrived in Baton Rouge, and he couldn't leave. (Later he went on the road alone, and unsuccessfully tried to work with his handicapped hand.)

I conferred with Sam Ball and Guy Foley, who were much more experienced travelers than I. We decided to head for Texas in the "klunker." The Dodge's transmission gear was "shot" and the car chugged along at about 25 mph — hour after hour. Shifting gears was difficult and a problem in the cities, but the 1925 model revolted only once in 1,600 miles of my use of it. That happened when a Texas belle at a country filling station poured some oil into the crankcase and didn't replace the "breathing cap." We discovered the omission later and plugged the oil entry tube with a rolled newspaper. The engine conked out. Sam Ball said the engine had to "breathe," so he fashioned an air vent: no further trouble.

The night of our departure from Baton Rouge we idled along until daybreak and reached Lake Charles. No work. Most chapels in Texas had "funds" for travelers. We had no "stake" or capital but were able to buy cheap Texas gasoline, and we slept in beds every night except the first two, and we didn't go hungry.

We reached Beaumont that next afternoon, but no hiring. Perhaps we slept there, I don't recall. I do remember a side trip to Port Arthur. The daily there published large special editions on paydays of the giant oil refinery there, usually hiring extra subs, but Foley, Ball and I missed out—too early or too late. Back to Beaumont.

I "passed my traveler" among the fellows at the *Morning Advocate*. The chairman was off that day, so the head apprentice did the honors while the men were at lunch in the locker room. One so-and-so set his cup of coffee on top of the card, spilled some, and the beverage washed most of the handwriting off. I was unhappy, humiliated, and I received nothing for my embarrassment. In all of my card passing activities I've reaped a total of perhaps five bucks, and maybe the same from "chapel funds" but I suppose I've contributed several hundred. In the Depression days prices were affordable: a bed could be rented for 25c to 50c. A good meal cost 25 cents. Bowl of chili, 15c. At Galveston, the three of us "ate great" in a union cafe for 25 cents each: fish, a large slice of roast beef, three vegetables, and a couple of other side dishes, dessert, large glass of milk or unlimited coffee. And NO TAX OR TIP. We bought gasoline for the klunker at 10 cents a gallon.

Between us we all solicited the chapel funds for several gallons of petrol. The two sheets in Beaumont, a.m. and p.m., were a hodgepodge of confusion, semi-mutiny and disgust. About 40 "office rules" were posted on the slipboard. Getting fired was easy. There was no contract. A sit-down strike and other stoppages and slowdown had occurred. Two or three journeymen were constantly stirring witches' brew. The paper had just put up a large new building: a "half-million dollar building and a 25-cent composing room," as Foley put it. The equipment was terrible. A year later I subbed there for two or three months.

The third night of the tour was really memorable. Sam Ball and I drove almost all night on the narrow asphalt road to Houston. Guy Foley wouldn't take the wheel. A "pea-soup" fog plagued us all the way; visibility was almost zero. The old Dodge chugged on at about 10 to 15 mph, now and then slowing almost to a walk as we encountered patches of even thicker fog.

As we drove along Foley regaled Sam and me with choice reminiscences. One story was about the time he "hitched a ride" with a man somewhere in Texas who tried to hire Guy for a "torch" job, to commit arson on a building.

Well, it took most of the night driving through the thick fog to make Houston. When we arrived, we visited all three papers, *Chronicle, Post* and *Press*. No work, but we scored for a few bucks. I believe we flopped there the third night and then headed for Galveston.

Galveston has streets named with letters of the alphabet, plus short ones with addition of "1/2". Foley renamed "M-l/2 Street" as "Pica-and-a-Half" Street, or "18-Point" Street. Peculiar conditions prevailed at the paper. The two papers with single ownership, like the *News* and *Tribune,* were evading the Union's new five-day law whereby sit holders were obliged to hire subs. Prior to that subs could be hired at will, but the superintendent, Joe Mulina, I believe, had posted the ultimatum that anyone giving out his or her sixth day would be fired. Chairmen [day and night] were keeping score, and several hundred sixth days hadn't been "given out." The printers at the paper were afraid of Mulina; he was known to slug people.

Meantime, old Charley Burton of Fort Worth—whom I knew well and had worked with in scale negotiations at Monroe—was the ITU Representative. He had been to Galveston to referee the mess. The super's main gripe concerned "department heads" giving out their days. He insisted that there were 13 departments, and therefore 13 department heads, which was ridiculous and reprehensible, of course. Charlie Burton contacted Charley Howard, then ITU President, and was instructed to compromise. So much for that.

With no chance in Galveston, we headed for San Antonio. There I caught some days on either the *Light* or the *Express,* piecework, and earned some nice money. When that was through we drove north to Austin. No work, and I got 35 cents by passing my card at the *Statesman* and nothing at the *American.* We visited the University's printing plant; we got nothing from the guys, but one of them took our cards into the superintendent's office and brought out 50 cents for each of us.

Until we reached Waco, we saw no chance of catching work. "Wild Bill" Caldwell was ramrod in Waco. He had foremanized in Shreveport years before, a loud talker, semi-tough. He had signs on "dark" machines: "If you can't or won't set 2200 lines, don't turn the light on."

Foley caught a shift, and Sam lucked into a stretch. So Guy Foley and I proceeded to Fort Worth and Dallas. We visited the Dallas *Morning News* where Foley made some modest "scores," receiving a fiver from "Tex" Barton. Then we caught on the Fort Worth *Star-Telegram,* more piece-work and good money, while it lasted.

So I left Foley in Fort Worth, and headed back home to Louisiana. It was an unforgettable odyssey in search of work, but very unprofitable. For a single man, it would have been fun, but as a family man, it just wasn't worth it.

I recall seeing "Gulf Coast" Foley 40 or 50 times after our trip, and worked with him in several shops. I've had a total of only 20 traveling cards in 45 years, but Foley usually "showed up" in all the towns where I worked. One of my most vivid memories revolved about that week I spent with Guy Foley and Sam Ball.

Freight Trains and Hitch-hiking

Leo L. Baker, of Nevada, Iowa, recalls that in his span of 50 years at the trade he never rode freights, but he did a lot of hitch-hiking in the Depression years. But some trampers back in those days used boxcars regularly, cooked in hobo jungles, anything to get to the next town. They would hit the weeklies on press day, usually Thursday. They'd help put the paper to bed and maybe stick around for a day or so to distribute the type. Most of them knew their stuff . . . from Linotypes to cylinder presses, could set rollers and make press repairs. Leo retired in 1976 from El Paso #370 and returned to his hometown in Iowa.

❊❊❊

Los Molinos News-Herald
from David Stryker, Cambridge, Mass.

I started in the trade in 1933 at age 15, part-time during school, then in 1934, in the early years of the Depression, I found a full-time job ($4 a week and room and board) with the local country weekly in Los Molinos, California (Tehama County). In the early days on the Los Molinos *News-Herald,* we had a couple of colorful tramp printers come along.

The one I remember most was called "Lazarus" and I don't think I ever heard his real name. He had a well-worn clipping he always carried, listing himself as having been killed in an elevator accident in Montana, and he gloried in the fact that he had "risen from the dead." I thought him ancient at the time, but he must have been 65 in 1934. He was always promising to teach me to run the press and operate the Linotype, but of course he never did; that would have meant he couldn't work there anymore. I finally learned the Linotype at age 16 on my own, while Lazarus was out to lunch. After a couple of days I guess he found out what I was doing, then it took me a couple more days to find out where the keyboard lock was. He traveled a route up and down the west coast, and could be counted on to hit our town for three or four weeks in the spring.

The second tramp printer, whose name I forget, was very much a wino. Part of my duties involved prodding him out of bed in the hobo jungle, getting him full of black coffee, sobered up, and to work at a reasonable time. (That so soured me on liquor that I didn't drink until I was past 21, but that's another story.) Anyway, these two were very much part of the tramp printer era—clean, fast and dependable while they were on the job and sober, but you had to watch for the bottle behind the type case. I learned a lot from both.

After about six years I graduated to the county seat daily at Red Bluff, where I became a real swift on the Model 8 Linotype. The operator at the machine beside me was a union member and he convinced me to join the ITU in 1941. All in all, I would say I've worked in nearly 100 shops up and down both coasts—newspapers and job shops—and in 50 years of working I only lost one day of work when I wanted to work—and that was between jobs. I miss the freedom of traveling cards, but on the other hand, I am going to call it quits one of these days.

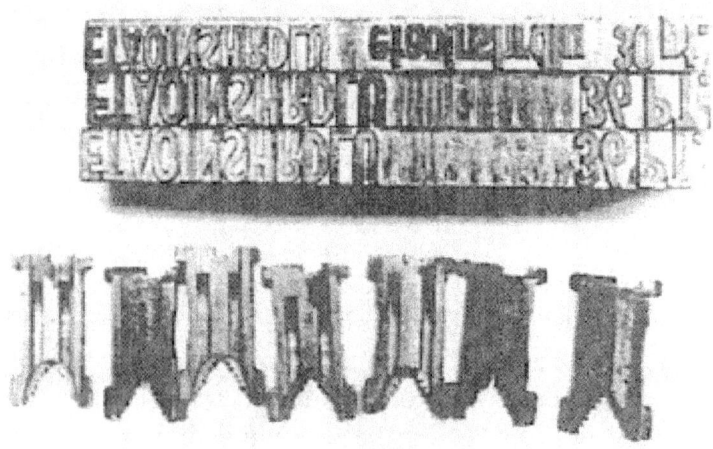

POST-WAR BONANZA

THOSE TRAVELING after the end of World War II, probably enjoyed the easiest traveling, with unlimited work, and were the best-paid of any travelers in printing history. The authors fell into this category, and most respondents to our questionnaire agreed that their best time in the printing business came after the end of the war.

Business was booming, advertising heavy, as the nation began a climb from the pre-war depression into the heady world of prosperity and full employment. For the first time in decades, there was actually a shortage of printers instead of an over-supply. Substitutes were placed on regular situations the minute they walked into a shop to look at the slipboard. Several hours a day overtime became the norm for many places, and regular situation holders went pleading for substitutes to allow them a day off once in a while.

These were halcyon days for union and non-union printers alike. Because union printing offices were short of help, any printer who could prove competency was invited to join the union and enjoy good wages and working conditions. Non-union shops were forced to pay higher wages and treat employees well, or they wouldn't have workers. ITU membership grew steadily.

For the incorrigible tramp printer, the world was wide open. Because of the vast amount of overtime posted on slipboards around the country, the tramp was assured of work almost anywhere he pleased. And, with all that overtime, few newspapers could keep up with the reproduction (bogus) that kept stacking up. That further guaranteed work for substitutes. The minute a tramp wandered into the composing room and started to look at the slipboard, the foreman would try to catch him with an "office hire" before the regulars could get to him. In fact, "bumping overtime" became a rare occurrence, because the newspapers needed all the printers they could hire.

Riding boxcars or hitch-hiking became a thing of the past. Postwar tramps drove reliable used cars, or new convertibles. Some traveled first-class on trains, others rode Greyhound buses and some flew TWA from one location to the next. It was no longer necessary to go north for the winter and south for the summer to catch hires, not when work was so easy to nail down wherever you chose to show up. This was the era of the "snowbird"—the printer who traveled to Miami for sunshine in the winter and north to Oregon for salmon fishing in the summer.

The problem for tramps became, not how to find work, but how to *avoid* being placed on a situation with regularly scheduled work days and days off. In order to "control their slip" (that is, work only those starting times and shifts that appealed to them), many tramps were in the habit of "pulling their slips" (quitting) at the end of every shift, and then making themselves available when they decided it was time to work again—maybe that would be the next day.

Tramp Printers' Little Black Book

In order to force substitutes to take regular situations rather than choose their starting times from day to day, the ITU gave newspapers permission to fire substitutes who refused a situation when others weren't available for the job. The foreman had the right, in such an instance, to place a six-month bar on the offender. This didn't faze the dedicated tramp printer one bit. He simply kept track of the places he had been fired and made note not to waste time coming back before his six-month bar was up. Those who traveled a lot found it difficult to remember details about various shops and often kept a notebook with information on each place they'd worked. They recorded the places worked, dates, the names of the cash-in man, the chairman and the foreman, and noted the dates they had been fired and barred (either for refusing a situation or for cashing in through the office) and when the bar would expire. An example of this is my personal black book for the year 1955, and I think I might have other notebooks for earlier years.

In chronological order, my list went like this: Detroit Post

Printing Co., Detroit *News,* Toledo *Blade,* St. Louis *Post-Dispatch,* St. Louis *Globe Democrat,* Chicago *Daily News,* Detroit *Free-Press,* Detroit *Times,* Cleveland *Plain Dealer,* A & L Typesetting (Detroit), Abbe Press (Detroit), Dayton *Daily News,* Indianapolis *Star,* Terre Haute *Star,* Evansville *Courier,* Memphis *Press Scimitar* and *Commercial Appeal* (two chapels), Little Rock *Gazette,* Houston *Post,* Houston *Chronicle,* San Antonio *Light,* El Paso *Post-Times,* Tucson *Citizen,* Los Angeles *Examiner,* Compton Printing Co. (LA.). and Monson Type (L.A.). That was the list for one year.

A couple of the shops listed above saw me slip up a couple of times that year. This was one of my better years, since I had decided to try out the West Coast and was pulling a 36-foot trailer (big in those days), and leisurely worked my way west, accompanied by my wife and children. Maybe zig-zag is a better description than leisurely.

Teletypesetters and Automation

Those truly free and easy times stretched on through the late 1960s. Until that time, the only cloud on the horizon had been the growing use of teletypesetters to set news type. Instead of a Linotype operator manipulating the keyboard on Mergenthaler's invention, an operator perforated paper tape which was then used to automate an already automated machine. Until the introduction of computerization of tape perforation, the net impact of teletype on a composing room was an increase in the number of printers needed to put out a newspaper. Instead of a skilled Lino operator turning the clock,[1] or at least maintaining an average of 250 lines an hour, a good TTS operator had to work hard to turn out 200 lines. Because of the complicated and haphazard way the TTS tape operated the Linotype, corrections were horrendous. Sometimes one fourth of a galley of type needed to be reset (by a manual operator) to correct the output. Small wonder that composing rooms grew during the time of the Teletypesetter.

---

[1] Linotypes were equipped with a measuring device, known as a "clock," which counted the number of lines set. The clocks registered to a maximum of 2500 lines, then reset to zero. Turning the clock past 2500 to zero, was known as "turning the clock."

The computer changed this. At first the changes weren't drastic. TTS operator still had to perforate the tape on a keyboard, but instead of adjusting the output to justify each line, the computer automatically broke the lines and inserted necessary letterspacing. Now a TTS operator with ordinary skills could produce as much type as a hot metal "swift." The only limitation was the speed at which an operator's fingers could fly. Corrections were still plentiful, but production of type rose dramatically. For the first time since the introduction of "new processes," newspapers were able to effect reductions in their workforce instead of a steady increase. Substitute lists grew longer. Overtime became an emergency situation instead of an every day affair.

Post-War Tramp Case Histories

An extremely valuable source of information about this booming post-war period came from questionnaires sent to over 100 printers who replied to requests printed in the *CWA News* (which replaced the *ITU Journal*) and *The Printer,* a newspaper of letterpress and typography nostalgia published by Michael and Sally Phillips, of Findlay, Ohio.[2]

The questionnaires showed interesting patterns in backgrounds, attitudes, and careers. As we hypothesized, most tramp printers eventually settled down, and used the skills gained "on the road" to become successful members of their communities. Most assumed leadership by being elected as union officers or being selected for management jobs. Many did both; most of those answering our questionnaire at one time served the union *and* management. (Hopefully not at the same time!) Several who returned our questionnaires ended up owning their own printing establishments. Others started and operated businesses in other fields of endeavors and became quite successful.

Examples of tramp printer success stories are many. John Hatfield used to alternate between positions as mechanical superintendent, president of the union, foreman, chapel chairman,

---

[2] *The Printer,* 337 Wilson Street, Findlay, OH 45840

and traveling printer. Rocky Stremming and George Story worked as foremen and mechanical superintendents at various newspapers after careers as tramp printers. Rocky retired as mechanical superintendent at the Hawaii newspapers. John Howells was foreman in several newspapers and managed a commercial printing plant.

The following is information extracted from our questionnaire. The respondent in this case is Roy Carter, who left tramp printing to become owner of a successful printing plant.

From Apprentice to Tramp Printer
from Roy Carter

I had dropped out of school at age 15 and held various jobs—filling stations, foundries, lumber yards, and construction labor. None of these jobs appeared to have much future. Then my father, who was a printer, got me a job as an apprentice at the Cleveland *Plain Dealer*. I could readily see a great future in this opportunity. I was not quite 18 years old at that time.

My duties the first year were mostly pulling proofs and sorting name slugs at the Cleveland *Plain Dealer,* which at that time was Ohio's largest daily and Sunday newspaper with about 450 situations and maybe 30 or 40 subs. The longer I was on the job the more tramp printers came through Cleveland, and I listened to the travelers' stories with interest. The more stories I heard, the more I developed a wanderlust. I couldn't wait to get my union card so I could "hit the road".

Some names of tramp printers in Cleveland I recall are: "Dirty Shirt" McKnight, Bob "Shotgun" Chutijan, Jack Finch, Horace G. "Stuttering" Walker, Lester Bungard, Marvin M. Manning, "Cactus Jack" Crawford, "Snuffy" Smith, Junior O'Malley, "Toad" Millbauer, George Story, Rocky Stremming, Henry Lipschitz, Scotty Dunn, The Wandering Jew, and numerous others who have slipped my mind.

The *Plain Dealer* was a nice place to work, but I could hardly wait until I got my journeyman's card so I could "hit the road." Deo Padgett was composing room superintendent at the time. He was a genuinely nice guy. However, that happy Sunday afternoon when I got my union card, I went up to quit my job and clean out my locker. Deo Padgett approached me and offered his congratulations.

I responded by telling him "Deo, there's something I've been wanting to tell you." He said, "What's that?" I said "Fuck you, I quit!" Deo grinned and said, "Roy, that's probably the best move you'll ever make."

A few minutes later I found out I couldn't get my traveling card until my ITU registration number came in. So I slipped up at the Cleveland *Press* and worked there for a couple of weeks. One Friday night, after I had already agreed to work four hours overtime, I had a phone call. It was the secretary of Local 53 who told me that my registration number came in and he could issue me a traveler in the morning. I quit that job right on the spot, went to the rooming house where I was staying, packed up, and went to Union Headquarters. I slept in the car that night so I wouldn't miss making connections with the secretary. I had my first Traveler!

I drove to Toledo and located the Toledo *Blade*. I was very nervous. After serving my apprenticeship on the *Plain Dealer,* an admittedly easy place to work, I wondered in my own mind if I really was a competent printer. When I told the chairman that this was my first traveling card, he said, "Don't worry about that, Kid, I'll take care of things for you." And he did. I worked in Toledo until I was deemed competent, then I quit. I went to St. Louis and slipped up on the *Globe Democrat*. In about two weeks they posted a situation, so I quit.

In the next few weeks I worked in Des Moines, Omaha, and Cheyenne and never had any problems proving my competence. I was on my way! I fell into the easy company of the fraternity of tramp printers. Some memorable tramps I ran into from time to time were:

Lester Bungard: A nice little guy with a drinking problem. Lester was from Akron and did a little traveling. He wouldn't get too far from home. Maybe Detroit, Pittsburgh, Columbus. Lester had a little notebook and always wrote down who he'd borrowed from, and how much, when he was on one of his binges. When he was tapped out, he would go back to work and get everyone paid back. Lester died maybe 15-20 years ago. He still owes me 5 bucks!

Dirty Shirt McKnight: The name says it all! I remember one time in Cleveland, Herb Kunmiller, the night composing room foreman, told Dirty Shirt he couldn't come back to work until he cleaned up. The next night he came to work wearing a new T-shirt stained with after shave lotion. He sought out Herb and asked him: "How do I smell now?" Then he proceeded to spill the balance of the lotion all over Herb. I think Dirty Shirt got fired.

Toad Millbauer. Toad also worked on freighters on the Great Lakes. I don't know why, because if he wanted to work all those hours, he could have made a lot more working at the printing trade. Toad borrowed $20.00 from me when I was still apprenticing at the PD. He left town without paying me back. Three or four years later I heard he was working at the Kansas City Star. I stopped by and inquired as to whether or not Toad was there. I was told he was in the proof room. I walked in and he immediately recognized me and said: "Roy, I know I owe you $20.00, I haven't got it but you can sleep with my daughter tonight!" I told him to forget it. I doubt if he even had a daughter!

Horace G. "Stutterin" Walker: I was sitting on the front steps of the Bakersfield *Californian* the day Marilyn Monroe died and I thought I recognized the shuffle in the walk of this guy who was entering the newspaper. I didn't know for sure until I asked him if he was slipped up in the composing room. When he spoke I then knew who he was. He replied, "No. I'm going to Sacr-, Sac-, Sac-, Sacra-. I'm going to Reno." (I hope you can imagine how funny this sounded.) He just couldn't say Sacramento!

The other tramp printers were always helpful, always full of tips on different places to work, shops to avoid and places where lots of overtime was available if one needed a "stake." I kept listening and learning. I kept a log of starting times of day and night shifts, financial weeks, vacation credits, cash in men, chairmen. I soon discovered that most travelers were far better printers than the regular situation holders. Homeguards may have been better at certain jobs—because they may have been doing the same routine for 20 or more years—but tramp printers had to be consistently proving their competency. (And the foreman was often looking for an excuse to fire a tramp.)

I always went to work with the idea I would give my employer a fair day's work. That way, if I ever came back looking for work, I knew I'd be hired. I always got along well with homeguards, too. Quite frankly, a lot of the homeguards were envious. Lots and lots of times, homeguards and I would share a few beers after work. They would talk about how they'd love to travel if only they could. And to be fair, the homeguards were the ones who saw to it that all the laws were upheld. Without overtime cancellation and "Deadhorse" [bogus], traveling would have been difficult. I doubt if we could have survived on only office hires. I'm sure the office hired so overtime wouldn't be bumped in a lot of instances.

Tramping was just a great way to get to travel. Who knows, I may never have left Cleveland if it weren't for traveling cards. I never would have met the girl I married 35 years ago, a beautiful lady from near Santa Fe, New Mexico. Linda and I were married in 1960 at San Juan, Pueblo, New Mexico. I had an old 1953 Buick and we went to Las Vegas, Nevada, where we bought a 19' travel trailer. I was 25 years old and Linda was 20 at the time. We appreciated that we were touring the country as young people, instead of waiting until old age. It seemed like everyone else was in their 60's, driving Cadillacs, and pulling expensive Airstream trailers, and popping who knows how many pills.

An experience comes to mind. In about August of 1960, we arrived in Long Beach, California with about a half tank of gas and less than $2.00 in cash. I found a nice little trailer park and told the lady that ran the park that I had a job starting that afternoon and I needed a place to park my wife and my travel trailer. She agreed to let us stay there but we couldn't hook up until I paid a week's rent—I think $13.00. I went to Long Beach Typo headquarters and was told I could start in the morning on the Long Beach Newspaper. I told the secretary I needed something sooner than that. He told me about a place in Signal Hill called American Typographers that I could possibly catch on the night shift. I showed up and got hired that evening and went to work about 11:00 p.m. About 5:00 or 6:00 in the morning, I asked if they had a coffee fund. The answer was yes. So I wrote an I.O.U. for $20.00 and took the cash. There was a little discussion but I won out convincing them that I had a full shift on the hook. I went back to work the following evening without incident. But, that night I found out that they held back a week's pay, so I quit and got a job the next day at the South Gate *Press*. About noon the third day there, I found out that if I quit, I could get my money immediately. So I cashed in. I chased the wolf away from my door.

Our son was born in November 1961, but we continued to travel in our small trailer. By the time my eldest daughter was born in April of 1964, we decided to move up to a 30-footer. At first, our daughter was sickly. Before she was a year old, we had her in hospitals in Santa Fe, St. Louis, Cleveland and Springfield. (She is now a 31-year-old-beauty.)

Of the "good" newspapers I worked on, St. Joseph, MO. *News-Press-Gazette* has to lead the list. The last hour or so of the shift was generally spent at the poker table. El Paso *Herald-Post* has got to be a close second. If only for its close proximity to Juarez. Chicago *Tribune* had the best shift. Something like 1:30 in the afternoon til about 8:45 p.m. You could stay out until daybreak and still get enough sleep for the next shift. Another thing about Chicago was that 14 days work was good for a vacation day.

Editor's note: When traveling became difficult, Roy Carter and his family settled in Springfield. He worked for the newspaper there, and as work became even slower, he decided to buy a printing shop. After this failed, he moved to a small, southern Illinois town, where he started a printing plant specializing in tickets and other jobwork using both Linotype and hand-set type. His plant now has seven offset and four letterpresses.

Eddie Hayes Interview

In an article titled, "Is He Betraying his Brotherhood?" The Santa Cruz *Sentinel* featured the following article that chronicled the life of Eddie Hayes, whose tramp printer career ended with a situation on the *Sentinel* in the California coastal city of Santa Cruz.

condensed from the Santa Cruz (California) Sentinel

Eddie, slender, with a bantam chassis, can't drink likker any more and actually admits to feeling settled in his small apartment over White & Wessendorf Mortuary.

You see, Mr. Hayes has put in 23 years as a tramp printer

throughout these United States, but over the past two years he's been held up in the *Sentinel backshop*. And that could ruin a tramp printer's reputation.

"I talk about hittin' the road, but, Santa Cruz is a hard town to leave," he says.

"I'm living a lot on my memories. Name most of the big papers and I've worked them. Tramp printers keep in touch. Got a call from one yesterday. Ol' Brice at the Atlanta *Journal*. Sounded gruff and drunk. He said he wanted to hit the road and I knew it was just talk, because we're changin' but it was an excuse to talk old times—travel, women, and the wild days."

Eddie was born into the news business. "My dad was editorial cartoonist with the Atlanta *Journal and Constitution* for 25 years and my uncle was a photographer," he explained. Eddie started as a copy boy, but took a six-year printer apprenticeship in Atlanta. It was this foundation that got him work at more than 36 different newspapers. This includes return visits; he worked at the *Sentinel* seven times over the years.

He never stayed long at one paper: a few weeks, a few months maybe. "Those were wild boozin' days. But in today's back shops," said Eddie with a wry smile, "a printer with a few belts stands out like a golf ball in a barrel of coal."

In the '60s he got off to a bad start. "After failing to pay attention to a marriage and its responsibilities, (two children) I was arrested at work for abandonment. The South was very hard on you and I spent nine months cleaning the highways. Drinking will do that to you."

Divorced, he decided to hit the road. From then on it was newspapers and Greyhound buses, or hitchhiking. "The Washington *Post* showed me the magnitude of the trade in the '60s. I showed up with 160 other extras and we all got work. In those days we set heads using individual letters. At the *Post* I met characters like The Red Baron, Ernie The Track, Dirty Shirt McKnight (ran into him again on the Monterey *Herald*), Bobby Who, Little Eva, Joe Williams (now also in the *Sentinel* backshop.)

"I fell in love with tramp printing. It was like a grand family," he said.

The Tulsa *Tribune*, Richmond *Times-Dispatch*, Fort Lauderdale *News*, Torrance *Daily Breeze*, Long Beach *Press-Telegram*.

"The tramp will get work if someone wants the day off, if the paper needs extra printers. If a union member has accumulated a day's overtime he must take it, allowing the tramp to fill in. If there was no work, I would pass around my Traveler's Card for donations to make the next town. Most tramp printers traveled broke.

"So before I'd start work, I'd call on the 'juice man.' He was a fellow who would loan you enough at two percent to get a drink, a room and something to eat for a week," said Eddie. "The two percent was worth it to be able to settle down on a barstool with other printers, play the jukebox and tell stories."

Greenville (SC) *News*, Mobile *Register*, Fresno *Bee*, Baton Rouge *Morning Advocate*, Watsonville *Register-Pajaronian*.

Eddie said that many a time, he'd arrive at a paper too late to set up a job. In that case he found that some newspapers on the floor served as an ample mattress. "A favorite spot was the ladies' restroom. .There was usually a couch." *[Note: Eddie Hayes' story didn't end with a "permanent situation" in Santa Cruz. About six months after this article was published, Eddie decided he couldn't stand working in one place any longer. He drew a traveling card and slipped up at the San Jose* Mercury News, *and before long, took another traveling card and was last heard of heading for Atlanta.]*

Working in England and Canada
from Junius P. Welch (ex-chairman, Houston Chronicle)

An ITU card was valid not only in the U.S. and Canada but was also interchangeable with European printing unions. A printer once told me of a time he used his card and worked in England. His story of the difference there from North American shops was amusing. He was working on a London paper as operator when he had a "roof stop." In the U.S. an operator either caught his own roof stop or, if the shop had a Linotype machinist, rang a bell or called for help. He was undecided what to do and asked the adjacent operator who replied: "You need to get the engineer. Come with me and I'll show you where he is." They walked quite a distance, entered a door marked 'engineer', and told the man at a desk what they wanted. The engineer took off his coat, put on a smock, accompanied them back to the machine, fixed the roof stop, and departed. Our tramp was impressed with British efficiency.

Before I settled in Houston I did have some time on the road. I worked briefly in Chicago and decided I would work my way to Halifax. I thought it would be enjoyable to see Canada. I worked a shift or two in Detroit and from there crossed the border into Canada. To my memory I was asked few questions by the border officer. I'm sure he failed to ask me if I intended to work in Canada. I proceeded on to Toronto and worked there about a week or so and then went to Montreal where I worked a few shifts. Showing up for the next shift I was surprised to be arrested by a Royal Canadian Police! He said I would have to accompany him to see the commissioner. Upon arriving at the police commissioner's office they announced that since I had not applied for a work permit when entering Canada and that I was in violation.

I stated that I was unaware that I needed one and explained my innocence. The commissioner said that I would need a permit to continue working. I asked him for one and he offered to send to Ottawa for one, but that it would take a fortnight, and I would not be allowed to work until it arrived. So, I returned to the paper explaining what had happened.

Over that night I considered what the commissioner had said and returned to his office the next morning. Making sure that I had understood correctly that I could not work for about two weeks I told the commissioner that with his permission I would leave the country and not to send for my permit. The commissioner was very nice and stated that there had been no real harm done, I was welcome to remain, and then work after obtaining m permit. But, if I insisted, I could leave. I did leave the next day.

After working in Toronto I visited the capital, Ottawa where there was a Royal Canadian Policeman standing guard in front of Parliament. He was dressed beautifully in his dress uniform with red coat, blue breeches with a yellow stripe running vertically down the sides. I regretted that the officer who had accosted me wore only his every day olive drab uniform.

John Hatfield
from John Howells

John Hatfield was one of the better-known of the Post-War tramps. Even in his thoughts of death, when he was dying of cancer, John Hatfield demonstrated the love to which he devoted his life: printing. He requested that he have a traveling card in his pocket when he was lowered into the ground. The Houston Typographical Union complied with his request and issued a traveler for the last journey he would ever make. Mary Lou Champagne remarked, "And when he slugs up you can bet he'll be the next chapel chairman!" (Mary Lou was well-traveled, perhaps not qualifying as a tramp, but certainly as lady traveler.)

John had a lot of friends and a few political enemies. (He was a staunch member of the ITU Independent Party.) I know from the sympathy cards his family received that even his adversaries respected his knowledge of ITU Law and his wisdom to enforce it.

I first met John Hatfield in Houston in 1952. I was working at News Incorporated (Shamrock publications, out on Harrisburg Blvd.), when Johnny and "Crippled Bob" Taylor came through. I only had my card about six months at the time, and was learning the ropes. We used to get off work about midnight, and many was the night we'd pick up a case of beer and go to George Dwyer's trailer for a prolonged chapel meeting which lasted until the beer was gone or until dawn, whichever came first. That's where I received my introduction to union laws, principles and ethics. George Dwyer's "law university," John Hatfield, "professor." George's trailer was only about 25 feet long, and didn't have a bathroom, so we had to go to the trailer park latrine, and we made numerous trips while finishing our case of beer. We all went at the same time so we wouldn't have to quit our discussions, arguments, and exchanges of personal philosophy. The neighbors didn't appreciate our nights there, because we'd never learned the art of arguing in whispers.

John Hatfield knew his lawbook. No question about it. I had read through the book many times, long before that lucky day when I got my card, but it was Hatfield who made it come to life for me. We would talk about a section of the law and then he'd give examples about how the law was applied, and give case examples. He introduced me to the idea of case law, using the *ITU Bulletins* as a basis for interpreting the Book of Laws. This came in very handy in later years, when I was a union officer and contract negotiator.

Many beers were consumed over his lectures on how to travel correctly, the proper way to treat fellow travelers, and how to handle hostile foremen and "overtime hogs". Johnny had a strict sense of ethics, and impressed on me the importance of living up to your beliefs and the principles of ITU, even though it might harm you in the short run, because in the long run you gain respect.

I loved to listen to his adventures in teaching homeguards the meaning of the ITU General Laws, and handling belligerent foremen. I'm sure the local union power structure in some towns felt threatened when John Hatfield appeared, but when he left town, the local would usually be stronger for the experience.

I knew that work would drop off drastically after the Christmas rush was over, and suspected that Johnny's tips on traveling would come in handy. I was correct. He told me where the best chapels were on the way to Florida, who the chairman was at the New Orleans *Item,* Atlanta *Constitution,* the papers in Mobile, Pensacola, Birmingham, you name it. He presented me with valuable tools for traveling. I needed them, too, because my wife Dorothy and I were living from paycheck to payday, as most of us were in those days, and had a new-born son and a two-year-old daughter. John Hatfield had a deep sense of worth as a journeyman, and a fierce pride in being an ITU member. This confidence rubbed off onto me, and found I had no problems traveling wherever I damn well pleased.

If it hadn't been for Johnny's detailing the subtleties of ITU laws, how they work (and should work), I might have never sustained the interest, the almost religious devotion to the ITU and its laws that drove me through the years. I went on to become chairman in numerous shops, delegate to four ITU conventions, and too many elected jobs to bother mentioning here. One thing I will mention, however, is that I was president of San Jose #231 when Scotty (John and Helen's son) received his ITU union card. I obligated him.

George Duncan

A post-war activist printer who did a fair amount of tramping before moving up to higher office, was George Duncan. Wherever he worked, you could be sure George would be up to his ears in politics. His experience "on the road" smoothed the way for his climb into union leadership. Eventually, his political activities attracted the attention of the ITU Executive Council and they invited him to become an ITU representative.

George once wrote an article for the *Tramp Printers' Newsletter* about a political action group composed mostly of tramp printers. The scene was Cleveland in the mid 1950s, in the "famous, or infamous, as the case may be," *St. Regis Chapel*. The St. Regis was an apartment hotel on East 82nd St., convenient to both daily Cleveland newspapers, well known as a haven for subs coming through on the Cleveland-Toledo-Detroit-Chicago swing.

"Many, many ITU members got their inspiration and indoctrination into the history and purpose of the ITU in the St. Regis Hotel Chapel," George said, "There were some wild times there: poker games, political strategy sessions against the local president (Tony Satullo) and naturally, against the employers. Everybody went to union meetings in those days!

"Many excellent unionists came through that *chapel*, some going on to other locals to spread the idea of union solidarity, some staying in Cleveland. Among them were Joe Van Kralingen, Jim Harmon, Bill Fowler, Glenn Britt, Terry Brennan, Don Seibert, Bill Withers, Newell Frizzell, Frank Krutch, Art Gnass, Hank Simmons, Roger Earwood, and many more. And, printers had no monopoly on the tramp scene—some mailers became part of the Cleveland St. Regis Chapel.[3]

Marion Dearman

---

[3] George Duncan was elected Chapel Chairman at the Plain Dealer in 1957 and served in that capacity until he accepted a job as assistant to ITU Secretary Don Hurd. When he left the job as ITU rep, George ran for office as 1st vice president of the San Francisco-Oakland Mailer's Union, and later became the local's secretary.

Editor's note: As authors of this volume, and as bona fide ex-tramp printers, we feel entitled to enter our own stories here.

I became a printer as a result of that vast structural change that resulted in upward social mobility for the poor, the minorities, and women. World War II took millions of men out of vital positions in industry, service occupations, and professions. This created opportunities for people like me. I was the eldest son of an Oklahoma tenant farmer, who had four daughters and six other sons. One day my father read a classified ad from the local newspaper, the Okemah *Daily Leader*. He clipped the ad and showed it to me. It said "Wanted: bright, ambitious, young man to learn the printing trade." I was 15 years old at the time and busily instructing my younger brothers in the various arts of which juvenile delinquency consisted in rural Oklahoma circa 1942: smoking Prince Albert and Bull Durham, stealing eggs with which to pay for the tobacco, playing mumbledy peg with our pocket knives when we were supposed to be hoeing corn or chopping cotton—things like that. In any case, for once Papa and I agreed on something— getting me off the farm.

I applied for the job, got it, and soon discovered that what was really wanted was a country boy who would work long, hard, and most important, cheap. In that regard, I recall Mr. Gaines, one of the Linotype operators, used to say to me: "Junior (which everyone called me at the time), I don't know what they're paying you, but whatever it is, it's too much." It was twenty-five cents per hour, which seemed like a lot to me compared to working for my father for free doing work that I hated.

I stayed in a room in the Broadway Hotel, for which I paid $4.00 per week. That didn't leave a whole lot for everything else, so I worried about not having enough to eat toward the end of the week. I solved my problem by buying a big jar of peanut butter and a loaf of bread and stashing them in my hotel room.

But my life wasn't all deprivation. I dearly loved everything about printing, even the smells of the shop and the sounds of the presses and Linotypes. For about six weeks I tried both going to high school and working at the print shop. But it was too tough doing both, so I did the predictable: I dropped out of high school. As it turned out, that was the last I would ever attend high school, although I was much later to get a BA, MA, and PhD.

As a fulltime worker, I was given the opportunity to try my hand at a wide variety of printing specializations in the back shop. My job, at first, was stereotyper-pressman helper: melting lead and pouring the "pigs" (lead ingots to melt in the Linotype pots), casting the plates for the ads and news pictures, and putting the full-page forms on the press. These could be quite heavy, especially when we had "double-truck" (two page) display ads. This job required that I get to the shop before 6:00 a.m. to fire up the pot in which the metal from the "hell boxes" was melted. I enjoyed this, especially due to the fact that a next door restaurant always had fresh doughnuts and music by Tommy Dorsey, Glen Miller, and Bob Wills on the juke box with which to begin my day on a happy note. I also worked in the bindery some of the time, ran job presses, operated the "Wing" mailing machine, doing the "single wraps" (papers that had to be wrapped, addressed, and mailed), and carrying them in mail bags to the post office across the street. But the bulk of my work came to be assembling individual ads and pages. This was the part of the trade which I enjoyed most, which I usually worked at when I became a journeyman printer, and which continues to recur in a dream that I have which always finds me in an oldtime composing room.

A few tramp printers came through Okemah during the war years. They were not union printers; few rural printers were. But they had interesting stories to tell about traveling and I was their most avid listener. I could hardly wait to get on the road. My first trip, however, was three years later when I reached 18—draft age. It was not to another print shop, but to Camp Chaffee, Arkansas, a replacement depot where new draftees were assigned to basic training—my very first time out of the State of Oklahoma.

At the replacement depot, they asked me what I did in civilian life. Proudly I told them that I was a printer. "Fine," they said, "you'll make a good demolition specialist." Whereupon, I was sent to Ft. Lewis, Washington for basic and demolition specialists training. However, when I went overseas to Germany, I managed to get myself assigned to the Army newspaper *The Stars and Stripes*, located in a plant near Nuremberg, where Julius Streicher, one of the 13 top Nazis tried at the Nuremberg Trials, had published *Der Sturmer*, the notorious Jew-baiting, hate-mongering rag. We had a rather unusual composing room: all the hand compositors were American soldiers, while all the Linotype operators, who were Germans, neither read nor spoke English—talk about following copy right out of the window!

I was discharged from the Army January 1947. Two days later I started on-the-job training at the Wewoka (Okla.) *Times-Democrat* (a Republican newspaper) on the G.I Bill. The following August I entered the University of Oklahoma via GED test and the G.I. Bill, again. After finishing two semesters and starting another (during which time I worked part-time running a press at the Oklahoma University *Press),* I dropped out. I was supposed to be a journalism major and I thought of myself as a journeyman printer already, so I reasoned that I had little to gain monetarily by getting a degree. Besides, I felt very much lost and alone with the other university students; I felt much more at home when I went to nearby Oklahoma City and drank beer with the Indians, cowboys, and oilfield workers. I soon discovered that there were people who did not entirely agree with my assessment of my level of printing competency. This happened when I returned to Okemah and another job on the *Daily Leader.* After a couple of months, I noticed that the journeyman printers were making at least 25% more than I. Consequently I asked for a raise, was told that I "wouldn't even make a good two-thirder" (a term then in use in non-union shops to denote a learner who is worth two-thirds journeyman's pay). That's when I quit my job and got on a bus bound for Los Angeles.

That's when my career as a tramp printer really commenced. By the time it ended I had been issued 55 traveling cards and had probably worked in as many as 200 shops, covering most of the United States.

By the time the bus got to Flagstaff, Arizona I was extremely tired (I never could sleep in a Greyhound bus seat), so I got off the bus to get a hotel room. The next morning, while waiting for the bus to L.A to arrive, I dropped by the paper to visit the composing room. When I walked in the shop, one of the printers said, "You're a printer, aren't you?" I answered, "Yeah, how did you know?" He said, "*Old Annie* (the foreman's dog which slept inside the entrance of the shop) knows printers and firemen. She can tell them by the way they smell." The foreman, Wayne Shields, was also the assistant chief of the Fire Department in Flagstaff. He furthermore informed me that they were short a printer and that the shop even kept the rent up on a small apartment nearby in case a printer came through needing a job and a place to stay. I was happy about this turn of events, but concerned that I didn't have the required union card. The Chairman, Slim Slaymaker, told me that there would be no problem if I was a competent printer I would get my union card and the foreman would know if I was competent by watching me work for one hour.

I don't know if I was that impressive or that the Arizona *Sun* was simply desperate, but the result of the foreman's inspection was that I got the job. I was subsequently "obligated," sworn in as a journeyman member of the International Typographical Union by the Flagstaff chapel of the Prescott local. I was 22 years old at the time and one of the youngest journeyman members in the union.

Arizona local No. 375 was the largest local in area in the ITU's jurisdiction, covering all of Northern Arizona: Prescott, Flagstaff, Cottonwood, Winslow, Williams, Holbrook, Seligman, and Kingman. Monthly union meetings alternated between those cities' chapels. Attending a union meeting was often an all-day affair. For example, a meeting in Prescott required the Flagstaff printers to drive through Oak Creek canyon, Sedona, Cottonwood, up Mingus mountain via the old copper mining ghost town of Jerome, and on to Prescott. The round trip, meeting, and lunch took about 14 hours—quite a day, but the spectacular scenery and union camaraderie was worth it!

As much as I loved Flagstaff and appreciated getting my Union card, I began to feel an onset of the disease, itchy feet. Tramp printers came through Flagstaff from time to time. I especially remember Snuffy Bryant, an itinerant Linotype operator, who made traveling sound so exciting and alluring. His tales, plus an unhappy ending to a summer romance, soon made me restless. The result was that I drew my first traveling card September 16, 1949. I planned to travel for a while, then return to Flagstaff to settle down. Unfortunately, the local went on strike within a year of my departure and the union lost, not only the Flagstaff chapel but the whole local.

I deposited my traveling card in Los Angeles local 174 three days later. My tramp printing career had begun in earnest.

A great many newspaper workers, from reporters to mail room workers, are frequent drinkers. And, from my observations, most traveling printers were heavy drinkers. Life on the road is very lonely in many ways. You are away from home and kin on birthdays, Christmas, and Thanksgiving, for example. Most of the ephemeral friends met on the road were drinkers. So, when off duty, the thing to do was to go to the bar and mingle. This was also our prime source of female companionship. The consequences of this type of sexual fulfillment and emotional outlet I will leave to your imagination.

Some printers had difficulty separating their tavern life from their work, often blending the two. One printer was especially memorable: he supposedly had a chronic medical condition which required that he take frequent doses of different colors of medicine, which he kept on his work frame in plain sight. We noticed that he dosed himself with these "medicines" frequently during the work shift and subsequently exhibited behavior quite characteristic of a person getting drunk. Inasmuch as this happened every night of his work week and perhaps interfered with his work, the foreman decided it was best to test the ingredients of the medicine. Not surprisingly, it proved to be mostly alcohol, some type of high-octane booze, with various food colors added. I don't remember whether he was fired or simply moved on to another chapel, where he could treat his ailments until authority figures again questioned his medical techniques. Most of the printers, and there were quite a few, who could not wait for the end of the shift for a drink, were not so creative; they simply made frequent trips to their lockers for libations. The potion of choice was vodka because it was believed that it left no detectable odor on the breath.

Most of us restrained ourselves until the shift ended, which would be around 11:00 p.m. for the swing shift, unless we worked overtime. San Francisco had a night life second to hardly any other city, and we took full advantage of it. When the bars closed at 2:00 a.m., we would go to a hotel room or apartment of one of the guys and continue our drinking and talking. While we drank, we talked about printing; and while we printed, we talked drinking. If overtime caused us to miss closing time at the bars, there were always the after-hours places, which never closed. One that I frequented was called "the Pup," located in North Beach, the old International Settlement. I would go to the side door, knock, and say "Dearman, *Chronicle*" whereupon the door would open and I would join the other night people: off-duty policemen and bartenders, entertainment industry people, printers, prostitutes, and the like—all those people who had to work when most people (day workers) relaxed with their libations. True, the price of drinks was somewhat higher, but that was no problem: there was plenty of work, wage scales were high, and drinking was one of the major ends of our existence.

Dearman's Printing Background

(before membership in International Typographical Union)
Okemah (Okla.) *Daily Leader* (twice before Army) 1943-1945
Stars and Stripes, Altdorf, Germany 1945-1946
Wewoka (Okla.) *Times Democrat* 1946-1947
University of Oklahoma Press; Norman, Oklahoma 1947-1948
Okemah (Okla.) *Daily Leader* 1948

Initiated as journeyman printer in Flagstaff chapel of Prescott Typographical Union, #375, May 11, 1949

The following lists where I was issued traveling cards and where they were deposited. The number of printing establishments I have worked in far exceeds this number.

Granted Traveling card, Date	Deposited Traveler, Date
375 Prescott (Ariz.) 8/16/49	174 Los Angeles 9/19/49
174 Los Angeles 10/7/49	144 Fresno 10/11/49
144 Fresno 10/12/49	21 San Francisco 10/14/49
21 San Francisco 2/20/50	80 Kansas City 2/24/50
80 Kansas City 3/1/50	18 Detroit 3/3/50
18 Detroit 5/31/50	78 Fort Wayne 6/1/50
78 Fort Wayne 9/1/50	283 Oklahoma City 9/11/50
283 Oklahoma City 9/19/50	21 San Francisco 9/22/50
21 San Francisco 1/12/51	115 Salt Lake City 1/21/51
115 Salt Lake City 1/16/51	21 San Francisco 2/15/51
21 San Francisco 6/8/51	231 San Jose 6/9/51
231 San Jose 6/15/51	46 Sacramento 6/16/51
46 Sacramento 6/22/51	271 Boise 6/26/51
271 Boise 8/31/51	49 Denver 9/04/51
49 Denver 9/13/51	525 Amarillo 9/15/51
525 Amarillo 11/08/51	613 Enid 11/10/51
613 Enid 12/21/51	173 Dallas 12/26/51
173 Dallas 01/01/52	155 Shreveport 01/02/52
155 Shreveport 01/15/52	11 Memphis 01/16/52
11 Memphis 02/08/52	20 Nashville 02/20/52
20 Nashville 02/23/52	18 Detroit 02/26/52
18 Detroit 05/25/52	53 Cleveland 05/31/52
53 Cleveland 06/09/52	63 Toledo 06/12/52
63 Toledo 06/21/52 57	57 Dayton 06/22/52
57 Dayton 07/02/52	1 Indianapolis 07/04/52
1 Indianapolis 07/12/52	16 Chicago 07/15/52
16 Chicago 07/24/52	29 Peoria 07/25/52
29 Peoria 09/23/52	177 Springfield Ill. 09/23/52
177 Springfield 10/02/52	8 St. Louis 10/06/52
8 St. Louis 10/08/52	11 Memphis 10/18/52
11 Memphis 10/19/53	933 Las Vegas 10/25/53
933 Las Vegas 04/23/54	11 Memphis 04/27/54
11 Memphis 01/02/55	138 Austin 01/06/55
138 Austin 02/10/55	87 Houston 02/14/55

87 Houston 07/08/55	28 Galveston 07/09/55
28 Galveston 07/16/55	87 Houston 07/17/55
87 Houston 07/19/55	933 Las Vegas 07/23/55
933 Las Vegas 08/22/55	624 San Mateo 08/24/55
624 San Mateo 08/24/55	21 San Francisco 08/26/55
21 San Francisco 09/01/55	624 San Mateo 09/01/55
624 San Mateo 02/17/56	21 San Francisco 02/17/56
21 San Francisco 03/07/56	624 San Mateo 03/09/56
624 San Mateo 03/15/56	21 San Francisco 03/22/56
21 San Francisco 04/06/59	389 Vallejo 11/07/59
389 Vallejo 01/05/60 521	521 Palo Alto 01/05/60
521 Palo Alto 01/05/60	21 San Francisco 09/16/60
21 San Francisco 10/20/60	231 San Jose 10/21/60
231 San Jose 11/16/60	21 San Francisco 11/16/60
21 San Francisco 12/03/62	36 Oakland 12/05/62
36 Oakland 12/15/62	21 San Francisco 12/17/62
21 San Francisco 09/11/63	231 San Jose 09/18/63
231 San Jose 06/25/68	496 Eugene 06/28/68
496 Eugene 08/30/71	650 Long Beach 09/03/71
650 Long Beach 06/16/72	496 Eugene 07/06/72
496 Eugene 08/30/72	650 Long Beach 09/12/72

Issued Honorable Withdrawal May 20, 1974 (Coast Valleys #650—formerly Long Beach Typographical Union #650) after 25 years continual journeyman membership.

Bob Howells
from John Howells

Rather than write of my own exploits as a tramp printer, I'd prefer to tell the story of my brother Bob Howells, who was a much better-known, and more traveled printer than I. Actually, my tramp printing career spanned a short seven-year period. In all, I probably drew no more than 50 traveling cards, and worked on a total of 40 daily newspapers and 15 commercial printing plants.[4]

My entry into the world of tramping was a deliberate move, following in my brother's footsteps. But Bob Howells' entry was purely accidental. We both learned the trade in our family country newspaper, from our earliest years. But neither had any particular

---

[4] This once prompted Don Cleary to indignantly demand: "If you've only had 50 travelers, how the hell can you claim to be a tramp? You're only a *tourist!*

desire to work as printers. After high school, Bob entered Harvard as a pre-med student, intending to follow a medical career. When he was drafted, because of his outstanding academic record, the Army placed him in ASTP (Army Specialized Training Corp.) and assigned him to Western Reserve University to continue studying medicine.

After the war, Bob completed undergraduate studies at Harvard, and took what he thought would be a short break before he went for a doctorate in Anthropology. While hanging around our home in suburban St. Louis, he needed a temporary job, so he answered an ad for a Linotype operator. It turned out to be an organized shop and Bob was obligated to join the union. After while, he discovered that union working conditions were not only pretty good, but there was a benefit called a "traveling card!" That was the end of his academic career. He bought a Harley-Davidson motorcycle and began touring the country in earnest. That attracted my attention, too. I gave up all ambition to become anything other than a tramp printer.

Like many tramp printers, Bob Howells had a few weaknesses. His biggest problem was compulsive gambling. Since he was single and made good wages as a printer, he never saw gambling as a problem—except when he ran out of money. Because of his addiction to the crap tables, Bob spent much time in places like Reno and Las Vegas, sometimes holding a situation for long stretches. There he met other tramp printers with the same affliction, and he became close friends with Johnny Burt—a well-known tramp printer who liked John Barleycorn as much as he did blackjack. When their money ran out, Bob and Johnny Burt made a practice of going out into the desert to prospect for gold. This came naturally, for prospecting is another form of chance, and very attractive to compulsive gamblers.

One night Bob became wildly lucky at the crap tables; he won almost ten thousand dollars. He decided that the only way he could keep any of it would be to spend it all before the gambling houses could take it back. (He knew of course, they would.) So, he bought a new Mercury convertible, a travel trailer and a wardrobe. But there was still a little money left over, so he and Johnny Burt decided to spend it on enough food and beer to last them a month of prospecting for gold in Death Valley. They put on substitutes (they happened to be on situations at the time) and both headed for the desert.

Bob Howells' lucky streak continued, for within a few days he and Johnny staked out a rich claim: it was to be Jubilee mine. Not gold, but silver. It turned out to be the most productive silver mine in the state of California at that time. It also was rich in lead, producing two-thirds of that mineral that came from the state. During the just first year of production, 85 feet of tunnel yielded two million dollars. (They didn't receive it all, just royalties from the mine's leasee.) Production continued over a span of 16 years, with nice royalty checks coming in twice monthly. However, as you might expect, the money rolled across the green felt tables of Las Vegas just as fast as their paychecks used to when they worked as printers. It was just in bigger bundles.

Johnny sometimes lost so much that he had to work as a printer to pay back borrowed money. He could work as a ship's printer for the Matson lines on a run between Frisco, Tahiti, New Zealand and back. At the end of each trip the shipping line paid one paycheck for the trip, in cash: $8,000. Unfortunately, Johnny celebrated each return and usually managed to spend it all before he could return to Shoshone, where the partners had their Death Valley headquarters. When the money was gone, Johnny would call Bob Howells and ask him to drive to San Francisco and bring him home. The last time this happened, Bob was furious. He shouted, "You spent $8,000 in *one night*? What's wrong with you, Johnny? Why, $8,000 ought to last *anyone* at *least* a week!"

After 16 years of comfortable cash-flow, their luck ran out. The government closed down their mine in an ecological move to preserve Death Valley. No richer than they had been when they first found the silver mine, both partners had to go back to the trade. Johnny traveled about the country until he was about 80 years old, and the last I heard of him, he was living in Oregon. Bob traveled a lot through Montana and Idaho before settling once again in Las Vegas—to be near his favorite sports: gambling and prospecting. He died in 1982 after complications from a rattlesnake bite received in the desert near Pahrump, Nevada. He had forty dollars in his pocket, so at least he died "standin' pat."

FRIENDS AND ENEMIES

SEVERAL UNION composing room institutions made traveling exceptionally easy for tramp printers, but they could be perceived as obstacles, depending upon circumstances. Positive aspects were a sympathetic local secretary and chapel chairman, a fair-minded foreman and the presence of a "cash-in man."

Always on the positive side was the system of "cash-in," whereby pay for time worked could be drawn in cash at any time instead of having to wait for the regular payday, which could be a week away. Two weeks in the case of a company that paid twice a month. Armed with the knowledge that he could draw his pay at the end of a shift—in some newspapers, in the middle of a shift—traveling printers felt confident and secure. They knew there would be work in the next town—at least working on bogus or bumping overtime—and the cash-in man would make sure that he had enough to rent a room and have a few beers after work. Money was no problem!

A sympathetic local secretary also made leaving town a breeze. A "good" secretary would make sure the roadster would have his traveling card at the end of his last shift. In all but the larger ITU locals, the secretary usually worked on the newspaper or a nearby job shop and could write a traveling card upon request. The traveler could then "hit the road" immediately after cashing in, and not have to wait until the next day. The secretary could make a special trip to the shop to give out a traveling card, if he wanted to, or he could give it to the chairman to hand over at the end of the shift. However, an unsympathetic secretary could insist that a traveling card only be issued during certain hours, and refuse to write one over a weekend.

Another composing room institution was the chapel chairman, whose duty was to enforce the rules and make sure everyone received equal treatment. Depending upon the circumstances, the chapel chairman could be viewed as a positive or a negative factor from the perspective of the tramp. Those chairmen who were sympathetic, who enforced ITU and chapel laws strictly, were good friends to the traveler. Those chairmen who reluctantly enforced the rules, or who were outright hostile to tramp printers could make it difficult if not impossible to find work.

The chairman's counterpart, the foreman, was rarely on the side of the traveling printer, and was generally viewed as an obstacle, if not an enemy, by travelers. The better foremen tried to be more or less fair in their dealings with travelers—especially those foremen who had done their share of traveling early in their careers. But many foremen were dictatorial and harsh with regular printers as well as antagonistic to tramps, apparently believing that it was the role of a foreman to be ornery.

Many foremen hated the idea of their regular workers having to give out overtime to the transient printers. From a foreman's perspective, overtime was a reward, a carrot on a stick, which could be granted to his toadies and withheld as a punishment for non-favorites. A tramp printer "bumping" overtime turned those bonus hours into a penalty rather than a reward. Even worse, a tramp printer could even bump the foreman himself—for a working foreman was not exempt from the overtime law. But whenever a foreman gained recognition as a friend to tramp printers, his name became hallowed with praise.

The Cash-In Man

A custom dating back to the benevolent societies in Colonial times was the system of "cash-in" that enabled union printers to move effortlessly from print shop to print shop. In the Post-War period, many larger newspaper chapels, as well as some smaller composing rooms, supported a fund which was administered by a chapel member who would lend money to other printers working there. Sometimes this was a formal arrangement, with chapel dues financing a fund for "cashing-in" a printer's paycheck. The interest collected was added to the chapel treasury, and could amount to a considerable amount of income. Money was usually lent at 1 or 2 percent interest for one week. Or, paychecks were cashed as a convenience for regular workers, with a 1 or 2 percent deduction for the service. Over the course of a 52-week period, the revolving fund would be greatly augmented by 52 to 104 percent interest rates.

The general rule was that a cash-in man would advance a day's wages at the end of the first shift a printer worked in a shop. After that, he could only cash in at the end of a financial week or when he terminated. Some cash-in men would also offer cash at lunchtime of the first shift worked, just in case the worker needed money for food. Other cash-in systems allowed daily drawing of wages. The most famous cash-in system was at the *Kansas City Star*, where a full-time cash-in man had his own office in the composing room. He would fork out a day's pay (less commission) at the end of any shift, or a week's pay at the end of the week. Some employees at the *Star* never saw a paycheck; it was easier to collect from the cash-in man than wait for a check and find a place to cash it.

Sometimes a cash-in man was privately financed or was operated by an independent credit union outside of the chapel structure. Some private cash-in men expanded their operations to become regular bankers. At least one we are aware of could finance cars, boats and even make loans on homes.

The key to a cash-in fund was management's cooperation in allowing the cash-in man prior right to a paycheck of a debtor. It would seem odd that a company would encourage such a practice, but a look at typical union contracts explains why. The company saved a lot of paperwork, bookkeeping and hassles through this system. Since all union contracts insisted that a printer be paid his full wages upon termination of employment, this meant having to write a check in the middle of a financial week, and extra bookkeeping tasks to figure out accrued vacation time, and the like. By allowing a cash-in man to pay the wages, the payroll office was spared a lot of work. After all, in larger composing rooms, printers were quitting daily. There would have to be a full-time payroll clerk to accommodate the drifters.

When newspaper management didn't cooperate with cash-in men—and some refused to—the way printers were discouraged from demanding their paycheck before payday was by placing a six-month "bar" on them. In effect this meant the quitting employee was fired and unable to return to work for a period of six months."[1] This didn't stop most tramp printers. As mentioned in the last chapter, tramp printers often kept track of the places where they were barred. They would just keep a notebook of places where they couldn't work, and when the bars were up, then visit when the coast was clear.

❇ ❇ ❇

from Chris Frisch

Following are some stories about famous cash-in men around the country.

During my somewhat wide roamings in the 20s and 30s, I came in contact with many of these gentlemen, and although they were frequently called "shylocks," they often saved me much time and trouble. Of course, I am referring to the "legits", those who operated under the ITU law.[2]

Two of these legit cash-ins stand out in my memory. One was on the Pueblo (Colo.) *Chieftain*. My folks lived in Denver, where my father held a sit on the now-defunct *Times*. It was my custom to visit them about once a year, mostly in the summertime, and I frequently lower-cased in from the south. I always stopped in Pueblo to replenish my purse and I never missed catching a shift (or more if I wanted them). When I walked into the composing room it seems that before I could say, "Hi," I would be sitting at a machine, knocking out type.

Soon a tall, slender man would come up and say, "Hello, Chris." It was Ernie "Two Percent" Brame. (Ernie didn't care for the appellation, but he would smile and let it pass.) He would hand me a night's pay in cash, less two percent, and I'd sign a cash-in slip. It saved me time and money, as I generally freighted or hitched out early in the morning. Ernie held this thankless job for many years,

---

[1] Six months was the longest period of time a printer could be prevented from showing for work in a union composing room, without special permission from the ITU.

[2] ITU law allowed cash-in funds, but prohibited interest of over 2 percent on the transaction. When a fund charged over this, it was not considered "legit."

working for nothing, for all money went into the chapel fund for worthy causes. *Bless you,* Ernie, wherever you are!

The other cash-in I especially remember was a society organized for that purpose at the Tulsa *World*. Many towns, unless you found a printer with money, which was seldom, you would have to cash-in through other sources, often at 10 percent or more. But Tulsa was a stop for the coast-to-coast trampers and many would put in a shift or two, want to leave, but be forced to wait hours to get their pay through the office. To correct this, several printers organized a society for the purpose of cashing-in trampers and also to relieve financial distress among regulars between paydays. Two percent was the lawful charge.

This fund was a great convenience to many. One sit-holder told me he hadn't received a paycheck from the paymaster for over five years! He didn't cash-in because he needed the money, it just saved him the trouble of making a special trip to get his pay. John Rawlins was cash-in man in Tulsa for many years. He was always obliging and often stretched the rules some to help a needy member. Of course some called John a "shylock," but he could take it. Those holding shares in the society received good dividends from their investment. But he did all the work. On payday he was up early, went to the newspaper with his list of cash-ins (which were many), collected the checks from the paymaster, took them to the bank, cashed them, went to the composing room where the boys and (sometimes) girls would be lined up to collect the balance of money due them. It was sure more pleasant than waiting in line at a bank!

from Lonnie Coleman

At the Kansas City *Star* at one time, brother Sam Young (a floorman) was cash-in man, and another was a machinist named John Hartley. I did business with both. On the Denver *Post*, I think the money man was Linn (can't recall his first name). But the Local #49 secretary, Bill Marise was always a reasonably safe bet for me. I knew Pappy Johnson on the Indianapolis *Star* quite well; he was always good for $15 at lunch time. In Chicago at the *News* (on the river) McDonald never seemed to run out of money. On the Chicago

American the night-side news copy cutter (one of two brothers) had an unlimited supply of long green. On the *Sun-Times,* chairman Frank Koernff was my ace in the hole. I don't know if this happened to many readers, but it occasionally happened to me: The secretary's office would be closed; the chairman would have my traveler and I wanted to take off early. The chairman would say, "It will cost you a couple of dollars." So, he'd pay me out of his pocket, less two bucks. I won't name the towns, but one was in Ohio and one in North Carolina.

❄❄❄

from Lou Brueske

Cliff Hewitt and a couple others had cash-in on the Post. Cliff came to St. Louis out of the Chicago strike in the later 40's and later held offices in Local #8 and was on scale committee many times. Duane Richmond was a cash-in man on the Globe, also sold candy and peanuts out of his proofroom desk. Ralph Leezy (some called him Mr. Loosy) was the big cash-in man, he had a setup that he would cash you in on all three places and some job shops. He made a fortune. In the mid-50s, Wally Reed tried cashing-in, but didn't last long and lost a bundle.

❄❄❄

from John Howells

The San Jose *Mercury-News* used to be a good place for travelers to stop over for a few days and get well after spending all their dough in Reno or Frisco. The chapel cash-in man was the chapel secretary (elected job), and the 2% went into the chapel fund. The pressure on the cash-in man from the regulars and travelers was tremendous. He would spend the entire payday cashing checks. Upwards of $30,000 a month passed through the chapel fund, because nobody wanted to go to the bank to cash their paychecks. They would simply stand in line by the slipboard and receive greenbacks for their check for the moderate sum of 50 cents.

The San Jose *Mercury-News* chapel was one of those where you were permitted to hit the cash-in fund but only once a week. Some of the drinkers found this inconvenient; they would have drawn their pay daily if they could. When they needed money, some would try every trick in the book to get cashed in more than once a week. One night as I was leaving the composing room, the phone rang; it was Ben Satterfield asking for the cash-in man. I called Bob Burgess and started for home. On the way out, I saw Ben Satterfield talking on the telephone in the hall. He was saying, "Honest to God, Bob. I am stuck over on the other side of town and my car is broke down. I need some money for a taxi."

I wheeled about and went back to the composing room and whispered to the cash-in man what was going on. He grinned and said, "Hold on a minute, will you Ben? I'll be right back." And he walked out into the hall where he found Ben holding the telephone. He pretended to be surprised and said, "My, you sure got here fast, Ben!"

Satterfield looked indignant and said, "Bob, I am really disappointed in you. How could you pull a dirty trick like that on me? And I thought I could trust you!" He hung up the phone and stalked out of the building, mumbling about cash-in men that he couldn't count on.

The Chairman

The chapel chairman could make a traveling printer's life easy or miserable. A good chairman would welcome the traveler, and make him feel wanted when he came in to slip-up. He would explain the slipboard and overtime situation (honestly) and predict the chances of catching work. He would recommend reasonable hotels and which restaurants served edible food. A "good" chairman would make arrangements with the cash-in man or the company bookkeeper to get your pay ready for you at the end of your last shift.

A "bad" chairman would refuse to reveal the overtime list, would not bother to help a new substitute get his or her feet on the ground and was usually pro-company. (Sometimes, a chairman figured that if he played his cards right, management might boost him to a supervisory job.) When a chairman was hostile to substitutes, it was often a token of the chapel's attitude. When members of the chapel hated substitutes because they wanted to keep their overtime, they would elect a chapel chairman who looked out for their interest. In cases like this the chairman and other printers did all they could to make things difficult for a sub. However, because the substitute had appeal to the local and International unions, a chairman was limited as to what he could do. Because most traveling printers were highly competent and knew ITU and local laws so well, they could handle hostile situations far better that those who had never moved from one shop to another.

Tramp printers often became the "bad" chairman's nemesis, for they knew ITU laws intimately and knew how to achieve enforcement under ITU law. Usually just a hint of trouble would be enough to force a chairman to disclose the overtime records. While it would seem that a troublemaking tramp printer would find little sympathy among chapel members, that was not always the case. Quite often the bad chairman worked hand-in-glove with the foreman and was given the lion's share of overtime as a reward. Therefore the chairman was intensely disliked by some composing room workers (if for no other reason than envy of his lucrative overtime). Since this individual usually had the highest amount of overtime, he was most vulnerable to being "bumped." Under ITU law he could be fined a day's pay for not hiring the first available sub to cancel his overtime. If a local did not assess the fine, a member could appeal to the ITU and a fine could be assessed against both the local and the member by the ITU. This gave a tramp printer a powerful weapon against "overtime hogs."

The composing room foreman, who by contract had to be a union member, was also subject to the overtime laws if he actually worked as a printer and didn't confine his work to administration. Often he had the most accumulated overtime of all. Therefore, when a traveling printer came to town and forced the chairman or the foreman to lay off overtime, some in the shop were gleeful and encouraged the tramp to stick around and continue the fun and mischief.

Some outstanding chairmen that respondents mentioned were: Lou Stacy and Bill Hall of the Cleveland *Plain Dealer,* Gary Sampson of the San Francisco *Chronicle;* Harvey Landford and N. Dennit Lee of the Washington *Post;* Bob Cummins of the Chicago *Daily News;* M. M. O'Neil of the Baltimore *Sun,* and Cliff Mitchell of the Buffalo

Courier-Express.

Good and Bad Foremen
from Jack Renter

Oscar Gebler was one of the best foremen I ever worked with in all my 30+ years on the road. I also remember Deo Padgett from the Cleveland *Plain Dealer* and Jim Goad of the Albuquerque *Journal*. Oscar Gebler used to have a habit, when he was "unhappy" about a man's work: he'd hold his cigar about two inches from his mouth, and roll it between his fingers while telling you what was making him unhappy. Another habit he had was in his dress. He came to work in a suit, changed into work clothes. Then at lunch, he'd dress to go out to eat. After lunch he'd change back to work clothes. Oscar was never seen entering or leaving the building in his work clothes.

I wonder how many of the guys remember "Pearshape" Presley on the El Paso papers? He was general foreman for a while. After he left El Paso, he showed up in Chicago, and made the mistake of bragging about how many subs he'd run out of El Paso. Needless to say, he didn't "catch" in Chicago. When he was foreman, he was the type who would pretend to be hung over and sick. If a guy felt sorry for him and would offer a drink, he'd go to the locker room for it, then fire the good Samaritan for having booze in his locker.

Getting fired was no big deal during Depression years. A sub showing up for work knew that if his slip was no longer on the board, he'd been fired for something or another. He'd shrug his shoulders and move on, often without bothering to ask why he'd been fired.

The foreman of the Louisville *Courier-Journal,* had a reputation for pulling slips and scattering them like confetti at every starting time. He was reputed to have pulled 2,000 slips during the early 1930s. He was proud of a book he carried which contained hundreds of names of printers he had fired during his career as supervisor, with the dates and reason for discharge. Then suddenly, a college-boy management type fired *him!* As a traveling journeyman, he toured the Midwest, searching for a day's work here and there. I am told that he was so well-known for pulling 2,000 slips that no one hired him if they could help it. Legend has it that he had a mental breakdown and was finally confined and died in some forgotten asylum.

When the subject of "good foremen" comes up, the name of Deo Padgett (Cleveland *Plain Dealer)* inevitably surfaces. Deo Padgett was a 66-year ITU member who died several years ago in Florida. Most tramp printers who hit Cleveland will remember Mr. Padgett, and few ever had any bad things to say about him. He was an honest, caring human being, as well as a professional superintendent who knew how to get things done. Deo had foremanized in Wichita, Milwaukee, and Omaha before he finally settled down at the Cleveland *Plain Dealer.* Deo trained many foremen and superintendents through his career.

Some of Deo Padgett's protégés who worked as foremen or mechanical superintendents were: Merle Wilson, Charlie Colin, Lester Welch, Rossi, Samson, Meverdin, Wilhite, Bob Rapp, Claire Mann, Hosmer, Bud Drefahl, Bill Gordon, Paul Radda, Eda Pugh, Mrs. Patterson, Tellafiero, Bill Maxwell, Gene and Tommy Leddy, Kit Carson.

Another well-known "good" foreman was Warren "Rocky" Stremming. Rocky had been a tramp printer for several years as he moved from newspaper to newspaper—deliberately learning and observing—for his goal was to become a foreman or mechanical superintendent some day. As he traveled, he learned ITU laws and their application, just as any tramp printer would; this knowledge made him especially valuable when he applied for supervisory positions. He understood contracts and union laws, so he was in a position to save management many headaches and labor problems. Because he traveled and worked so many newspapers as a substitute, Rocky insisted on treating his composing room staff as he had liked to be treated. He also demanded that substitutes be handled fairly and that overtime be given out in strict accordance with ITU rules.

This had a dramatic effect on production when he took over in one composing room and insisted that printers give out their overtime when substitutes were present. Until that time, the crew customarily dragged the work out so they could earn an extra five or six hours of overtime every week. But when they discovered they'd have to give it out as soon as they got it, the printers began hustling to avoid working overtime. Management was astounded at how the payroll dropped as soon as Rocky became foreman. He was considered a magician!

❈❈❈

from Tom Holson . . . Bakersfield, California (written about 1972)

A name that will ring a bell in the memories of old-timers all over the west and beyond: that of Elmer Forgy. Elmer arrived at the Bakersfield *Californian* in 1912 and remained to make life miserable for printers for the next 52 years.

He soon became foreman on the then-small daily and job shop combined, and later was promoted to mechanical superintendent. But this new job didn't keep him from continuing to act as foreman. He dictated all hiring, firing and composing room procedures, not letting the skipper make decisions. Needless to say, no foreman endured this for long and there was a procession of them over the years.

Elmer was a burly Irishman with blue eyes who started out in Alton, Ill. He wore a felt hat indoors and out, evidently as the badge of the man in charge. He maintained his membership in the ITU for more than 60 years.

The *Californian* was and is the only shop of any size between Los Angeles and Fresno and consequently was a way station for many a roadster. Elmer lurked behind his foreman to keep tabs on every new hire and if he didn't measure up he would mutter to the skipper to pull his slip. If the sub chose to argue and express his views, Elmer would pull his hat down over his eyes, look grim and confront the complainer without saying a word. When the one-sided contest ended he would turn and walk away. Of course, some firings were reinstated on appeal to the chapel.

Elmer was given a free hand in the composing room by Alfred Harrell, the courtly gentleman who owned the paper (and whose descendants still do). He never forgot the early struggles of the company to make money and long after it became highly profitable he continued to buy used equipment and stint on supplies. He kept old monotypes casting headlines and ad type until long after they had been replaced by modern equipment everywhere else. The machinists were kept busy maintaining the junk Linotypes until after World War II, when the business manager woke up and went over Elmer's head to order some new late model machines. He once ordered a machinist to repair a worn cam by fastening a thin strip of spring steel to the cam with machine screws. Some time later the screws gave way and the shim shot across the composing room and crashed into a type case. Fortunately no one was in its way or he would have been mangled.

When I slipped up at the Cal in 1938, an old-timer told me, "You are not working on a newspaper—you are working on a blankety-blank book." I soon found out what he meant. Elmer had a style book of 128 pages with rules for everything you ever heard of. Reading matter was to be spaced out with 1-point leads—and how the casting room hands cried about having to cast them. Every headline and style of makeup was dictated and monitored by Elmer, although from the background. Everything had to fit. There were no three-line fillers.

Word division was a fixation with Elmer. Every take of 7-point on 8-lead was slugged with the machine number, of course, and Elmer was known to find a doubtful division in the paper, look up the proof, identify the operator and instruct the skipper to give him hell about it.

Every machine had a clock and the operator kept the readings on the back of his time slip. The clocks were read at the end of the shift and an office girl made a record for Elmer. Occasionally this was used to harass or fire someone. Eventually this irksome business was ended by union negotiation.

My first job at the Cal was the lunch relief, a nice little plan dreamed up by Elmer. The day shift started at 7 A.M. At 11 A.M. I relieved the first operator to go to lunch and worked on his machine for 30 minutes until his return, then jumped to the second machine and so on until I had covered seven machines for a half hour each. By then it was 2 P.M. and I went to lunch myself, then finished my shift just before the night crew arrived. Furthermore I had to read all those clocks, keep a record of my string and inform each operator of how many lines to subtract from his number. This form of cruelty was finally halted by union contract, and lunch periods were extended to 45 minutes

Elmer gradually lost some of his iron grip and retired in 1964; he died a few years later. I remained on the *Cal* slip board for more than 30 years and survived all of Elmer's antics, retiring in 1969.

Tramp Foremen

It wasn't only journeymen who traveled around the country; foremen also moved about in response to newspaper failures, mergers or to accept better job offers. Management could fire a foreman as quickly as a foreman could fire a journeyman. Some foremen gained a reputation for cost-cutting or for solving production problems and were in demand by publishers. Below is the fascinating story of a self-styled "Tramp Foreman." Ted Morse was one of the more prolific contributors to the *Tramp Printer Newsletter*, and passed away about 1980. Before he died he wrote:

"As a 59-year ITU member, I thank you for circulating some of my memories of 60 years past in the *Tramp Printers Newsletter*. Made into a book, or just as they are, they might help erase my kids' admonitions that their dad was just a hobo. The Great Depression, mergers, strikes, bankruptcies and a dying industry is beyond their ken." Then after Ted passed away, we received the following letter from one of his daughters:

"I've just read my first *Tramp Printers Newsletter,* passed on to me by my stepmother, Leona Morse (widow of Ted G. Morse). In it you had an article about my dad. Yes, we'd come to that conclusion long ago, that our dad wasn't just a hobo. Our 'hobo dad,' you see, took us three girls after mom left for greener pastures and he was forced to settle down and make a home for us. By the time I was nine, I can remember Omaha (where I was born), El Paso, Chesterton, Pa., Albany, NY, and quite a few other places we had gone as a family. When dad had us girls dropped in his lap, so to speak, he bought 31 acres in Zanesville, Ohio, took a job as a Linotype operator at Mercury Match, and became a 'solid citizen.' After we three girls had married and moved on, dad took up his own life again, got married to a lovely lady and went to work for the Chicago *Tribune* until retirement. Then he and Leona moved back to the only place he ever had a home, Zanesville., He continued in his heart as a news printer until the day he died. I wish you could have known him. Thanks so much for the articles about dad—a tramp printer in his heart forever."

❄❄❄

from Ted Morse

Editor's note: This is one of the last articles Ted wrote for the Tramp Printers' Newsletter".

As an 80-year-old journeyman (now pensionless), a survivor of the Great Depression, Butte winters, Omaha mergers, picket-lines in Chicago, Philadelphia bankruptcies, Albany consolidations, Chester Guild strike, El Paso chicanery; and technology changes, I suppose I am doing as well as most oldsters!

The unforgettable thrill of hand-setting my first line of perfectly spaced type that would "lift" is never lost. It was from an oldtime news case with caps, small caps, lower case and symbols, double mounted above cases of display types.

With a shop-apron made by my mother (still cherished) protecting my front, a stick in hand and pica-pole ruining my right back pocket, I finally graduated from galley boy to distributor. A paragraph of type, whacked with a wet sponge to hold it together, was balanced in the left hand and each letter clicked into its proper box in the case. I did distribution for a long time before I was permitted to achieve actual composition. The hand-set job shop proprietor finally became aware of my ability. He gave me a dummy Linotype keyboard to take home to practice on. I was on my way to becoming a journeyman!

I wanted to travel. In that frightful age of 1922, few descendants of widowed immigrant mothers would realize their dreams. I wanted to see the world, and printing did it for me!

Omaha was my starting point. Towns in Nebraska, Illinois, Indiana, Tennessee, Virginia, Iowa, Indiana, Montana, Wyoming, Colorado, New Mexico, Texas, Florida, Pennsylvania, New York and Ohio all became 'home towns". Brief forays into Kentucky, Missouri, Alabama, Louisiana, the Carolinas, Georgia, Maryland and Delaware were short stays and not counted. I achieved my dream of travel!

Thus, after years of purposely traveling as a tramp printer wanting to "see the world," I matriculated to being a "tramp foreman" with a wife, three kids and an aging mother to care for. Although the foreman's job paid more money, it afforded much less security than a regular journeyman's position. According to ITU law, newly-hired foreman or superintendents were denied priority standing in the chapel.

Printing-house bosses like myself, upon disagreements with college-boy purchasing agents or business managers, were frequently fired. This placed them at the bottom of over-laden slipboards by local union law. The alternative to starvation was to look for another foreman's job.

Old-time printers in Omaha, Sioux Falls, Des Moines, Wichita, Enid, Kansas City, Salt Lake, Butte, Billings, Casper, Cheyenne, Huntington, Fort Wayne, Chester, Philadelphia, Albany, Albia, Ottumwa, South Bend, Michigan City, Zanesville and Chicago might remember Ted Morse, the "Tramp Foreman."

PRINTING POTPOURRI

MOST TRAMP PRINTERS prided themselves on their ability to walk into almost any print shop in the country and immediately begin turning out quality work. It was a gratifying experience to begin the shift under the skeptical, sometimes hostile eye of a foreman or proprietor, and before the shift was half over, having him slapping you on the back, telling you what a wonderful town this is, and urging you to take a regular situation. (That's happened many times to both authors of this book.)

"I prided myself on my ability to size up a shop before I started to work," one ex-tramp said with a mischievous smile. "I observed where they, stored borders, leads and slugs, stereo cuts, and analyzed the system they used to handle ads or galley pages. If I were slipped up on the machine side, I would memorize the location of the swing magazines and knew where to find sorts. When the shift began, I always kept an eye on those working around me, to make sure my production was obviously higher than the regulars. If I noticed another sub having a problem 'making his string,' I'd slug his name on a take or two, and then work a little faster to make up for it.[1] A good tramp printer knew how to keep ahead of the homeguards, put out more work, and above all, make it look easy. The secret to making it look easy is to do everything with minimum hand motion, maximum efficiency, and plan every move in advance so as not to waste energy or look nervous."

The following stories about different composing rooms about

---

[1] Type used to be measured with a string laid across the type columns, and a Linotype slug with the printer's name placed at the top. A *take* is a piece of copy set into type.

the country may not be of interest to those not familiar with the variety of machinery and processes in old-time printing. Of necessity, there's a lot of jargon used, but in order to tell the stories properly, the words have to be from the mouths of the participants. But those with a curiosity about how it was to work as a printer in hot-metal days might want to browse through the following stories.

Printing Skills Of Yesterday
from Ted Morse

Journeymen were trained to set and distribute type from "news cases" brimming with foundry-cast type, handle Simplex and Unitype machines, Linotypes, Intertypes, Linographs and Graphotype. They knew makeready, paper cutting, stone work—along with proper display, punctuation and spelling. They made flat casts to be nailed to lumber-yard boards and cut them to size on Miller saws. They fed Chandler Price presses by hand at 3,000 whomps per hour. They made up page ads at one per hour, they re-shuffled columns of type four times nightly to "catch trains" with editions.

Afternoon and evening home-delivered newspapers with 8 page Sunday "funnies" and supplements meant day work for printers and gold-mines to Saturday-night subs. Home delivered six afternoons and Sunday mornings for 10c a week. New York City had 11 popular dailies, Chicago seven, Omaha five. The little county seat at Wabash, Indiana had four daily papers, the big town of Lima, Ohio also boasted four dailies.

A printer "on tour" could go a couple of blocks to leave a dull saw or some other inconvenience and go right to work. He had training and skills the employers couldn't do without.

Now it's all replaced by paste-up and TV news which brings the latest into everyone's parlor while the shots are still being fired.

Worst Commercial Shop
from a retired printer in Garland Texas

The worst commercial shop, by far, that I worked in was Dayton Typographic Service, Dayton, Ohio. It was so bad that no local person would work there. They found printers by running ads in publications all over the country. I worked there for a year, 1961-62. It is the only place I worked that treated employees like they were nothing. It ended up non-union.

The first thing they did after pressuring employees to decertify was cut their pay 15 per cent. I liked typesetting shop work. I had 10 years of it in New Orleans. So I tried Dayton Typo. Stood it a year and went to the newspaper where I spent 21 happy years.

Another shop I enjoyed working in was Montgomery & Co., printers of *The Daily Court Record* and of law briefs. I spent five good years there and especially enjoyed setting legal copy. Off and on I had set brief and transcript for quite a few years. In the New Orleans typesetting shop I spent some time setting the type for the quarterly *International Journal of Leprosy* for five years. I set virtually every line of it. Also set part of *The Jewish Ledger,* a weekly circulated throughout the South, for 10 years. We set a lot of different publications and miscellaneous jobs there. These two shops were in New Orleans.

Detroit Rotary Plants

Many tramp printers knew about overtime work to be found in the "Rotary Plants" in Detroit. These plants printed weeklies for towns and neighborhoods around Detroit: Royal Oak *Tribune,* Post Printing, Abbe Press, Michigan Rotary, etc. This was always a good place to make a lot of money and get caught up on the bills before striking out again. Three to four hours a night overtime was common, plus an occasional sixth day of overtime. Management in these plants felt it was more economical to work two 12-hour shifts than to put on more workers for a third shift, or to invest in additional equipment.

Don Cleary remembered working in a rotary plant when he was locked out on the Detroit *News (when* the pressmen went on strike). He showed up at the hiring hall and was told to go to Post Printing and work for a regular that night. Since it was the situation holder's night off, it was considered a sixth shift for Don. After he had been at his machine about 20 minutes, the chairman came around and asked him to work 5 hours O.T. The same thing happened every night thereafter. Talk about a big check!

"Then a couple of weeks of that, I pulled an "E" card[2] Washington *Post*. At that time I was on strike in West Palm Beach, locked out in Detroit and working in Washington, D.C.!"

Tough Places To Work
from Al Reed

Just thought the brethren might like to compare different types of "tough" jobs they may have been called on to set either on the Lino or by hand. Several of mine come to mind. One of the most demanding was in a commercial shop in Louisville, which compiled two insurance volumes, a fire insurance compendium of 800 pages and a life volume of 1,200 pages. The type was stored in galleys in a huge basement, mostly in agate tabular and was constantly being corrected, so operators had to go over the galleys one by one, hunting the lines to be reset, taking proofs and reading them. Wow! Another job on which I worked was setting the Arizona State school budget in agate tabular, full page, much of it butted slugs clear across the page. A top Mexican operator and I did the whole job, he on the night shift and I on days. Another nasty one was setting the Yuma, Arizona telephone directories in a shop with a tin roof, no air conditioner and the temperature 116 degrees! In one way it was not so bad, as it was cantaloupe season and dozens of carloads were being packed in ice for daily shipping and they gave away all the overripe ones to anyone who would pick them up.

And how about setting ad guts, night shift, on the San Antonio *Light,* walking six blocks to lunch, eating, and getting back in 30 minutes?

(*Editor's note: Yes, but I seem to recall some compensation for working the San Antonio Light, night shift. The YWCA was right across the street and many of the girls didn't bother to pull the shades in the hot Texas summer.*)

---

[2] "Emergency" traveling cards were issued during a strike, to allow union members to work elsewhere for the duration.

✣✣✣
from Don Cleary

Al Reed wants to hear about "tough" jobs. Seeing that he put quotes around "tough jobs" shows that he knows that there were really no tough or hard jobs in printing. All printing was and still is just "picas & points." Picas & points, ems & ens, picas & points. It just took longer to accomplish some jobs than others.

When working on the ad floor, you'd face Walgreens and other drug store ads, full page shell casts with a hundred million holes in them, at angles.. Boxes, lines, and sometimes just a price to put in a hole. The #!@!! angles were all different, of course, and a lot of the "picas & points" was the time you spent lifting the cast on and off to see if the @#!%!! angles you'd made matched the ©#!%!! angles in the cast. Of course, some guys would cut a Linotype slug shell cast high and stick it in the hole with tape. That was cheating.

One time, when I went back home to visit the old folks and other relatives, the newspaper was on strike. So I went to Griffiths job shop and found a circus of things I didn't know existed. They printed a newsletter for a "Camp Dudley" somewhere in the Adirondacks. Old Dudley thought he was the second coming or nearabouts. He must have been a retired "General Halftrack." They also published a biology magazine and a chemistry and other technical journals. A night's work at the machine often consisted of a little better than 3/4 galley of type, single column.

When I left that much type in a galley for a night's work that first night, I figured I might as well not show up the next night because I'd surely be fired. They didn't fire me; they wanted me to stay around. Almost all of the work was setting formulas that had parens, inferior numbers & letters (both caps, small caps), superior numbers and letters, caps, lower case and upside down and sideways. And, as with most small job shops, much of the time was spent looking for that *one* mat that they had somewhere in the shop.

Some time later after working at that shop I was having a half dozen cans of Bud with my friend Earl Norris who was living on Signal Mountain outside of Chattanooga. He was telling me about the job he was working on at a job shop in Chattanooga where they were doing a job for the TVA. They had a formula for every time the water went up or down a foot above their dams. It was similar to the stuff I had been doing. It was driving him crazy. He wanted me to slip up at his place for a couple of weeks to help him out. I told him, "Earl, remember, it's just 'picas and points, picas and points'. And, cold weather is chasing me south to all that straight matter at the Palm Beach *News*"

Chicago Tribune
from Frederick G. Schmidt

My first visit to this noteworthy establishment was when I was making a quick trip to Toronto from California. As I did not have enough money to complete the trip, I slugged up on the *Trib* and mentioned that I wanted to work only three days. This statement lifted a few eyebrows, and while they had to give me the work, due to the fact they hired the entire sub board every night, you can be sure they watched carefully as I operated the Linotype. They had not to watch long, however, as I was certainly more than competent. The *Trib's* composing room was one of the best organized places mechanically that I have ever worked in. When a Linotyper found the name of the paper in the copy—which was often—it was required to be in caps and small caps, which was not to be found on all type fonts. What was found, though, in your thin-space box was a complete logo of the paper's name, divided into syllables that you placed in your assembler. Neat! Also, when one was given tabular matter to set—stock market quotations, whatever—they had the column heads already set in type for you, with a sample listing. Neat, neat!

The *Tribune's* building is absolutely stunning and needs to be seen to be appreciated. It has embedded in its outer walls stones from important edifices around the world, even from Blarney Castle, would you believe? The Trib's building fronted, or backed, on Lake Michigan. Ships could unload paper right near the point of usage. It is something to speculate that this system might be impervious to striking Teamsters.

A visit to their press room would be similarly awe-inspiring. The many eight-page units seemed to extend to the horizon down there, and then some, at least two rows, if I remember correctly. A stereotyper acquaintance of mine from Texas spoke of going up to Chi to work on the *Trib*—casting plates hard by the presses. Reporting to the stereo foreman, he was told: "Number free, over dere."

Yesterday's Technology
from Tom Holson

Does anyone remember the Linograph Typesetting Machine? Produced in Davenport, Iowa, the Linograph was a marvel of its day. It had 15 vertical magazines easily available on one machine which could be changed by the operator sitting in his chair. It cast lines of type eight per minute, had 3/4-size matrices cut deeply to produce type images 5-points above the slug's shoulder. Matrices were advertised at four to seven cents apiece. The Linograph was a great improvement over Mergenthaler's best. But it was a wonderful machine produced at exactly the wrong time—the Great Depression squelched the Linograph along with many other brilliant concepts of the 1920s.

The Bristol Va.-Tenn. *Herald Courier* in the 1920s went along with new technology in the ad-room. This plant was one of the first with factory-mitered brass rules and borders. All leads and slugs were also brass. Everything was quickly distributed while very hot after baking in stereo steam-tables. Apprentices and ad-men developed leather-thick calluses on hands and fingers from handling the hot brass.

Who remembers the chalk plate? Perhaps some do, but for those who don't: it was a metal plate coated on one side with about six points of firm, white chalk. A design could be sketched on the chalk, then engraved with a sharp tool. The plate was then cast just like a stereotype mat. Anything that was cut through to the metal base would print.

The only time I ever saw this process was when I visited a small shop in New Mexico in the early '20s. An elderly printer of the old school was getting out a weekly paper with equipment whose only concessions to the post-Gutenberg era were a four-page flatbed press, a snapper, a Model 15 Linotype and a casting box.

I suppose the chalk plates were still available from Western

Newspaper Union. The old fellow would design a logo—or more likely, a cattle brand, which had to be published as a legal when they were registered—and then skillfully engrave it in the chalk. He was an artist in his way.

The Model 15 was the only one of its kind I ever saw. For those who haven't heard, it was a junior Lino, about two-thirds the size of a Model 5. The short magazine channels could carry only 15 mats. I heard that the Merganthaler Company tried to trade or buy back all of them, to get them off the market because of their numerous shortcomings.

from David M. Stryker

On the Linograph: It was my pleasure some years ago as a student at California Polytechnic College, to operate one of those machines. That bank of magazines hanging over your head could be intimidating, but it was a beauty to operate. The mats on this model were shorter than standard Linotype mats, about one inch in height, otherwise the same. It is possible that the machine mentioned in the article was a later model if it took standard Linotype-Intertype mats.

from Jim White

The G 4-4 Intertype was a very interesting machine; I worked on many of them. The sweetest I ever ran was a pair at *Southwest Magazine* in Grand Prairie, Texas. They were brand-new and gave very little trouble. The "big job" there was page mats of grocery ads for Kroger Co. We never did any actual printing; we just shipped the stereo mats out all over that part of the country. Machine work was mostly two- and three-line process—seemed like millions of them. Many crap machines had a 30-pica shelf at eye level on which you put your overhang line, then a pointer attached to the assembler slide was supposed to line up the second and third lines. This never worked for me. Like most crap operators, I cast a slug in 10-pt. nut-1, nut-2, nut-3, etc. to calculate the number of quads to drop for the lineup. Most operators I knew preferred Intertype over Linotype; they were simpler and more precise in many respects, like the spaceband box and the double-black safety.

But let's hear it for the Model 26 mixers. Lots of operators never even saw one—it was a peculiar machine and you had to understand it to love it. It had two distributors and the mats ran over a bridge. Mats not cut for the upper distributor engaged the blade on the bridge and dropped into a funnel (believe me) and fed into the lower distributor box. The magazines were shifted by pump handles. I learned to set "bean" ads[3] on a Model 26 at the Albany (NY) *Knickerbocker-News,* then graduated to the Blue Streaks, which were just coming on the scene (at least in Albany). The News used the band saw Don describes; the tit was formed by a hole in the back of the left-hand Jaw.

Model 25's (without auxiliaries) were the primary machine at the California State Printing office in Sacramento. Bills were printed in (I'm pretty sure) 10-pt. Devinne roman, then as the Legislature made changes any part to be dropped was set in strikeout and anything added in italics. As I remember it, the top magazine carried roman and italics; the second magazine roman and strikeout characters.

We don't bigawd do things like that!

First time I ever worked at the St. Louis *Post-Dispatch* and *Globe-Democrat* was about 1958 or 1959; they were just in the process of moving to the present building. The news machine I operated was on the floor below the composing room, and I had to take a freight elevator up and down to dump takes and grab copy off the hook.

For some reason they wanted a thin-space left and right, and I struggled with it for a couple of shifts. The first thin-space would pop out of the assembler about every third time, and the last one would lean over and hang up on the spaceband chute finger. I got a new starwheel but it didn't help much. The assembler spring detent were about as sharp as a baseball bat. Then a light dawned. I was setting 8-pt; So I backed the spindle off two points and jammed a two-point lead back of the right-hand jaw. It worked great. I set type like that for a week or two, avoiding tight lines and always remembering to disassemble the rig before quitting time.

One night I came back from lunch and there was a grim-looking

---

[3] Full-page grocery advertisements.

assistant, assistant machinist leaning on the first elevator. Well, I was terrified as you can well imagine. He explained firmly that "we don't bigawd do things like that!" I tried to make a deal to keep the spindle backed off and just drop the right-hand thin space, but he was like steel, so I went back to picking thins off the floor.

❊❊❊

from Lou Brueske

The only Linograph I ran into was in Rapid City, S. D., but didn't operate it. Wonder how many remember the Model 30 Linotype mixer for ads, or the APL line casting machine (All Purpose Linotype) which was used for heads and base material? I started learning to operate the Linotype when I was about 12 years old, on a country weekly. A rebuilt Model 5 with a gasoline burner (high test gasoline), it had a tank and I had to pump the air pressure with a bicycle pump. There was a small cup under the mouthpiece in which we burnt alcohol to heat it before turning on the gas. Had to change liners for every measure by hand, plus the machine had to be backed up and set a certain way before you could change the ejector blade by hand. It had one magazine, so we had to run out the mats and put in another size. Had three type sizes 6pt, 8pt and 14pt. We had no saw of any kind except a regular hand saw to cut down typehigh cuts (along with several files). Brass rules were used for column rules, 6 points wide, and all cutoff rules, etc., were brass. We used a slug breaker to cut down Lino slugs. All display type was foundry or wood, and we saved all leads and slugs and used a lot of wood reglets and wood furniture to build ads.

Journey Through the Alphabet
Norman A. Sinowitz

In the days when Linotype machines set most of the text type for all printed matter, there were many specialty shops that handled the typesetting and updating of the white page telephone directories. Some of those shops handled the "yellow pages" also, but where I worked from until that last day—on Nov. 10, 1983—we only handled the white pages. On that date, the composing room closed, and phone books were done by computers.

Every day, segments of the various books would be lifted out of the galley racks by the men as they stood lined up behind each other at the galley racks. The pages would be laid out on the tops of the racks in perfect numerical and alphabetical sequence. Large books like Miami ran in segments for the phone company.

Disconnected or otherwise altered phone numbers would be removed from the pages in the form of kills. These kills would be shown on various mark-out sheets received from the telephone company each day in addition to the copy from which the new listings were set. The kills would be gathered up, placed on long galleys and proofed on a Vandercook for checking against the kill listings.

About four or five Fairchild ITS machines punched tape for the new listings. The tape then ran through a primitive computer which would decide whether a list would fit in one or two lines. The output tape would be run into the Linotypes. Those machines were three Comets and a Model 31.

Making the kills was referred to as "plucking" and inserting the new type into the pages was called "stuffing." In between "book closings" or printing, the pages were kept five columns to a galley to allow room to take old listings out and put new listings in.

When it came time to get a book ready for publication (closing time), a cut-off date would be established to stop further inserting of new listings, and the book would be ready to make up into four columns per page. The columns were 14 picas wide and 63 picas deep. Make-up would begin only after all corrections were made and the folio numbers checked, so that each galley page was laid out in perfect continuity. While one person laid out the pages another came behind and justified the page with 2-point leads.

Over the years, setting type, proofreading, making the kills inserting the new lists, the page makeup which went from one end of the shop to the other, and the alphabetical sequence checking of countless telephone page proofs were like one long "Journey Through the Alphabet." But now, because of computerization the journey has ended. Along long with others who worked the hot metal telephone directories I am drifting into other fields of work.

Legislature Sessions

One type of specialized printing that meant big money for tramp printers was setting type for state legislature sessions. A daily record of everything said, bills presented, and all actions taken at a state legislature had to be set into type and published by the next day. A group of traveling printers made an excellent living by showing up at printing plants that held contracts to cover the session. Extra help was always desperately needed. The better known legislature sessions were in Louisiana, at Baton Rouge; Florida, at Tallahassee, and California, in Sacramento. There were others, but those printers who worked them tried to keep it secret; too many printers might spoil it for them.

Legislature sessions lasted two to four months. Journeymen worked from 12 to 16 hours, six days a week—sometimes seven days. Those who remained for the entire session were given a bonus.

The legislature sessions attracted a different type of traveling printer, and created a unique snowbird type. For one thing, this was not a place for tramps who couldn't handle alcohol or hard work. Being at your machine or makeup stone was critical, and being able to turn out high production for hours on end essential. Many of those attracted to the sessions earned enough money to "retire" for the rest of the year, until the next session started. Some went to Mexico and lived well on their stake. Others traveled to Europe and occasionally worked there. Several English-language newspapers there, such as the Paris *Herald-Tribune,* hired traveling printers.

Legislative sessions weren't the only source of lucrative paychecks for these printers. Someone who wanted to earn an extra half-year's pay had several options. Some printing plants had contracts to produce yearly updates of mail-order catalogs, telephone books or newspaper anniversary editions, which always meant large amounts of overtime. These plants depended on traveling printers, because once the "big job" was complete, they no longer needed the extra help. So traveling printers would learn of a work abnormality in some shop or some city and work there as long as the "gravy" lasted, then gravitate to another such place.

Hartford, Kentucky
From Jack Renter

It's been said there were really no "tough jobs." I agree, they weren't tough, just some took more thought and skill. Most of the old-time tramps walked in, slipped up and told the foreman, "I can do anything you want done." Probably the roughest job I ever tackled was on the *Hartford Messenger* in Hartford, Kentucky. Percy Landram, publisher at that time, called my home local #622 in Owensboro for help. The local president asked me to go. It was a "combination" job, a one man composing room, a weekly paper and job shop. I was green (just got my card) and the butterflies damn near carried me away. What made the job so rough was the fact that he had so few mats for the machine — like two or three "e's" or "i's". Some lines had to be set two or three times and cut and butted. Don't guess there's any shops like that left. Incidentally, that was the first job I ever quit in the middle of the shift. We delivered a job to the next town, a full page form (heavy!), and he told me to carry it into a print shop there. I told him I hired out as his printer, not his delivery boy and I walked off. Caught a bus home and the local #622 president called the publisher to get my money for me.

As I said, I was young and didn't know the ropes, so I took my problems to the local president. It didn't take long on the road to learn to fight my own battles—foreman or publishers didn't scare me after I began to learn my way around. For a long time, I was one of those guys that carried an ITU Law Book and asked for a chapel law book at each new place. I soon learned to "read a board" and see for myself how work was going, who was catching what.

from John Howells

The first union shop I ever worked in was a small job shop in Toledo. It was a one-man composing room, all handset, with the owner of the shop doing the presswork. I was to replace a printer who had worked there for 28 years and suddenly died, inconsiderately leaving the shop without a typesetter. The local secretary gave me a work permit and sent me out on the job. In those days, you were sent to the toughest shop in town to prove your competency before you were allowed to make application for membership. I suspect the secretary knew he could never hope to supply that shop with a printer any other way. But I didn't care, I just wanted a chance to prove myself and to become an ITU member.

The shop was dark, musty smelling, cold. The owner made Scrooge look like a Good Time Charlie. He fired the stove frugally, to a point where one's fingers were a constant blue. The shop boasted several hundred cases of type— a nice selection in fact—but the problem was that the printer who worked there before me hadn't bothered to label the cases. This wouldn't have been so bad if they were in some kind of order. But his logic had been that point sizes should be in order, rather than fonts. Therefore, all 10-point type cases were in one rack, and 8-point types in another area of the composing room, and so forth. After 28 years, he had no problem.

The owner almost came unglued when he saw me pick up a lead and slap it in a dusty slug-cutter to trim it to fit. He shouted, "These leads and slugs are the original ones my father bought when he started this shop 50 years ago," he informed me with an indignant glare. "Don't you dare destroy them."

When I tied up a job, he watched closely to make sure that I found a skein of string just the right length. When I asked him if the string was original too, I received an malevolent stare for a reply. I've always believed that at least some of that string was 50 years old!

It was tough to qualify as a journeyman in those days. But it was worth it. I'll never forget that day I was obligated, that feeling that I had finally proved myself to be among the best, that I had earned the privilege of working alongside the best printers in the country. My next greatest thrill came about six months later, when I had that first traveling card in my pocket and the overwhelming sense of freedom of knowing I could go anywhere in the world I damn well pleased.

Union Training
from Ted G. Morse

For over a hundred years, the ITU prided itself on producing skilled journeymen. Young printers, trained in small shops in far-away places "slipped up" to become reliable makeups, operators, proofreaders, markups, admen and foremen in the nation's best newspapers. I remember many from those old days, such as "Rome Blackie" and "Piggy" Feeney in Albany; Lester "Turkey" Welch from Wichita; Wilhite and Wilson from Kansas City and Pueblo. They were good craftsmen.

Floormen Gene Hadley and Billy Britt from Oklahoma could produce page ads at one per hour in almost any newspaper ad room. Tom Leddy could "turn the clock" in such tough shops as Corpus Christi and Baton Rouge (where the chairman had to make them wait 'til lunch-time for an interview).

Some of those old print shops were adventures in themselves. In Tallahassee, they were equipped with racks of pre-Civil War handset types. This certainly gave journeymen headaches! Also at the Springfield, Ill. *Register* job shop, the handmen were faced with type racks stacked ceiling high with ancient type. They had to approach them on ladders. Just think of duplicating exact replicas of 1860 legal forms while standing on a ladder, handsetting 11-1/2 point forgotten type faces into an old-time stick!

Bisbee Arizona
from Reuben F. Slattery

At least one article on Bisbee ought to be in order. Even in the 1930s there was usually work in Bisbee. Printers would stop a while, make a stake, then wonder what they were doing way down in that corner of the country, and move on. They were continually short of help. The first time I showed up on the Bisbee *Review,* in '35 or '36, the chairman wanted me to work a double shift all week. I didn't go for that, so we settled on a shift and a half per day for the week.

The main street of Bisbee wound up a canyon. At the bottom, Brewery Gulch Street intersected the main street. Brewery Gulch was aptly named. The buildings were all connected and about every other one was a saloon. Beer was 10 cents a glass. If you ordered a beer the bartender would ask if you just got off shift. If you said "yes" you were entitled to a shot *and* a beer for the 10 cents.

There were four machines at the Bisbee *Review* to get out a daily paper, so it was a struggle. The machines ran plumb awful, short of mats, etc. So the operators kept hammering away, hoping that their proofs wouldn't be too bad. The editors of the *Review* read proof. One day I wondered why my proofs kept coming back consistently okay. The composing room was on the second floor overlooking Main street. As I was looking out the window I noticed the editors making numerous trips across the street to the bar. "Aha," I thought, "the mystery is solved. There is the reason for my okay proofs!"

Dr. Miles Nervine
from John Howells

Printers who worked in old-time country shops might remember using "Dr. Miles Nervine" proof presses, type fonts, and miscellaneous printing equipment. They knew it was of Dr. Miles Nervine origin because the name was imprinted somewhere on the item. Many today wonder what all of this meant, and what Dr. Miles had with printing. After all, this was the manufacturer of Bromo-Quinine, Bromo-Seltzer and Alka-Seltzer.

It turns out that during the depression, when advertising money was almost non-existent, country weeklies were willing to do anything to fill up their pages. So when Dr. Miles Nervine company offered to pay for their advertising with printing equipment and supplies, the small publishers readily agreed.

At that time, in the early 1930s, my father had just bailed out of a partnership in a country weekly in Lancaster, Missouri (or someplace like that), and was looking for a way to make money. So my father—Owen F. Howells—took a sales job with the Dr. Miles Company. The deal was that in return for running Alka-Seltzer and Bromo-Quinine ads, a publisher would receive a drum-roller proof press, or German foundry type, planer blocks-and-mallet sets, or other low-quality equipment. And the salesmen received a commission from Dr. Miles company.

It wasn't difficult to convince a publisher to go for the deal. Dr. Miles furnished the ads in the form of boiler plate, easy to slap into a page, filled up space, and made the paper look as if there were at least some advertising.

My father was assigned everything west of the Mississippi, and another salesman everything to the east. The pay was small, but the two of them put their heads together and soon figured out a way to make the work pay off handsomely.

The plan was: they also became salesmen for Meyer-Both stereotype mat service. The only way my father and his partner would offer a publisher the opportunity of running Alka-Seltzer ads would be if the newspaper subscribed to Meyer-Both service. Since country weeklies couldn't survive without a mat service—for ad illustrations, fancy display types and graphics needed to dress up the paper—they readily agreed to switching to the Meyer-Both service. Didn't cost any more.

The commission money rolled in from both companies, and the cheap printing equipment rolled out. My dad was making $200 a week, when $40 was considered an excellent wage. This went on for a couple of years, until Dr. Miles management discovered how much money their salesmen were making. The company split the territory into several pieces, upon which the two original salesmen quit. By that time, my father had enough money to purchase a healthy weekly newspaper in Salem, Missouri, and later a successful one in Ferguson, Missouri.

Tramp Printers' Chapel Meeting

The idea of a newsletter to gather stories from the remaining tramp printers was hatched one day in the cafeteria of the San Jose *Mercury-News*. Denny Gatzmeyer, Johnny Burt, John Howells, and several other ex-tramp printers enthused over the idea, and thus the *Tramp Printers' Newsletter* came into existence. Much of the material from this book was excerpted from the *Tramp Printers' Newsletter*.

One consequence of keeping the old-timers in touch was the clamor for a reunion. The perfect opportunity presented itself in August of 1983, when the International Typographical Union's annual convention was held in San Francisco. It turned out that many ex-tramp printers were delegates to the convention and others were in the habit of attending conventions for recreation.

Through the columns of the *Tramp Printers' Newsletter*, a meeting was scheduled on a free afternoon of the convention. It was to be called: The Tramp Printers' Chapel Meeting. Appropriately enough, it was held at Jerry and Johnny's Bar, an old-time favorite hangout for San Francisco printers, very convenient to those who worked at the old San Francisco *Examiner*. The long-time owner, Jerry Hansen, had always been a friend to newspaper workers, and he particularly enjoyed traveling printers. "They were among my best customers. They added color to the joint," he said.

About 40 people attended the meeting, most of them well-traveled printers. The article below is reprinted from the *Tramp Printers' Newsletter* of September, 1983. Although everyone enjoyed themselves immensely, any relation between actual events that occurred at the Tramp Printers' Chapel Meeting and reality are purely coincidental.

Official Minutes, Tramp Printers Chapel Meeting

"SAN FRANCISCO (Aug. 7, 1983) — Tramp printers from various parts of the jurisdiction—from the United States, Canada and Texas—held their first annual chapel meeting this afternoon. The tramp printer chapel members assembled at Jerry & Johnny's Bar, an historic newspapermen's shrine just down the block from the old S.F. *Examiner*. As the members sipped drinks and waited for the meeting to convene, they remembered the many good times printers had in this bar, and all the impromptu chapel meetings of years ago. Some recalled how often they slipped away for a drink without Bill Ferregiario catching them. But the *Examiner* is gone now, moved away to merge with the *Chronicle* on Fifth Street. Might as well be in China as far as how many printers visit the bar today.

"Denny Gatzmeyer (acting chapel chairman) called the meeting to order at 1 p.m. A motion was made to adjourn. Jim Joly raised a point of order to the effect that since the motion was made by the bartender, who was not a member of the chapel and who hoped to get rid of the noisy crowd and go home early, the motion should be out of order.

"The motion to adjourn was defeated by lusty cries of '*No!*' '*Nay!*' *Never!*' and, '*Who took my drink?*'

"Minutes of the meeting were taken by recording secretary Johnny Howells, who transcribed them with a black felt pen on a damp bar napkin. The minutes looked marvelously like Chinese calligraphy and almost legible for a time. But someone spilled a gin and tonic over the napkin towards the end of the meeting, so it didn't matter anyway. Therefore this report was transcribed from memory a day or so later, when the fog cleared. The problem being that the secretary's memory became somewhat like Chinese calligraphy towards the end of the meeting. Therefore, any resemblance to accuracy herein is purely coincidental.

"Gary Stiggers made a motion that the Sergeant at Arms, Terry Brennen, buy a drink for the house. The motion was seconded by Faye Shaw and a host of others. Jim Joly raised a point of order to the effect that Terry should order *two* drinks for the house. Terry threatened to remove Joly from the meeting for being disorderly and ruled the motion out of order or else he would throw *everyone* out. The bartender vigorously nodded his head in approval of that idea.

"Jerry Hansen, proprietor of Jerry and Johnnys Bar, was proposed for honorary membership in the Tramp Printers' Chapel. The bartender attempted to raise a point of order. The bartender was once again shouted down. Speaking on the motion to make Jerry Hansen an honorary member, several recalled Jerry's 48 years on Third Street and his friendship with printers. They recalled how he started work as a bartender at Green's Bar and then later, when he opened his own bar at this location. They testified how Jerry was a friend to all newspaper workers, but particularly to traveling printers. A typical example was when Denney Gatzmeyer recalled the time Tommy Neal (the Silver Fox) wired from Chicago or somewhere, needing getaway money for a ticket to Frisco —Jerry wired it to him, no questions asked.

"The motion to make Jerry an honorary tramp printer was carried unanimously. The bartender again tried to raise a point of order after which Sergeant at Arms, Terry Brennen, chased him down the bar.

"A resolution was offered and passed unanimously, to condemn the practice of keeping ITU locals closed to travelers on an almost permanent basis. It was pointed out that many locals have been closed for years, with the homeguards often working scads of overtime. Some remembered the depression years when work was scarce and recalled that ITU locals stayed open; work was shared with brother members.

"A resolution was presented approving of the *Tramp Printers' Newsletter* and encouraging people to subscribe. A point of order was made by Johnny Howells, who objected that: the more subscribers, the more stamps he had to lick, and his mouth was getting gummy. He explained, 'M' tongue's stickin' to the roof of m' mouth, as a matter of fact.'

"Brian Maloney bought Howells another drink, causing him to forget what point he had raised. The motion passed with Howells voting affirmative. Maloney took back his drink.

"A motion was made to declare Jerry and Johnny's Bar an historical monument for ITU traveling printers and mailers. Since Jerry had just bought a drink for the house, the motion passed unanimously.

"A motion was made to adjourn to a committee of the whole, and to reconvene at the earliest opportunity, and to keep the Tramp Printers' Chapel a viable unit. The meeting closed with each member mentioning a departed tramp printer friend, and all stood for one minute of silence in the memory of our departed brethren.

"Most agreed that the meeting was a success, even though one member claims he was injured while attempting to make a motion. It seems that while he was trying to get the floor, Sharon Longley inadvertently stepped on his fingers. Jerry Hansen did a lot to make us welcome, and he obviously enjoyed talking to his old friends. Some thought it would be a good idea to meet at Jerry and Johnny's on a regular basis. The bartender considered this a lousy idea, and threatened to quit if too many tramp printers came to destroy the peace and quiet of his workplace.

"After the Tramp Printers' Chapel Meeting adjourned, Jerry Hansen brought a real piece of nostalgia from his back room. How many remember the "slip board" he used to keep on the back wall? Well, he still has it, with names yellowing on the cardboard slips but most still recognizable. We crowded around the board and searched through the slips, catching many well-known tramps' names.

"Among others, I recognized: Jumpin' Joe Owens, Bob (Shotgun) Chutijian, John Head, Guy Foley, Glen Hurse, Gene Marsden, James Leslie, Ed Whiteley, Otis Cook, Buzzy Eckert, and Kokomo Joe Philips. Jumpin' Joe Owens had *two* slips on the board, one which bore the notation "See Foreman." He probably jumped the job again.[4]

"There were a hundred names or more on the slipboard. Some were reporters, stereotypers, mailers and pressmen. But Jerry seemed to know them all, and had fond stories to tell about each. He told the members how he opened this place in 1935, and probably knew more tramp printers than all of us put together, for most passed through his Jerry and Johnny's at some time or another. Many needed help from time to time and they knew they could count on Jerry Hansen. 48 years of printing history.

---

[4] Customarily, when a substitute was fired for something done (or not done) on a previous shift, his slip was marked "unavailable" and "see foreman."

EL PASO, TEXAS

DURING THE YEARS the *Tramp Printers' Newsletter* was being published, we asked printers all around the country to send in their stories, experiences, and observations about tramp printers. We didn't want stories exclusively from tramp printers themselves; we encouraged homeguards to become involved in the project. The reaction was gratifying, for our mail box was flooded with letters.

A surprising development was the large percentage of the stories written about one town in particular: El Paso, Texas. Both tramp printers and those who only made one trip in their entire career—and happened to stop off in El Paso on the way—wrote about their experiences in this Texas border town. Several special conditions account for this, conditions which weren't duplicated in many other places around the country.

For one thing, El Paso was considered a prime stopping-off place for ITU printers traveling from one coast to another. A tramp knew he could probably catch a few days' work, enjoy meeting old friends, and take a few trips across the Rio Grande (to the Mexican city of Juarez), before getting ready for the long trip between places to work. From El Paso east, the next large newspapers were in San Antonio, and to the west it was Phoenix or Tucson; both a two day drive, much longer hitchhiking or by freight car.

It wasn't just tramps who laid over in El Paso. Young printers with families, on their way to California to begin a new life in the Golden State, found it convenient to stay a few months here to replace money spent on the trip so far. Those who towed mobile homes behind their autos appreciated a rest-stop in El Paso. They would work a few weeks, a few months, sometimes a few years before moving on.

Juarez was, of course, one of the main attractions for single printers. (Some married printers loved it as well, much to the chagrin of their wives.) It isn't surprising that many stories about El Paso involve Juarez to some degree or another. Because the night shift on the El Paso newspaper took an hour and a quarter lunch break, many printers hustled off to Juarez to drink their lunch. Occasionally, they failed to make it back, to the dismay of both the chairman and foreman. Many slips were pulled"[1] because of this infraction of the rules. Juarez bars were open 24 hours and printers had several saloons they patronized, places where the owners and patrons watched over them and kept them out of trouble to some extent. One tramp printer reminisced, "I remember a place in Juarez where you could get three shots of tequila and a plate of tacos for a dime!" And during prohibition days in the United States, Juarez was exceptionally popular, for Mexico never adopted such impractical and unenforceable laws.

But neither El Paso's location, nor the attraction of Juarez can totally account for the town's popularity with union printers. It turns out that the two newspapers, both printed in the same plant, followed union rules and customs diligently, more so than many other isolated cities like El Paso. When a substitute showed up for work, there was no question about "bumping overtime," or working on "bogus." If a day's work was available, the substitute would work. Because regular printers also liked to visit Juarez, many hires were made because a regular either wanted to visit Mexico for the night, or perhaps because he neglected to return in time for work.[2] The chairman would automatically hire a sub for any absent situation holder.

Another explanation why El Paso printers were so open to travelers and tramps was that most regular situation holders had been in that position themselves at one time or another, and many felt

---

[1] When the foreman ordered a sub's slip "pulled" from the slipboard, the sub was fired, with a six-month bar against working in that composing room.

[2] If a substitute were available to cover for an absent printer, the regular wouldn't be fired. But if the situation went "dark," a discharge was inevitable.

great empathy for the roadsters. After all, had it not been for the strict enforcement of substitute laws and the friendly solidarity of the homeguards, they would never have had the opportunity of working in El Paso themselves. Most had experience in other locals where the chairman, homeguards and the foreman teamed up to discourage subs from showing up to dilute the work, to cut into the overtime—or even worse: bumping overtime! Also, many employees were self-styled "two-city tramps," in that they would work in their home towns for half a year and head for El Paso for half a year. These regular situation holders were also understandably sympathetic to travelers and tramps.

Furthermore, a large percentage of *El Paso Times* printers were Mexican (some citizens, some not). They recognized that their jobs, good pay, and equal treatment were due to the union contract and the chapel's strict enforcement of contract and chapel laws, without which they could have been subject to the rank discrimination prevalent in other trades along the Mexican border. Therefore the Mexican-Americans were also supportive of traveling printers, and often accompanied them on their escapades across the river.

A further explanation for the solidarity and openness to traveling substitutes: the El Paso newspaper composing room probably had a larger percentage of tramp printers working at any given time than any other newspaper chapel in the country. El Paso was so attractive and enjoyable that tramps tended to stay a while. The town kept them from the road for months, and sometimes years. In fact, one of the more famous tramp printers, John Hatfield, settled here for some time, alternately working as a floorman, as chapel chairman, or as foreman. At times, he was president of the local and on occasion he was management's mechanical superintendent. He gained the respect of workers and management alike because his experiences "on the road" provided him with intimate knowledge of contracts and ITU laws, and he knew how to apply them in a way which benefited all parties involved.

Leo J. Barry, from Michigan once wrote, "Of course, El Paso was a favorite place for travelers! A fine bunch of regulars there made the sub feel welcome (I worked there several times myself). There was Virgil "Pop" Hatfield, his son Johnny Hatfield, "Cactus Jack"

Crawford, the three Bob Taylors: Big Bob, Little Bob and Crippled Bob), Wilhelm, Dave Bates, Don Seibert, Frank Graham, the Case Brothers (Upper and Lower), 'Jumpin' Joe' Owens, Pete Peterman, and many more.

El Paso in the Old Days
from Tom Holson

I subbed in El Paso for a while, and being too sober or too tight-fisted to do much drinking, I managed to stay on the job and pick up some shifts from those who preferred the watering holes of Juarez to working. There were three papers in El Paso then, the *Times*, the *Herald* and the *Post*, each with its own shop, which gave a lot of opportunity for work. I guess we thought the good old days would go on forever. Eventually they merged into one composing room, with two editions a day. They formed two chapels, the dayside and the nightside.

❊❊❊

from Ted Morse

As a tramp foreman, I thought I had seen it all, but in 1937, in answer to an ad in *Publisher's Auxiliary,* a Jewish publisher by the name of Morris J. Boretz in El Paso gave me a job as foreman of Spanish-printed *El Continental*. Neither the publisher nor I knew Spanish. So blanket-stealer stories appeared on society pages, funny comics were mistranslated into tragedies, and Hearst-like 144-pt. extra-condensed 8-col. front page "screamers", promoted Juarez bullfights. Yet, the *El Continental* somehow prospered. It was the most amusing publication since the days of P. T. Barnum.

"Old Man Brooks" who worked at *El Continental* had over 2,000 jealously guarded Mergenthaler and Intertype border slides and casting blocks saved up for his old age. Already in his late 70s, Mr. Brooks confided in me that if he ever retired he would install a Linotype machine downstairs where he lived that would have 'everything' Mergenthaler ever sold, on one unit. He and I used to visit the abandoned *El Paso Times* building to search through tons of discarded fonts of Linotype matrices for "sorts." His assistant machinist, Manuel Munoz was once Secretary of the Treasury in Pancho Villa's provisional government in revolutionary Mexico. His name appears on all currency issued by General Villa—now on sale as souvenirs throughout the Southwest.

Linotype metal, costing 20c a pound in Depression days, was always a problem; we never had enough. One day, while searching through junk-yards, we discovered that *El Continental's* Negro "metal-man" (the guy who melted the Lino metal and poured them into pigs) faithfully took one Monarch pig daily to the junk-yard—just enough for one 12-oz. bottle of sotol, or a half-bottle of mescal. Four pigs would get him a bottle of tequila. Believe it or not, the publisher, Mr. Boretz, forgave the black man's sins, and even raised his wages. He never stole again.

Eduardo Aguirre, an *El Continental* makeup man who married a Guatemalan woman, lived near me, just off Piedras avenue on the road to rattlesnake-infested McKelligan Canyon. We would often picnic in the canyon, along with Wilhite (the *Herald-Posts* chief makeup and one of the world's best chefs), and 'Frenchie' and his wife from Matamoros. Fortified with a couple of cases of Mitchell's El Paso beer, we never roasted less than a 15-lb chunk of beef flavored with garlic, oregano and parsley. We always left McKelligan Canyon well filled! I generally found that the Latin Americans basically are family-loving, hard-working and loving people always struggling for better lives.

Sanitation in El Paso print-shops in the 1920s was crude by today's standards. To keep cockroaches in check, apprentices with oil cans loaded with kerosene put a few drops in each type box in every case. The hand-man setting type into his stick was thus protected from composing bugs into lines of type. Usually, the toilet facilities were "out back". However, El Paso's *El Continental,* where I was foreman for a time, boasted "hot and cold running water" for washups at the communal, one-faucet sink. When the summer sun got the thermometer up to 120 degrees indoors, printers scrubbed up in hot water... when freezing desert winds blew, the faucet ran ice-cold.

❈❈❈

Most stories about El Paso involved incidents that occurred during excursions across the Rio Grande to Juarez. The names of several bars kept cropping up in the stories. Most mentioned Fred's Rainbow Bar, or the Cadillac Bar, or El Conquistador.

Fred's Rainbow Bar and Other Joints
from Don Cleary

Do I remember Fred's Bar? On my slide night,[3] my wife Greta would fold down the back seat of our 1955 Ford Ranchwagon, make up the back end into a bed for our two girls, Naomi and Colleen, and tuck them in. Then we'd drive from the El Rancho Grande Trailer Park in El Paso over the bridge, and around the corner to Fred's Rainbow Bar. When our "green machine" eased around the comer by the bar, a Juarez cop would wave us to a parking spot. I would slip him some peso notes and he would sit on the fender of the station wagon (with his .45 in full view) and be our babysitter while we went into Fred's for some Cruz Blanca beer. Can you imagine that happening today?

❋❋❋

from John Howells

One morning after an all-night revelry at Fred's Rainbow, four of us were an our way across the bridge to face the sunshine and our wives' fury at having spent another night 'across the river.' The Immigration Officer asked the usual question: "Are you American citizens?" The driver of the car answered in Spanish: "Si, Jefe, soy Tejano" (sure, boss, I'm Texan). His companion in the front seat nodded his head, too strung-out answer. The immigration agent recognized both of them, so things seemed to be going smooth enough. He looked at me, and I managed to say "Yep" without a hiccup. But my friend (whose name I won't mention) focused his eyes with some difficulty and asked, "Who wants to know?" It took an extra hour to cross into the United States that morning. Our wives were a little more angry than usual.

---

[3] A regularly scheduled day off from work was called a "slide day" or "slide night."

❄❄❄

When the Rainbow Bar's owner, Fred Menendez, passed away he took with him the charm of the place. A lot of us 'Juarez hands' were going to the Arco Iris (Rainbow) before Fred bought and built it to what it was. Fred knew how to treat people and make them want to come back. He was truly a friend to the printers, stereotypes and reporters. His place was the place for all of us in the newspaper business. Fred passed as a Mexican, but the truth was, Fred Menendez was Italian and was originally from Chicago.

The Rainbow was a meeting place not only for printers, but pressmen, stereotypers, editorial writers and reporters as well. The customary class distinctions between workers seemed to dissolve in the friendly, other-worldly atmosphere of Fred's Rainbow Bar. A news anchorman from the newspaper's television station could be found arguing philosophy with a stereotyper while a tramp printer and a sports reporter might be discussing the merits of squeezing lemon juice into their bottles of Carta Blanca beer. Because the Rainbow was open 24 hours a day, it became a recognized meeting place and social center for newspaper workers of all descriptions.

Juarez Cops
from Jack Renter

The Juarez jail was occasionally a trap for printers who were prone to commit indiscretions. Actually, the police were fairly tolerant, but outrageous behavior could draw their attention. When a printer ended up in the Juarez Hoosegow[4] the jailer would notify the Secretary of ITU Local 370, Bill Etter, who would go over the river to retrieve the errant "knight of the road." One morning, Bill got a call from the Juarez jail and he asked me to go with him. Another printer, Clay Lee, asked to go along as he was new in El Paso and wanted to see the place. The jailers located the prisoner, who was unfamiliar to us, and got him as far as the turnkey. Bill Etter was starting to pay the bail, when he discovered that the prisoner wasn't a local member.

---

[4] Actually, the word "hoosegow" comes from the Spanish word "juzgado" which, when pronounced with the soft "d" sound common along the border, comes out as "hoos-gao."

Suddenly, a bell rang with Clay. He asked the guy, "Didn't you work as a strike-breaker in Wheeling, West Virginia?" The prisoner said, "Well, yes, but I *am* a fellow printer!" We all three of us replied "You are not a fellow printer to us! You are a strike-breaking rat!" We left him, as the jailers were dragging him back to the lockup.

Another time, a carload of us turned into Otumba Alley with Milton Roberts driving, and he hit a Juarez police car. Bob Ariza, one of the Mexican-American printers from the shop, talked to the cops in Spanish and finally got us out of it. He told Milton, "Everything's O.K. Let's go!" But when Milton backed up to get around the damaged police car, he smacked into another cop car. It took Bob some time to talk us out of that one!

Another morning I was driving out Mejia (Juarez) and a cop stopped me. I had been dodging pot holes. He claimed I was drinking too much, and I explained about the potholes. He said: "But Senor, you was staggering with your truck." A couple of bucks and it was O.K. to "stagger with my truck."

El Continental
from Ted Morse

ITU Spanish-printing *El Continental* printers in the 1930s converged frequently at Honest Dan Arnell's Shamrock Inn, a couple of blocks away from *El Continental,* which was across the street from the city jail. "Honest Dan's" place featured "fixed" slot machines, booze and food where you could sign a tab until payday, and where forbidden cartoon movies were shown in the highfenced adjoining yard.

In the depth of the Great Depression, streetcar trips to Juarez cost 3c; and three printers could be fairly well plastered if three dimes were available. Close to the "zona tolerencia" was Pancho's back-alley drinking place—a room with a few battered tables and chairs. Pancho brought in a small plate of sliced limes, lemons and pineapple and a 12-ounce bottle of sotol along with three shot glasses. The cost was a dime. Passing the bottle around, Ted Morse, Milton Roberts and Lester Green would share the liquor amidst mouthfuls of citrus. By the time the third dime disappeared, they would be Texas-style borracho! Can you imagine quenching three printers for 30 cents today?

Lester Green, a young writer and editor at *El Continental,* was married to a beautiful Monterrey (Mexico) woman. He claimed that for five cents American daily he could live well anywhere south of "Rio Bravo". He spoke Spanish fluently, having lived in Venezuela and Panama before 1930. He confessed to me that being married to a Spanish-speaking Mexican beauty, and "sleeping with the dictionary" helped his career greatly.

I remember Mitchell's El Paso Brewery—"Gordo" Salas, the world's most artistic newspaper pressman—other typographical wizards coming from the Las Cruces *Sun,* Hobbs *Daily News,* and Chihuahua—the 8,000 "horse soldiers" at Fort Bliss with their polo games on Sunday afternoons (no more horses, now there are 50,000 anti-aircraft personnel)—In those days a 7-ounce bottle of Carta Blanca cost 5 cents American and you could give an old troubadour a few coins and he would trail the printers from bar to bar in Juarez, singing Cielito Lindo all night long.

The Plaza de Torros in Juarez, 50 years ago,[5] was a wonderful amusement for printers and other tourists. We could always get passes to sit in the sun and watch Brazilian toreadors with their $6,000 horses, while "barritos" of tequila passed around the printers. But the "Escusado para Hombres" was strictly taboo to knowledgeable gringos like myself. In semi-darkness, guided by a dim light-globe, a dumb-ox tourist often stepped into a quagmire of excrement. This was almost as bad as staying overnight in a Mexican jail, then brought before a local "jefe" sans shoes, belt and most clothing, to plead innocent of being "borracho" the next afternoon!

❊❊❊

from Jack Renter

El Paso! Late one Sunday night the ad crew and a lot of the makeups went to Juarez for "lunch." Ed Cady was on the wagon and was the only ad man to return. (It was partly the newspaper's fault; they shouldn't have given us an hour and a quarter to drink our lunch.) Some of us didn't get back for a couple of days. That was the

---

[5] Written around 1980.

time Mr. Frishe (he was always Mister to me) announced he was a bird and stepped off the rail up on Scenic Drive about daybreak one morning. He was pretty well scratched up from his roll down the mountain! As you know, Frank Graham has many nicknames. One of them was "La Luna." One evening while visiting the Indian ruins in Casa Grande, Mexico, Frank and I were following the old Mexican custom of walking around the plaza. We were the only two Gringos in town that night. Several small boys were behind us, giggling and having a good time, when one of them got brave, pointed at Frank's bald head and said: "La Luna" (the moon), and then took off running. Everyone got a good laugh.

❊❊❊

(The following article was printed in the Tramp Printers' Newsletter, but we are unable to determine who wrote it. If you know, please let us know.)

You mentioned El Paso being a "favorite place for travelers." During the 9-month strike in Detroit in '68, I traveled throughout the country and only there did I realize that we are a true "brotherhood." I slipped up just prior to Labor Day and caught maybe a couple of shifts the preceding week. I was told not to bother showing on the holiday because they only worked a half-shift and likely no one would lay off. But I showed anyway and as luck would have it, someone called in and hired the "bottom sub" (me). After working about 2 hours, the chairman John Guarilla invited me to the annual chapel picnic immediately following shift's end at noon. He knew I had my wife and 1-year-old baby with me. Being on the road for 3 months, I didn't have too much cash and a picnic lunch sure sounded inviting. But the picnic lunch turned out to be a banquet!

My Mexican-American pals asked me to make sure our steaks were cooked just the way we wanted them. The chapel wives provided tables upon tables of south-of-the-border ecstasy. After eating the guys brought out their guitars and we had a good old sing-a-long and then we struck up a football game. Guess who they made quarterback? I'm not kidding, they treated me like — well, like a brother. Upon returning to Detroit I sent back a postcard thanking them all for their hospitality and graciousness. Since then Zeke Galvan, an El Paso native, showed up here and let me know my postcard was received and appreciated.

If brotherhood in the I.T.U. existed throughout the entire U.S. and Canada the way it does in El Paso, we'd have already attained the dream of our founding fathers: true fraternalism.

THE TRAMP PRINTER

ANONYMOUS

He used to call around and borrow
A dollar;
There was grime and printers' ink upon
His collar;
At times he used to get quite drunk—
They said it was
To indicate his strong contempt for Editors;
He used to eat tobacco at his case
And, what is more,
He spat quite freely anywhere
Upon the floor;
I haven't seen him since the latter 80s.
The foreman couldn't even tell you
where his state is;
Perhaps he's gone the way of all the earth—
Mayhap to jail;
But if he ever shows up here again
He will not fail
To have on that same
Collar
And strike you for the
Dollar;
And he doesn't get it
From me.
Not this time!
See?

Inland Printer, Vol. 29, 1902, page 254
(C)Poetic Printshop Past-Times,
Graphic Crafts, Inc. Lancaster, PA

END OF THE TRAIL

TRAMP PRINTING didn't die a slow death; it happened suddenly. It took printers quite by surprise. Ironically, it came not from the continual, vigorous anti-union activities of publishers and printshop owners, but from the swift, relentless advance of technology. The death blow came from computers: that fourth invention that we must append to Francis Bacon's list of world-shaking breakthroughs in human ingenuity. The computer marked the end of the trail for traditional printing processes, and the end of an era for tramp printers.

The revolution started slowly. The original phototypesetting equipment upon which printing management pinned hopes turned out to be very cumbersome and labor intensive; composing room staffs actually increased to cope with it. The quality often left much to be desired. By the mid 1960s, all major daily newspapers were running Linotypes via teletype tape. Although many publishers refused to recognize it, a teletype operation required more employees, and the corrections were costly. Printers continued to be smug and secure about their jobs and the chances of being replaced by machines. Teletype tape produced the straight matter type needed for a daily paper, but almost as many Linotype operators were needed to make corrections as were needed before to set the type. The more astute tramp printers learned to punch TTS tape, and continued to travel at will—some doing traditional printing jobs, and others punching TTS tape—their mobility curtailed somewhat, but to no significant degree. The worrisome thing was a lowered level of skills needed to operate a Teletypesetter.

The introduction of photo-composing machines to replace hot metal production came as a shock to printers. At first used only on ads, it reduced the time needed to set the type and lowered the skills necessary to assemble the type into ads. Now the sub boards became as loaded as they had been back in the depression. There were no more smug faces in the composing room.

However, the end of the trail became obvious with the introduction of computers for typesetting. IBM was probably the first to enter the field, around 1968, with Compugraphic not far behind. At first it was a rather simple concept—although at the time it seemed revolutionary: computerized justification of TTS tape. Instead of a TTS operator tediously spacing out lines so they would justify when the tape ran through a Linotype, the computer figured out the spacing on the TTS operator's output and then generated a new, justified tape to run on the Lino. TTS operators could simply type away at full speed with no interruptions. Production matched and even exceeded the publishers' expectations. A TTS operator's production was limited only by his or her finger speed. Skill levels of TTS tape punchers dropped drastically. Jobs for tramp Linotype operators began disappearing. The survivors switched over to monitoring the TTS-operated Linos, setting corrections, or else they learned paste-makeup. Traveling became a bit difficult, but it still could be done. At this point, many tramp printers decided to hold onto priority, and try to land a permanent job. Few were willing to brave the shrinking priority lists in newspapers around the country.

The next step was to adapt punched tape to operate photosetting machines. Previously, manual operation of one of these hybrid mechanical-photographic monsters, took a highly skilled operator. Computer programs were becoming more intelligent by the month. Next, optical character recognition (OCR) devices hit the market; there were machines that could recognize typewritten pages and convert them into teletype tape which in turn operates Linotypes and phototypesetting machines. News stories, columns, and even advertisements could now be sent directly from the newsroom or the ad department to the typesetting devices, totally bypassing printers. This eliminated TTS jobs. Tramp printers lost yet another category of work to which they could apply. More of them gave up notions of traveling, preferring the boredom of a steady job to the uncertain future of a tramp printer.

Things moved fast now. The trail became shorter month by

month.

The final blow came with the introduction of video terminals which directly linked the newsroom with the photo-composing machines. Now the reporters, editors and anyone else who knew how to type, became typesetters. The composing room was bypassed, with work limited to making up ads and news pages and setting occasional corrections.

Even this work disappeared with pagination. Now editors and writers could make up pages on a computer screen. The computer held articles and ads in memory until needed, and the entire newspaper page was spit out in one piece, ads, news, comics and all, directly to the laser printer. The need for typesetters, makeups and ad floormen evaporated overnight. Even proofreading was not required; newswriters did their own proofreading. Clearly, tramp printers were no longer needed, in fact *no* printers were needed.

Composing room work forces were chopped to the maximum allowed by union contracts—which usually provided for "lifetime jobs." Eventually the remaining printers were given retirement incentives, moved to other departments or otherwise coaxed into leaving. Non-union composing rooms simply disappeared. Linotypes were sent to the junk yard, replaced with high speed photocomposing machines. Machines that cost $50,000 each just a couple of years earlier were given away to whoever felt like hauling them off. Better and less expensive laser equipment came out monthly.

End of the International Typographical Union

Non-union printers were dismissed without formality as their composing rooms vanished. But the strength of the ITU and the solidarity of its members were remarkably tenacious. For several years local unions were able to maintain contracts in the face of job losses, further automation and employer pressures. A good deal of this can be attributed to the "lifetime jobs" which most locals managed to negotiate during the early days of automation—when employers originally shared workers' doubts that the new equipment would work as well as the salesmen predicted. Most publishers preferred to work with the union, content to watch printers retire and die off, rather than replace them under the threat of strikes and retribution. Attrition was doing the job, and it wasn't worth the expense of a strike to throw the few remaining printers into the street.

However, the terrific loss of working members and the incredible success of new processes pushed the Typographical Union to the verge of collapse. It was finally forced to merge with the Communications Workers of America (CWA), rather than fold entirely. This left the militant printers' union without its traditional base of old-style unionism and rigid structure of laws, rules and custom. The dwindling membership lost its basic strength.

Publishers and commercial employers around the country saw their chance to rid themselves forever of the annoying Typographical Union. For commercial printing establishments it was easy; the new processes had eliminated all but a handful of ITU members years earlier. The few shops that retained union members, simply refused to renew contracts, confident that the union was too weak to put up a fight, and that employees would drop their union membership before taking a chance on losing precious jobs by going on strike. In the old days, they knew that if they lost a job, there would be another, just as good, down the street. No more.

Newspaper publishers began calling "decertification elections."[1] These "decerts" followed a clearly defined pattern as employers vigorously campaigned to persuade employees to dump the ITU in favor of the benevolent protection of the publisher. Below are two examples of how the system worked, and typical results.

Autopsy of a Typographical Union Local

In November 1988 Harry L. Hendriksen, ITU Reg. #191577, filed petition for union decertification with the NLRB. On December 1, 1988, the membership voted 31 to 50 in favor of the company, thus ending 94 years of union representation in the *Albuquerque-Journal* composing room.

---

[1] Under National Labor Relations Board rules, if the majority of union members vote to decertify their union, the employer no longer has to deal with the union.

In contrast to the union, the company was aggressive in courting the members' vote. Management sent almost daily letters to employees, sponsored a $500 drawing, held closed meetings with attendees paid wages, and made many promises. Union membership would be optional, and no discriminatory action would be taken against those who kept their union cards. The terms of the old contract would be respected regarding priority (seniority), wages, working conditions and company benefits. The printers were assured there would only be changes for the better if they dumped the union.

The union's efforts to persuade the union members to reject the vote was pale in comparison. President McMichen sent a letter to chapel members reminding them that, if they voted against the union they would lose, among other things, their right to hire substitutes. He obviously didn't realize the right to hire subs had already been given away in the last signed contract, on January 1, 1986. Vice-President Billy Austin and Carl Hatton, Administrator of the NPP did their best to stem the tide, but it was too little and too late. The vote came as no surprise to many as the contract had expired in September of 1987 and little progress made toward a new one.

One of those who voted in favor of the union said, "We ITU members now wonder what benefit the ITU's merging with the CWA brought us. We feel abandoned. Disillusion with the merger is as much a reason for the result of the election as anything else."

However, those who voted in favor of the company—confident that little would change and that promises would be kept—were in for a shock. A mandatory meeting was held to announce changes concerning company policy and benefits. During the first two months of company control, the following changes were made:

- Payday was changed from weekly to twice a month. Priority was ignored by hiring low-priority subs for regular jobs.
- Substitutes had to show up, ready for work, five days a week in order to hold priority. Some had been hired but one day in February and had to drive 25 miles each way to receive that.

By March 1, only 21 dues-paying union members were left in Albuquerque. The company gave the promised 4 percent pay increase—which they had agreed to previously in contract negotiations, before the decertification vote—however it was not retroactive. They had previously agreed with the union to make the raise retroactive back to September 1987.

Some subs began leaving after showing in the composing room seven days a week for over two months without working while regulars worked six days a week plus overtime.

By February 1, 1991, about two years later, conditions were as follows:

- No pay raises for two years, since March of 1989; all wages and hires now frozen.
- Overtime rate was paid only after a full week (37-1/2 or 40 hours), when previously it had been paid for any time worked after the hours of a regular shift.
- The night substitute board cut in half. Ten printers were laid off from the day shift (one third of the shift) cutting back 15 years in priority, to those hired from 1976 on.
- No severance pay was given (as had been agreed to in the expired union contract).

The company discontinued its traditional yearly bonus. Deductions for medical insurance doubled, to $45 a week for two in family. Medical co-payment to doctor or hospital doubled, and prescription costs jumped one third. Management offered to pay $100 a month extra if all insurance is dropped. Sick leave policy modified to suspend pay for first three days of illness. Subs were not covered.

Priority was being routinely ignored when convenient. Regular workers bypassed for training in new equipment, with lowest priority substitute given training and a situation in computer and plate making. Unskilled workers were hired at $7 an hour to work longer hours than regulars to do work they normally performed at $13 an hour.

A general campaign of harassment was instituted, with workers being suspended for minor reasons. Substitutes who were not available at least five days a week were permanently removed from sub board (even though there were very few hires). Editorial workers began doing work traditionally performed by printers, such as making up pages.

By that point in time, there were only ten union members left at the *Albuquerque Journal,* six on the night shift and four working days.

On April 5, 1991, management decided that all subs must be available *seven* days a week. They had to report in 45 minutes before shift to see if they would be needed. Additional $7 hour workers were being hired.

In June, the entire night sub board (eight workers) was terminated and nine removed from the day sub board. Two people quit and six regulars (mostly the last of the union supporters) were given incentives to leave. The pay scales that had been promised at the time of the decertification election were now being ignored, with company offering jobs at reduced pay, depending on the work category.

Two days later eight more dayside regular workers were laid off and considered to be substitutes, and two were removed from the night shift, told to be available seven days a week, even though they would probably only be hired for three days. Priority was not considered in laying off workers.

To sum up: the autopsy of this newspaper went as follows:

- No raise since March of 1989.
- All wages and hires now frozen.
- Pay day twice a month.
- Overtime rate paid more than a full week work of 40 hours instead of more than 8 hours in one day.
- Night sub board cut in half.
- One third (10 sits) laid off the day side. Back to 1976, no severance pay.
- No future yearly bonus. Subs got $25 less deductions.
- Medical insurance withholding doubled. $45 a week for two in family.
- Company will pay $100 a month if all insurance is dropped.
- Medical co-pay to doctor or hospital has doubled.
- Prescription cost up one third.
- Workers hired at $7 an hour as trimmers (40 hours a week).
- Lowest priority sub trained in computer and plate making.

- Priority ignored when convenient
- Suspension for minor reason.
- Pay suspended for first three days of illness. Sick slip required. (Situation holders)
- All subs must be available five days a week or be removed from board.
- Some news editors paste-up own pages.
- Six union members left on night side, four days.
- April 5, 1991: All subs must be available *seven days a week*. Call in 45 minutes before shift. Additional $7 hour workers being hired.
- June 15, 1991: Entire night sub board (8 people) removed or laid off—fired. Ditto 9 on day board.
- Two people quit.
- Six bought off with $12,000. Oldtimers, union supporters, union president, etc.
- $7.00 hour trimmer fired. Job to be filled by regular.
- Day sub board to cover all shifts.
- Pay will be according to work category.
- After first of the month company will offer jobs at reduced pay in certain areas.
- Approximately 45 people to handle all composing work, camera including process separation and plate making. Most ads camera ready.
- New, lowered wage scale.
- Effective June 17, 1991—Eight more dayside regulars placed on sub board. Two more from night side, out of priority. Three categories. Dayside make-up, night side make-up and ads to be made up by subs on 3 to 11 shift. Call in 1:00 pm. Must be available seven days a week. Ad flow is Wednesday through Friday. The best a worker could hope for was three days a week. By October 1995, there were almost no union members still working at the newspaper.

Autopsy, Twin Falls, Idaho

Robert Johnson was foreman at the Columbia Basin News in

Pasco, Washington when I and my wife Dorothy went there in 1957. It was a Unitypo paper, and we all worked hard trying to make a go of it. Unitypo was an ITU corporation that was started as a weapon against struck newspapers. When a publisher employed strikebreakers, the ITU financed a competition newspaper to employ the printers on strike and to damage the publisher's monopoly in the field. This was a very controversial move on the part of the ITU and arguments among rank and file ITU members still surface concerning the question of Unitypo's effectiveness. This author's personal belief was that it sharply discouraged other publishers from attempting to break the local union because of the high cost of losing the monopoly on the newspaper field in that area. Many ITU members will disagree about the wisdom of Unitypo; it was one of the most divisive issues in the ITU's political process.

When Bob took over as mechanical superintendent, I moved into his foreman's job for a while. It was a very unusual place to work in that if anyone tried to goof off or give the company a screwing, the others would criticize him as not being a good union man. After all, we were working for the ITU, indirectly at least, for the *Columbia Basin News was* in direct competition to the *Tri-City Herald*, the non-union newspaper across the river that had locked out its union printers and replaced them with strikebreakers. The pay at the union paper was low, the equipment pure junk, but the morale was high.

Eventually, the union newspaper surrendered to the determination and higher finances of the non-union chain newspaper. It folded after a number of years of semi-success, and the ITU members scattered to the four winds. Robert Johnson, the mechanical superintendent of the *Columbia Basin News,* ended up working for the union newspaper in Great Falls, Idaho.

As luck would have it, he was caught in one of the many decertification campaigns, and was thrown back into an unwelcome battle of union vs anti-union publisher. He wrote the following poignant letter about his plight, back in 1982:

"At age **60**, and **40** years as an ITU member, I am one of four who try to maintain some form of a union here in the wilds of Idaho. The employer has taken all the work he can away from us, promised us that we may work until death or retirement 'with a reasonable adjustment of wages and conditions,' such as reducing our holidays from seven to five, and then working at least a half shift on those remaining holidays. When a wage increase is announced for the plant, the union members are excluded 'to make the adjustment in equal wages.'

"Each member who left or died was replaced by four part-time girls who will work 60 hours a week for 30 hours pay. Part-time workers receive no company benefits such as sick leave, health care, pension, or holidays—or even Idaho unemployment benefits. If the company can just get out of the social security payments, we may see the ideal non-union operation."

End of an Era

In one sense, we tramp printers had "no house, no place, no people of our own." But in another sense, we had "family" everywhere we traveled; in every chapel throughout the ITU's jurisdiction, we found our brothers and sisters ready to help and welcome us. In addition, the ITU's laws and traditions gave form and meaning to the life of the tramp printer. His law was the ITU book of laws and the chapel laws; his norms and values were those he shared with both travelers and homeguards. Every ITU traveling printer knew what the expectations were for his behavior on the job and with his fellow printers. They were his family and his community. This relationship was no mere veneer either; we tramp printers felt such a deep attachment to the union and the craft that it represented that we mourn its passage like a person who has lost his entire family in a fatal accident. The end of the composing room closes an era that began centuries ago and will not likely ever return.

SOCIOLOGICAL POSTSCRIPT

Marion Dearman

WE HAVE COMPILED this book in order to preserve the memories of experiences of what many would label "the golden age of printing." But like the "golden years" of our lives, it is probably a misnomer: these so-called golden years shortly precede our deaths. So, too, the last few decades of tramp printing were followed not only with the demise of the practice of tramping, but with the total destruction of all the craft printing trades and the disappearance of their powerful, militant unions. A way of life that had been more or less continuous and virtually unchanged since Gutenberg revolutionized the reproduction of the printed word circa 1430 is now extinct, like dinosaurs and dodo birds. However, this epitaph would not be complete without recognition of the many interesting sociological features of the culture or institution of tramp printing. Some of these practices may be useful in today's chaotic employment situation, while others are of antiquarian interest only, destined to be dumped in the dustbin of history.

A few of the many sociological concepts which appear applicable to the materials in this collection are presented in the following, concluding paragraphs of this addendum. Some of these apply to the union and others to homeguards, tramp printers, or both classifications.

Regarding solutions to present employment problems, we must again call attention to the network of practices in the ITU associated with worksharing. These included overtime posting, reproduction clauses, mandatory short hours, militant enforcement of ITU laws, identification with the Union, not the local or employer, and—most important—establishment of the slipboard and control of hiring by the Union. Taken together, these practices resulted in very critical controls involving equalizing of employment opportunity and elimination of greed. While they did not always perform perfectly, as many of the accounts presented in this memorial demonstrate, they were virtual lifesavers during hard times, especially in the Great Depression.

Altruism involves the unselfish concern for the welfare of others; in ethics it would demonstrate the doctrine that the general welfare of one's society is more important than an individual's comfort, security or—in extreme cases—even life. Does this apply to tramp printers? A good case could be argued either way. On the one hand, the willingness of the tramp printer to give up the security of a steady job helped the family man who had to stay in one place keep his job. The homeguard more than reciprocated in this exchange, however, in that he gave out his overtime, hired travelers to substitute for him, often for long stretches, gave money when travelers passed their cards, and voluntarily assessed himself in order to fund travelers, whether the travel was forced by economic circumstances or was voluntary. It is a matter of considerable argument as to whether the system of reciprocation was balanced or not. My feeling is that the traveler gave as good as he got in the exchange.

But there is another side of the argument. Overtime was not noted or registered on traveling cards, despite numerous efforts to institute such a practice by some ITU locals. Consequently, the traveler could accumulate considerable overtime in one or more locals and cancel, or "kill" it simply by drawing a traveling card, instead of having to hire a substitute, as was the case with those who didn't move around. It was possible, also, for travelers to work many days in a row—sometimes more than one shift in a day— without either getting time and a half for it or posting it as overtime. This circumvention of the rules certainly flies in the face of this type of traveler's often heard boast of how great a union member he was. This violation of the "five-day law" was entirely possible in certain geographical areas—two that come to mind are the Great Lakes area and the San Francisco Bay Area, both of which had several locals in close proximity. In these areas, a traveler could finish a shift of work in Detroit, for example, and in less than two hours begin working in

Toledo. After working five days in Toledo, he could move on to Cleveland and continue working without a day off—even catch beaucoup overtime at the Cleveland *Plain Dealer*. This is the type of me-first individualism which was abhorred by the union purist. However, the traveler would argue that you have to get it when you can, because who knows when you are going to be thin-spacing again due to a shortage of work.

Another consideration regarding the altruist-individualist discussion involves a certain type of tramp: the "swift" (or merely "swift wanna-be's"). While it was customary for most printers to restrict output to a certain extent, the swift liked to demonstrate his skills by producing far more than anyone else. If he was an operator, he would be likely to show that he could "hang the elevator" on just about any kind of line of type. Floor men or makeups would produce more pages or column inches than any of the homeguards—I have been guilty of this, myself: I remember having foremen in Galveston and Las Vegas tell me that if I ever wanted to come back and they didn't have a job for me, they'd make one—oh, how I loved that flattery! But a good union man, many believed, kept his production down to a reasonable level which would allow even the slower compositors or operators to keep their jobs without unfair comparison. Only in sweat shops did printers work at full speed for the entire shift.

Many tramps traveled alone, drinking their way from city to city. They had complete freedom or autonomy. But this situation is almost a sure-fire recipe for anomy. While not a precise sociological definition, the dictionary says this is as "lack of purpose, identity, or ethical values in a person or in society; disorganization, rootlessness, etc." Without strong social bonds, customarily supplied by the family, community, tribe, society, or some such social group, there is a much greater probability that the individual would experience some degree of personal disintegration. This happens to people on the road. The anonymity of city life where no one knows you leads to temptations which would be unthinkable in a community where one is known. What gave tramp printers a surrogate family was the union: the members were his brothers and sisters, a degree of protection against anomaly. But anytime the tramp printer wanted to run away from himself, he could do so—or thought he could; but in fact, he always took himself with him!

Perhaps more apparent than real, at least to ITU printers, is the potential conflict between loyalty to one's employer and loyalty to the union. For the traveler this was not an issue: he was loyal to the union, first and always. This did not mean that he did not think he owed his employer a good day's work, as attested by many in the anecdotes we've presented in these pages. But anyone who has traveled knows that homeguards quite often felt different about loyalty to employers. However, when push came to shove, when a strike occurred, for instance, very few union printers ratted (crossed the picket line), even though going with the union often meant losing the home and community ties established for many years.

Culture can be briefly defined as "the ideas, custom, traditions, skills, arts, language, belief systems, etc., of a given people at a given time." Those who practice these shared ways of life are said to be a culture; elements within that culture who share that culture only partially or who actively oppose it can be called a subculture, in the first instance, and a counterculture, in the second. Tramp printers certainly demonstrated many elements of a subculture: while they were union members, they were certainly different from the homeguards, and proud of it. Sometimes they even behaved like counterculture members, actively opposing the homeguard way of life and belittling the fellow who could not or would not give up his steady job and hit the road. In any case, the tramps had a close affinity for fellow tramps; when we slipped up in a new chapel, it was the tramp or ex-tramp whom we sought out for advice and companionship. The homeguards, too often perhaps, were thought of as the out-group, some were decent fellows, but on the whole they were not to be trusted. If you had not traveled, no matter how skilled you thought you were, you were only good in that one shop; you had to travel to prove yourself on the road; you had to show that you could perform in all kinds of shops under various conditions. So said the itinerant typographers.

In many ways printers differed from their blue-collar brethren in other trades, as well. For one, printers acquired wide, if unsystematic, knowledge through their work: they were better educated than the average member of the working class (don't challenge an ex-proofreader to a game of Trivial Pursuit!). Additionally, printers were more likely to work different hours, which insulated them from interaction with other workers. Metropolitan daily newspapers operated twenty-four hours a day, three shifts a day: day, swing, and lobster (graveyard). As taxicab drivers, policemen, prostitutes, pimps, and printers well know, night workers live in a different world than day workers. The newspaper printer was also likely to work Saturdays and Sundays and have, say, Tuesdays and Wednesdays as his slide days. As a consequence, printers tended to associate only with other printers, on the job and off, and developed thereby a distinct way of life. Neither exactly working class nor white-collar, printers were marginal (a marginal man in the sociological sense does not fit in) like the Japanese-American who is not fully a part of either Japanese or American society, the printer falls between the blue-collar workers, on the one side, and the arts and professions on the other. In the newspapers, he felt himself a cut above the pressmen and stereotypers, but was not accepted as socially equal by the journalists or advertising sales staff.

If printers were marginal in the foregoing sense, tramp printers were doubly marginal. Like the wanderers in the Robert Service poem quoted in the early pages of this book, the tramp printer didn't fit in anywhere. He had rejected the community in which he was reared, his nuclear and extended families, his civic responsibilities (he didn't vote and many did not file income taxes—they moved around too much for either), and even did not entirely trust the bulk of the ITU's membership: the homeguards. Other tramp printers were his primary or reference group. He associated with them as much as possible, lived with them, traveled with them occasionally, and sought their advice regarding working conditions, the foreman's stoolies in shops, availability of work, cheap hotels, bars that stayed open after hours, and other information vital to the traveling printer. Although he valued his International Typographical Union membership, he was most proud of his credentials as a tramp printer. He could even acquire a certain amount of "derived status" by traveling with a tramp "super star," like Sunshine Wilson or Gulf Coast Foley.

Tramp Printer is an achieved status, esteemed by many, envied by some, and scorned by others. The attitude depends in part on whether one has traveled or not. We have not determined how much traveling is required before we can claim to be tramp printers. I have had over fifty traveling cards, which my relatives thought was far too many, but I feel like a "homeguard" compared with the numberless traveling cards claimed by the likes of Nate Bergman (the Wandering Jew), Jumping Joe Owens, or the others I've named "super stars."

The role of the tramp printer required regular travel. As Sunshine Wilson used to say: "I came here looking for work; I found it; now I've got to go somewhere else and look for work." One could not rest on one's laurels and remain a tramp printer. The demands of the printing trade required both homeguards and tramps. Certain manifest functions and latent functions resulted from this institutionalized system of traveling. The former is "a functional relationship having a recognized value . . . which contributes to the adjustment, adaptation, or well-being of the individual or group." For tramp printers, these would include freedom, autonomy, new experiences, adventure, seeing the country, and so forth. For the homeguard, they offered a source of leisure—he could hire the traveler to work for him, sometimes for long stretches (and hope the tramp didn't "jump the job" during the stretch). For the employer, he was a flexible labor source when the need arose, or a pest, bumping overtime and demanding to be hired to set accumulated reproduction ads (which the employers called "bogus" or "deadhorse"), if he was not needed. Whether these manifest functions were deemed positive or not depended on the definition of the situation by the various parties doing the defining.

Latent functions are neither intended nor recognized. For example, tramp printing, we have argued, contributed to the ITU member's feeling of solidarity with the union as a whole, rather than merely with his own chapel or local. Whether he traveled or not, the ITU printer, partly due to the example of tramp printers, never had to feel like a wage slave: his boss did not own him; he could always draw a traveler and hit the road. Travelers also ensured that the ITU laws and contracts were enforced and obeyed by employers and homeguards. This was often done for selfish reasons, of course, and was sometimes deeply resented, but it resulted in a proud, militant International Typographical Union, with fairly consistent working conditions throughout its jurisdiction. Traveling also improved the skills of both homeguards and tramps and spread innovations widely.

It may be difficult to agree on what the norms were for tramp printers. To sociologists, a norm is "a rule or standard of behavior defined by the shared expectations… regarding what behavior is to be considered appropriate" in relevant situations. For the traveler, these would certainly include doing a good day's work, covering the job for which he was hired, staying sober on the job, paying his union dues, and helping fellow travelers in need. For tramp printers, or anyone for that matter, there is often a wide difference between stated norms and actual performance. Alcohol was most often the culprit for the traveler. The stories in this collection certainly highlight the central position of drinking in the life of the traveling printer. It may be noted, as well, that recollections of their drinking episodes are usually presented as uniformly high good times—read the anecdotes about life of tramp printers in El Paso, for instance. Perhaps others were more successful drinkers than I, but I remember a number of occasions when my drinking resulted in black eyes, busted teeth, and being slammed into jail. Other horror stories come to mind readily, but you will be spared the details; after all this a festschrift honoring the past.

Perhaps the central concept that is the stock in trade of sociologists is institution and its accompanying verb form institutionalization. Institution is defined as "an interrelated system of social roles and norms organized about the satisfaction of an important social need or function." Institutionalization is "the development of stable patterns of social interaction based on formalized rules, laws, customs, and rituals." The vast system of interrelated norms, traditions, customs, measurements, language, technology, meanings, arts, skills, attitudes, and values that constituted the printing trade, used in the widest sense, came into being over the past five and a half centuries by the process of institutionalization. It is what William G. Sumner called a "crescive institution," as compared to an "enacted institution." It "developed slowly and spontaneously through the gradual accretion of social norms." When I was obligated into the International Typographical Union in 1949, it seemed like it had been in existence forever and no one had even a hint that it would ever end. But after the decades or so that it took to perfect the computer and adapt it to various forms of typesetting, tramp printing, the printing craft, and the union which sustained us abruptly ended. The climax of our craft came about, as T. S. Eliot said of the end of the world "not with a bang but a whimper."

We were the last generation of printers who used real type. We were the last of the "knights of the road." Although I am grateful to have had the privilege of being a part of the venerable institutions of printing and tramping and I know that I should go quietly and not make a scene, I keep hearing the words of Dylan Thomas:

Do not go gentle into that good night,
Old age should burn and rave at close of day;
Rage, rage against the dying of the light.

GLOSSARY

ad alley – Section of composing room where display advertisements are marked up, set in type, and assembled.

ad man – Compositor (man or woman) who specializes in assembling display ads.

ad skipper – Assistant foreman in charge of ad alley operations.

apprentice – Trainee who is learning all phases of printing trade; usually mited to skills practiced in a particular shop; in ITU six years duration and coupled with ITU lessons in printing.

barnstorming – Traveling from shop to shop for the purpose of learning the Linotype or some other facet of the trade, often with the expectancy of being fired until gaining competency.

barring – Practice of discharging printers for certain infractions which were serious enough that rule forbidding reemployment could be enforced for a set period, usually six months.

begging off – Requesting permission to take time off without situation being covered by a substitute (see dark situation).

blacksmith – Unskilled, crude workman; the motto of a Linotype machinist 'blacksmith' would be 'don't force it - get a bigger hammer.'

bogus – Pejorative term for reproduction ads (see also chapel reset and deadhorse).

bumping overtime – Forcing a regular situation holder to hire substitute to 'lay off' one or more shifts of accumulated overtime.

calling in sick – Telephoning a message that one is ill and cannot cover job, even if no sub is available; sometimes foremen referred to this (at times correctly) as 'calling in drunk.'

card holder – 1. Journeyman member of the International Typographical Union with all the privileges and responsibilities adhering thereto. 2. Pejorative term for a union member whose loyalty is with the company, and has a union card only because he needs one in order to work in the composing room.

cash in man – Composing room person from whom an advance in pay could be acquired.

catching a stretch – Being hired by a situation holder or by the office to fill a dark situation for a substantial period of time.

chapel – A print shop within the jurisdiction of a local union; a chapel could vary in number of membership from two or three printers to several hundred.

chapel chairman – The ITU representative in a particular shop; this position is analogous to that of shop steward in other industries.

chapel meeting – Meetings held by chapel members; these could be regular monthly meetings or special meetings called for special purpose. For example, to consider appeal for reinstatement by member discharged for cause.

chapel rules – Special rules (other than ITU, local, or office rules) of the chapel: these, like the office rules, were posted in the composing room.

chapel reset – Another name for advertisements required by contract to be reset, were local ads; these were local ads originally printed from plates furnished from an outside source – This rule did not apply to national ads (see also bogus and deadhorse).

classification – Composing room specialty in which a printer claimed competency.

clock – Device on Linotype or lntertype to count number of lines set during shift.

column – A section of a newspaper consisting of a length of type from top to bottom of a page, varying in width from nine picas, for some classified ad columns, to thirteen picas or more.

composing room – Newspaper production department in which advertisements were marked up and assembled, typesetting and proofreading was done, and pages were completed. This work was all under the ITU's jurisdiction and was jealously guarded.

composing stick – Device in which handset type was assembled.

composition – All the work required to process copy from editorial room and display or classified offices into pages of type ready for platemaking.

compositor – A typesetter or printer, although usually applied specifically to hand composition.

copy – Materials such as advertisements or news stories to be set in type.

copy cutter – Printer who separated copy into segments (called takes) for typesetting. Usually a sub-foreman.

country printer – A printer who learned the trade in small-town newspapers and job shops and who usually confined his or her career to such shops; as a rule those working in country shop were not union members.

dark machine – A Linotype with nobody working on it. Ostensibly available should a substitute be needed for extra work.

dark situation – A fulltime composing room position which, because of illness or otherwise, was not being covered. This refers to a machine or ad frame with the light out because no substitute was hired to work there.

dead horse – Another word sometimes used for chapel reset (which see).

decertification – Process of voting out the union and replacing with nonunion shop.

departmental shop – Composing room in which competency and priority was claimed only in one printing specialization (see also vertical board).

deposit card – Process of presenting one's traveling card to chapel chairman or local secretary in order to secure a working card in that local.

discharge – Being fired for cause other than lack of work (latter called layoff).

distribution – Placing handset type into proper compartments in type case - This was done automatically by Linotypes and Intertypes.

distributor – Person or device doing the distribution of type or matrices.

double truck – A display ad consisting of two pages set as one double-wide ad.

dupe – Duplicate proof of printer's production required by foreman in order to establish competency. These proofs were put on "dupe hook". To be duped was this process of being watched and production measured.

elevator – Linotypes had two elevators: one in which the matrices were assembled and then "elevated" to the casting mechanism; then the "second elevator" would pick up the matrices and "elevate" them to the distributor bar to be redistributed in the magazines.

Elrod – Device used for casting spacing material (called leads and slugs) in long strips which were subsequently sawed into desired lengths.

em – Formerly the width of the letter "m" of any type font; more properly the square of any type size used as a measure or space.

en – Half an em.

etaoin shrdlu – The first two rows of a Linotype keyboard.

floor work – Hand composition; this included operation of typesetting devices, such as the Ludlow, for which the matrices were assembled by hand.

floor man – Man (or woman) who claimed competency or who worked only on hand composition.

font – A complete assortment of type in one size and style.

frame – Area where floor man assembled display ads.

flatbed press – Press which printed directly from typeset pages, as compared to rotary presses which printed from curved plates - Flatbed presses were used in small shops.

galley – Trays in which type was deposited after setting. Also used for storing type-set materials.

hand side – Floor work; the section in which hand composition was performed.

hell box – Wood or metal boxes in which discarded type metal was placed prior to melting.

homeguards – Printers who preferred to spend their careers in one place.

Independents – One of the two political parties within the ITU. Often considered more conservative .

ITU headquarters – The administrative center of the union, located in Indianapolis, the local designated Number 1 because of this.

ITU Bulletin – Union publication in which law decisions and appeals from local union decisions were announced.

ITU Journal – Union publication in which local news, help wanted advertisements, and other materials of general interest to union members was published.

itinerant typographer – A fancy name for tramp printer.

jetting – Rolling quads like dice in order to determine who gets to work a shift or for gambling.

job shop – Shop which specialized in general commercial printing.
journeyman – Fully trained printer supposedly capable of working in any print shop.
jumping the job – Failing to cover a position for which one had been hired and had agreed to work; this was sometimes an acute source of conflict between travelers and homeguards.
justify – Filling out a line of type to the end so that all lines are the same; also filling or tightening lines of handset type so that they would fit without falling apart.
kerning – The practice of cutting undesirable whitespace from between letters so that they would present desirable appearance.
Linotype – Brand name for typesetting machine invented by Ottmar Mergenthaler; also used as generic name for such typesetting devices.
lobster shift – (also called lobster run) Shift in print shops corresponding to what is called "graveyard shift" in other industries. Source of the term is uncertain.
local secretary – The official of the ITU local who issued traveling cards and collected dues.
lower case – The small letters (non-capitals) of a type face (see also upper case).
Ludlow – Typecasting device for which the matrices were assembled by hand and used primarily for newspaper headlines and large display type in ads.
machinist – Printer who specialized in maintaining and repair of Linotypes, Intertypes, and other machinery in composing room.
machinist-operator –A printer who both operated and maintained typesetting machines.
magazine – Part of Linotype machine in which the brass matrices were stored.
matrix – Brass mold for casting a letter of a type face.
makeup department – Section of composing room where ads and straight matter were assembled into pages; a makeup man (or woman) specialized in such composition.
makeup rule – A thin sliver of steel, approximately one column wide, used as an aid in hand composition.
markup man – Printer (man or woman) who designated type races

and measurements for display ads.

monotype machine – Typecasting device which cast one letter at a time.

obligation – Act of being sworn in as a journeyman union member.

office – The employer.

office rules – Rules posted in a composing room by the foreman, outlining conditions of work. Violations of these rules were just cause for discharge.

office man – A printer who didn't travel. Sometimes a printer whose primary loyalty was thought to be to the office, not the union - the opposite of "union man."

open shop – A print shop which did not have an ITU contract but which was not necessarily anti-union.

overtime board – Posted schedule of accumulated overtime for each member of chapel. The member was obligated to hire a substitute to -cancel this overtime.

overtime hog – Printers who desired as much overtime as possible; these types would sometimes drag their feet all during regular shift so as to create more overtime. They were famous for not wishing to cancel their overtime by hiring sub.

passing card – Practice of having traveling card circulated among homeguards in order to get donations when no work existed.

pica – Printing measurement about 1/6 inch.

pica pole – Tool used for measuring picas; a humorous name for line gauge.

point – A measuring unit for type bodies and printing matter, equal to about 1/2 of an inch; there are 12 points in a pica

printer's devil – Term used for apprentices and, especially, beginners at trade. More prevalent in open shops than union shop

priority – Term used in most print shops meaning seniority, length of continuous employment. The foreman had to hire substitutes in 'priority order"; the oldest first.

Progressive – A member of one of the two political parties in the ITU.

pulling slip – If done by the printer, he is quitting the job; by foreman, he is fired; sometimes there would be a race to slipboard to determine which was which.

quad – The square of a typeface ; see also em. A 12-point em measured 12x12.

quoin – A wedge-shaped wooden or metal device used to lock up type in a galley or form.

reglet – Wood pieces used for spacing material; usually of 6- or 12-point size.

reproduction clauses – Sections of ITU local contracts which required publishers to reset local ads which had been furnished in plate form (see bogus, chapel reset, deadhorse).

rotary presses – High-speed presses which printed from curved, cast stereotype plates.

scale – Contractual definition of minimum wage that could be paid for printer's labor in a local – Employers could pay over, but not under the scale.

shift – A contractually established definition of a day's work; it varied depending on the local, between 5 and 8;for the last few decades of ITU it was 7 hours in metro dailies.

situation – (also called "sit") – A more or less permanent position; sometimes situations were temporary, for the purpose of filling vacation stretches or for busy times of year.

showup time – Time required of substitutes to appear for possible hiring on each shift. Usually a separate showup time for each shift, day, night, or lobster.

sorts – Odds and ends for Linotype or hand typesetting which were not part of the standard requirements of a font.

slip – Piece of paper containing name of printer and placed on priority board when hired.

slipboard – Priority board on which names of printers were placed as they were hired; the last hired, the first to be laid off.

slipping up – Act of having one's slip placed on slipboard. Also called "slugging up".

slug – A line of type cast in metal from a Linotype; also used for name plates on priority boards in place of slips.

squirt – Hot metal squirting through a loose line of Linotype matrices. An operator could be severely burned by a squirt.

stone – Smooth, level surface of metal or stone, where type forms were locked up for press.

stone man – Printer skilled at lockup and imposition of printing forms, not a Neanderthal!

straight matter – Type used for news columns in contrast to "ad guts".

stretch – Hire a substitute or office extra for more than one day at a time.

string – The total galleys of type or column inches set by a printer in a shift. At one time measured by a string with knots tied in it

swift – A Linotype operator who could set type extremely fast and clean.

take – Long stories were clipped into sections to expedite production on daily newspapers; each part so clipped was called a "take".

teletypesetter – Automated Linotype machines which preceded computer typesetting; the fact that the type had to be manually punched limited its usefulness.

tourist printer – Could be a fancy name for tramp printer or pejorative name for "tramp printer wannabe".

tf – Abbreviation for "till further notice". Used to designate an indefinite length of hire. A substitute on a "tf" was responsible for covering the absent printer's job.

thin spacing – Literally putting in thin spaces to stretch out a word or line to fill space; often used to indicate that funds were in short supply and, therefore, need to conserve money.

thirty dash or 30 dash – A linotype slug with a long dash which was placed at the end of a story. Traditionally, a newswriter wrote "30" at the end of a story. "Thirty" therefore signifies the end of something, and was written: -30-. When written alongside someone's name on the slipboard that indicated the chapel member either quit or had been fired.

traveling card – When working in a local, printer had a working card; when he or she traveled, a traveling card was issued, which would be recognized by any other ITU local union.

turning off light – Being fired. If a foreman came to your Linotype machine and turned off the light, you knew you were fired.

union shop – A shop with a union contract, sometimes called a "closed shop".

Unitypo – Corporation formed by the ITU to serve as a vehicle for setting up competition in one-newspaper cities where the union printers had been on strike long periods. A controversial point among printers: whether to fund Unitypo.

up on charges – An individual could be accused of conduct unbecoming a union member, or some such charge, by another member, a chapel, the local, or the ITU itself – When this occurred, it was called being "up on charges."

upper case – Capital letters.

varitype – A form of typesetting used by newspapers in Chicago in the 1940s to try to break a strike by ITU printers.

vertical board – Slipboard on which all departments in a composing room were lumped together to determine priority, non-departmental.

TRAMP PRINTERS

BIBLIOGRAPHY

Articles:

Dearman, Marion and John Howells
1975 – *An essay: Computer Technology and the Return of the Printer-Journalist* Journalism History, Vol. 2, No. 4, pp. 133-136

1980 – *Computers versus Craftsmen: the Case of the International Typographical Union*, California Sociologist, Vol. 3, No. 1, pp. 44-57

Books:

Berger, Peter and Thomas Luckmann
1966 – *The Social Construction of Reality*, Garden City, N.Y., Anchor Books Executive Council of the International Typographical Union

1964 – *A Study of the History of the International Typographical Union*, 1852-1963, Volume 1, Colorado Springs, Colorado (ITU publication), 1967, Volume 2.

Harris, Marvin
1968 – *The Rise of Anthropological Theory*, New York, Columbia University, by Thomas Y. Crowell Company

Hicks, John Edward
1950 – *The Adventures of a Tramp Printer: 1880-1890*, Kansas City, Mo., Midamericana Press.

Lampman, Ben Hur
1934 – *The Tramp Printer: sometimes journeyman of the little home-town that come no more*, Portland, Oregon, Metropolitan Press, with the Craftsman Syndicate cooperating.

Lipset, Seymour Martin, Martin Trow, and James Coleman
1956 – *Union Democracy: the inside politics of the International Typographical Union*, New York: The Free Press

Nisbet, Robert A.
1966 – *The Sociological Tradtion*, New York: Basic Books, Inc.

Schneider, Louis
1975 – *The Sociological Way of Looking at the World*, New York: McGraw-Hill

Stevens, George A.
1913 – *New York Typographical Union No. 6: Study of a Modern Trade Union and its Predecessors*. Albany, N.Y., J.B. Lyon Company, State Printers

Theodorson, George and Achllles G. Theodorson
1969 - *A Modern Dictionary of Sociology*, New York: Thomas Y. Crowell Co.

Schlesinger, Carl

1989 - *The Biography of Ottmar Mergenthaler*. New Castle, Del., Oak Knoll.
1967 - *Union Printers and Controlled Automation*. New York: Free Press.
1978 - *Farewell etaoin shrdlu (last night of hot-metal typesetting at the New York Times)* documentaty movie, Museum of Modem Art, New York

Hoftzbert-Call, Maggie

1992 – *The Lost World of the Craft Printer*. Urbana, Ill, University of Illinois Press

Boudin, Otto J.

1970 - *A Catfish in the Bodoni*

INDEX

A

Aguirre, Eduardo, 247
Avery, Lydia, 110

B

Baker, Leo, 77, 90, 177
Ball, Sam, 13
Bamitz, Gerald, 150
Banks, O.T., 88
Bates, Dave, 246
Bergman, Nate, 49, 74, 75, 76, 270
Bishop, Charlie, 130, 131, 163
Boardman, Sally, 65
Boretz, Morris, 246, 247
Brame, Ernie, 208
Brennan, Terry, 193
Britt, Billy, 193, 235
Brohoff, Clarence, 69
Brueske, Lou, 68, 69, 82, 85, 210, 230
Bryant, Snuffy, 95, 197
Bunce, Bunny, 78
Bundick, Bill, O., 50, 51
Bungard, Lester, 183, 184
Burgess, Bob, 211
Burns, Scorcher, 151
Burr, Ed, 85, 86, 91, 151
Burt, John, 69, 98, 202, 238

C

Cagle, Lonnie, 95
Caldwell, Wild Bill, 176
Campbell, "Shad", 132
Cannon, Guy, 96
Carson, Kit, 214
Carter, Roy, 6, 108, 183, 187
Case Brothers, 246
Champagne, Mary Lou, 191
Chandler, Al, 91
Chutijian, 241
Cleary, Don, 6, 65, 67, 69, 78, 87, 118, 201, 225, 248
Clemens, Samuel, 24, 42
Col. Claggett, 86
Colin, Charlie, 214
Comfort, Shorty, 91, 111
Cook, Otis, 241
Crabtree, 96
Crampton, Simeon Wood Jr., 133
Crawford, Jack, 50, 90, 183, 246
Crews, Johnny, 173
Cummins, Bob, 212
Curtin, John Henry, 77, 78, 121

D

Dearman, Marion, 6, 33, 36, 88, 95, 120, 193, 199, 265
Desaulniers, Frenchie, 69
Doolittle, Jimmy, 95
Drefahl, Bud, 214
Duncan, George, 192, 193
Dwyer, George, 191

E

Earwood, Roger, 193
Eckert, Buzzy, 241
Emory, Marie, 13, 113
Ernie The Track, 188
Etter, Bill, 249

F

Ferregiario, Bill, 239
Fikes, Carl, 83
Foley, Guy, 13, 50, 80, 81, 82, 83, 84, 87, 173, 174, 175, 176, 241, 269
Fowler, Elmer, 193

Franklin, Ben, 33, 49, 81, 93, 103, 153, 166, 173
Fred's Rainbow Bar, 248, 249
Frishe, Chris, 74, 252
Frizzell, Newell, 193

G

Gaines, Burt, 150, 194
Gamble, Shorty, 132
Gatzmeyer, Denny, 238, 239, 240
Gebler, Oscar, 213
Gnass, Art, 193
Goad, Jim, 213
Gordon, Bill, 214
Graham, Frank, 66, 80, 81, 246, 252
Greeley, Horace, 25, 32, 132
Green, Lester, 250
Greenspun, Hank, 98
Grigsby, Judge, 126
Guarilla, John, 252
Gutenberg, Johann, 12, 20, 119, 227, 265
Guthrie, Little Richard, 69

H

Hadley, Gene, 50, 235
Hall, Bill, 212
Hanesworth, Le, 6, 115

Hansen, Jerry, 238, 239, 241
Harmon, Jim, 193
Hartley, Mose, 135, 137
Hatcher, Guy, 82
Hatfield, John, 96, 182, 190, 191, 192, 245
Hayes, Eddie, 187, 189
Head, John, 241
Herod, Walter, 96
Hicks, John Edward, 18, 38, 54, 60, 65, 66, 68, 125, 126, 127
Hodges, Gene, 69
Holderby, Pinky, 133
Holson, Tom, 52, 94, 215, 227, 246
Hosmer, 214
Houck, Charlie, 133
Howells, Bob, 201, 202
Howells, John, 6, 14, 17, 36, 70, 79, 85, 89, 96, 98, 183, 191, 201, 203, 210, 233, 236, 237, 238, 239, 240, 248
Hurse, Glen, 241

J

Jacobs, Byron, Jake, 69
Jerry and Johnny's, 238, 240, 241

Johnson, Pappy, 209, 262, 263
Joly, 239

K

Kelly, Tom, 50, 87
Koernff, Big Bill, 210
Kokomo, Philips, 87, 136, 137, 149, 241
Kralingen, Joe Van, 193
Krutch, Frank, 193
Kusch, Al, 69

L

Landford, Harvey, 212
Lazarus, Henry, 97, 98, 177
Leddy, Gene and Tommy, 214, 235
Lee, Clay, 249
Lee, Peter Bartlett, 54
Lee, N. Dennit, 212
Leezy, Ralph, 210
Leffingwell, Sam, 132
Legge, Felton, 82
Leo J. Barry, 245
Leslie, James, 241
Little Eva, 188
Longley, Sharon, 241
Luna, Amulfo, 95

M

Maloney, Brian, 240

Mann, Claire, 214
Marise, Bill, 209
Mark Twain, 24, 42, 124
Marsden, Gene, 241
Maxim, Shiela, 111
Maxwell, Bill, 89, 214
McCarthy, Mary, 106
McDonald, 209
McGowan, Dizzy, 97
McGowan, Mary, 110
McKnight, C.O., 183, 188
McWhiney, Bill, 134
Menendez, Fred, 249
Millbauer, Toad, 183, 185
Miller, Sol, 131
Mitchell, Cliff, 212
Mobley, Tex, 70
Morse, Ted, 104, 119, 135, 137, 155, 217, 218, 219, 222, 234, 246, 250
Munoz, Manuel, 247

N

Neal, Tommy, 240
Norris, Earl, 225
Norvill, Horace, 138

O

O'Donnell, Eddie, 82, 96
O'Neil, M., 172
Ormand, 13
Owens, Jumpin' Joe, 79, 241, 246, 270

P

Padgett, Deo, 96, 183, 213, 214
Patterson, Mrs., 214
Peterman, Pete, 65, 246
Philips, Kokomo Joe, 241
Presley, Pearshape, 213
Pugh, Eda, 214
Pyle, Chet, 76

Q

Quinn, Tom, 87

R

Radda, Paul, 214
Rapp, Bob, 214
Rawlins, John, 209
Red Baron, 188
Reed, Al, 210
Reeves, Gadget, 91
Reuter, Jack, 113
Richmond, Duane, 210
Roberts, Milton, 250
Rossi, 214

S

Sampson, Gary, 212
Samson, 214
Satterfield, Ben, 211
Schmidt, Frederick G., 226
Seibert, Don, 137, 193, 246
Shanghai Lil, 69
Shaw, Faye, 239
Shields, Mary and Wayne, 95, 196
Sieber, Dick, 83
Simmons, Hank, 193
Sinowitz, Norman A., 230
Slattery, Rueben, 235
Slaymaker, Slim, 95, 197
Smith, William G., 183
Stacy, Lou, 212
Sternes, Frank, 163
Stiggers, Gary, 239
Story, George, 183
Stremming, Warren, 183, 214
Stryker, David M., 177, 228
Swingle, Billy, 172

T

Taylor, Bill, 191
Tellafiero, 214
Tunnell, Martin, 96

W

Walker, Stutterin', 84, 85, 86, 88, 183, 185
Warden, Ralph, 151
Ware, Jack, 50

Welch, Junius P., 189, 214
Wilson, Sunshine, 13, 87, 96, 137, 269, 270
Wertz, Lester, 94, 96
Wesson, Emma, 120
White, Franklin M., 228
Whiteley, Ed, 241
Who, Bobby, 188
Wildman, W.O., 166
Wilhite, 214, 235, 247
Williams, 188
Willie, A.L., 49
Wilson, Merle, 214
Withers, Bill, 193
Wrongfont McGuire, 136

Y

Young, Sam, 209

TRAMP PRINTERS

www.ingramcontent.com/pod-product-compliance
Lightning Source LLC
Chambersburg PA
CBHW050626300426
44112CB00012B/1675